Asperger Syndrome in Adolescence

Living with the Ups, the Downs and Things in Between

Edited by Liane Holliday Willey

Foreword by Luke Jackson

Jessica Kingsley Publishers
London and New York

First published in the United Kingdom in 2003
by Jessica Kingsley Publishers Ltd
116 Pentonville Road
London N1 9JB, England
and
29 West 35th Street, 10th fl.
New York, NY 10001-2299
www.jkp.com

Copyright © 2003 Jessica Kingsley Publishers

Library of Congress Cataloging in Publication Data

Asperger syndrome in adolescence : living with the ups, the downs, and things in between / edited by Liane Holliday Willey ; foreword by Luke Jackson.
    p. cm.
  Includes bibliographical references and indexes.
  ISBN 1-84301-742-2 (alk. paper)
    1. Asperger's syndrome. 2. Teenagers--Mental health. 3. Teenagers with mental disabilities. 4. Autistic children. I. Willey, Liane Holliday.

RJ506.A9A86 2003
616.89'82'00835--dc21   2003041610

British Library Cataloguing in Publication Data
A CIP catalogue record for this book is available from the British Library

ISBN 1 84310 742 2

Printed and Bound in Great Britain by
Athenaeum Press, Gateshead, Tyne and Wear

Contents

Foreword

When I was asked to write a Foreword my first reaction was astonishment. Why would someone ask a simple fourteen-year-old to do a Foreword for a book with lots of big words in and by lots of famous people? Well, that was not exactly my first reaction – rather just one of them. My first reaction when I actually read the book was 'hallelujah'. (OK so that is a word, not a reaction but let's not be pedantic!) Anyhow, I was glad that finally, here was a book that dealt with the whole minefield of adolescence without missing out the difficult bits. I started out writing my *Freaks Geeks and Asperger Syndrome* book because although there were loads of books that talked about AS there were very few that dealt with the issues that I, and I am sure loads of others, were going through in adolescence. This book gives easy solutions on how best to help and understand anyone in adolescence with AS and believe me that is no easy task! Although this book is aimed primarily at carers, parents and teachers of adolescents with AS, people that are just interested in finding out about AS, and in fact any living being that even vaguely knows someone with AS, it would have helped me greatly to understand at least some things about others and myself.

I do have to admit that although…uh hum…not liking to boast (my family may disagree here!) I am a good reader and fairly intelligent, I did struggle to digest some of the more in depth stuff and that is how it should be because these are aimed towards adults working with AS adolescents. They give some accurate and valuable information and I particularly like the fact that there are many authors from many walks of life, all offering valuable contributions. That is how life is – not just one opinion, not just one type of adolescent with AS, or indeed adolescent without, but many variations all struggling to find our way in the world. This book will go a long way towards helping many do that.

As a teenager with AS myself I guess I am quite entitled to lose focus, get into moods, slam a few doors and generally be more of a pain in the...erm...*neck* than usual! This is where this book is invaluable. From all of those – shall we say – interesting topics of sex and other such seemingly unmentionables (though not in our house!) to cognitive behaviour therapy, it is unique in the fact that it covers many topics previously untouched; friendships, sexuality, depression, sensory issues, disclosure and most definitely issues about trying to retain a sense of identity in the midst of an alien world (well OK Mike Stanton didn't quite write that but that is paraphrased by Jackson!). Each chapter weaves its way in and out of the difficulties of adolescence and AS with amazing insight and as a teenager with AS myself, it is particularly good to read chapters from Liane and Stephen and know that they truly understand what I and others are going through.

I especially liked Richard Howlin's chapter, 'Asperger Syndrome in the Adolescent Years', and the way he summarized so perfectly how children form groups, almost wolf packs, where everybody follows a specific social role, and how he describes the confusion of being a teenager with Asperger Syndrome. That is exactly what life is like at the moment and a book which helps any of us deal with such stuff is long overdue and most welcome. I was amazed at how Jacqui Jackson (yep, that's right, she is my mum) could view our crazy household with such humour whilst also giving such useful tips on how to manage a family with more than one child and such a range of autistic spectrum disorders (I prefer to call them gifts!). I am very proud of her and also very surprised that her mind hasn't blocked all memory of certain events because of the stress!

Although I have only described a few of the chapters in this book, every single chapter goes towards making this book what it is. *Asperger Syndrome and Adolescence* will definitely help people to understand people with AS, or 'aspies' as Liane Holliday Willey calls us.

One thing that makes this book stand out from the rest is the fact that it acknowledges the fact that adolescence is a particularly difficult time of life for someone with Asperger Syndrome and aims to inform others on how best to help. Struggling through adolescence myself I can only say a great big 'thank you' to all the authors – we need all the help we can get!

– Luke Jackson

Introduction

Liane Holliday Willey

Adolescence: the period of human development, that begins at the onset of puberty and which will continue until maturity.

When humans grow, they quite literally begin in a crawl and then a toddle toward whom they will someday be. Little humans tend to be self-motivated and self-involved, and generally oblivious to the differences of those around them. They have not started to separate people by color, religion, gender or developmental progress. Life for these wobbly climbers and seekers is happily devoid of political correctness and popularity contests. There are no who's who, no peer expectations put upon their little hearts. True enough, they are self-centered creatures, but they are not selfish or narcissistic, at least not as we define those terms when applying them to people beyond the early discovery stages of life. When a person is a young one, self-centeredness serves as the catalyst for many important things like self-confidence, beginning autonomy, physical development.

After a child reaches her seventh or eighth year, she will typically have moved beyond the perimeters set by self-centeredness. Though this child will not be ready completely to sacrifice her own wishes for a bright and shiny spot on her peers' path, more and more, she will search for ways to satisfy others' demands and requests. Sure, the child will still be focused on what makes her tick, but she'll spread her horizons to include new hobbies, burgeoning responsibilities at school and at home, and activities anchored in particular skills. So too will she begin to look for the kingdom of friendship, for at this age, who you play with starts to become more important than who you are. What you are able to do on the playground or in the gym becomes far more important than the grade you received on a paper or the number of facts you can recite. While these things might impress your teachers and parents, chances are strong they will not do much to bring you the coveted attention from peers at the top of the popularity chart. Things grow fuzzy and confusing and the world starts to tilt.

By the time puberty begins to raise its curious head, the rapidly maturing eleven- or twelve-year-old child is more than on her way to a sense of personal identity and worth, be it good or be it bad. Other people's views mix with her own moral and ethical codes to firm up her 'Who Am I?' self-portrait. Ever increasingly, the marks left from previous experiences and encounters are either smoothing over to make way for new discoveries, or roughing up in an attempt to keep more bad things from rooting. Teams are formed. Groups divide. Not so invisible lines are drawn separating children by colors, races, creeds, abilities and even statures. Doors close. Few open. How you look, what you like to do and cannot do, how you handle yourself in public and what you do when you are not…these are the things that count now. The kindness of the heart and the depth of the soul are remnants left scrambling to make it through the wake of this roaring and hot period we call adolescence.

Each and every one of the above scenarios can punch each and every adolescent. The bigger concern becomes: will the punch merely knock the adolescent off of a square footing or will it knock her out and to the ground. Neurotypical adolescents are born with a bit of bounce and good balance. They are the adolescents who will most likely be standing the tallest once adolescence ends its course. Such is not the case for kids with Asperger Syndrome. They come into this world on less than square footings and it takes just one strong punch to knock them flat.

What then, can the caregivers and loved ones of the aspie* adolescent do to keep the playing field more even and the chances of a knock out far from becoming a reality? The importance of that question should be reflected in dozens and dozens of books on the subject. This is not the case. The well-stocked Asperger Syndrome library is bound to be filled with volume after volume of works that relate to the aspie child. This is well and good. In fact, most of the contributing authors to this book have written at least one such book and those that have not, surely could. There are oodles of general books that cover bits of most everything a parent would want to know about their aspie. In addition, there are books that cover in great depth and detail, the specific effects Asperger Syndrome can have on young ones. Yet, there are very few titles that cover Asperger Syndrome and adolescence. I cannot imagine why this is the case and it concerns me. Children with Asperger Syndrome face their fair share of challenges, and the more we share information on how to help those kids, the better. No one would deny those truths. But it is during adolescence when the deeply personal effects of Asperger Syndrome strike with real vim and vigor. I base that assumption on the reality that adolescence is, without a doubt, such a tumultuous and confusing time. Puberty, subtle changes in society's expectations and familial responsibilities, more challenging academic requirements, new myriads of choices that come with just being older, and worries and wonders about what will pop up tomorrow, all work together to create one heck of a messy mix. Let us see if you remember...

Turn back the pages of your life to a time when the face in the mirror was curiously caught between the innocence of childhood and the darkened realities of the almost adult. Can you recall the mashed up feelings running through your mind and showing up in your behaviours?

When things felt uncertain or numbing, sad or wearisome, what did you do? Did you scream and cry, or go quiet and mute. Did you fight the world head on or did you retreat to a safe spot. Did you have responsible friends and adults to turn to? Or were you like a fawn stuck deep in the woods with no hope of rescue?

No matter where you fit or how you handled your adolescent years, it has to be clear that you needed circles of care to see you through the sticky bits. Now consider the aspie adolescent. Circles of support are not enough for the aspie. He or she needs spheres of support. I know I did. I would have collapsed without my caregivers and I am not at all certain I would ever have rebuilt.

This book is intended to be one of the circles in the aspie's sphere. It brings forth a mass of information on Asperger Syndrome and the effects it can have on today's adolescent. It is a community effort, written by three somewhat separate, yet intrinsically connected groups of experts including: the top international researchers in the field; everyday parents whose widely respected ideas are frequently shared in their publications and lectures; and last but not at all least, a few of us Aspies. Together, we three groups have come to explore virtually every area of Asperger Syndrome that is likely to swirl about the hearts, minds and souls of adolescent Aspies.

Our book moves in and out of all sorts of Asperger Syndrome concerns, worries, hopes, dreams and possibilities. In fact, no other book on the subject contains the unique mix of subjects that our book does. It begins where it must, with a general explanation of what Asperger Syndrome is and how essential it is to provide a sound structure of support bricked with strategies mixed from modified cognitive behaviour theories. From there, it heads straight on to the heavy hitting issues – sexuality, friendships, inappropriate peer relationships and depression. And then comes a breather of sorts as it explores the rites of passage that come with new dragonesses, the realities of parenting neurotypical/Asperger Syndrome families, the possibilities of new social opportunities and the quest for continuing education choices. Ultimately we wind around the bend face to face with the issues of self-discovery and self-acceptance.

I hold the authors of this book in an esteem beyond all heights. They are not only gracious, they are also honest, open and truly concerned for our Aspies. I cannot imagine there is a better group of people to handle a book that covers the magnitude of issues this one does. I trust you will agree.

Note

*Through out my visits around the US, I have occasionally heard from those who dislike my calling people with Asperger Syndrome 'Aspies'. I regret this is so. When I coined the term 'aspie' in my first book *Pretending to be Normal: Living with Asperger's Syndrome*, I intended for it to connotate images of kind and caring individuals who live lives wrapped in different colors and fluffed with different stuffings. Moreover, I meant it to take away the stigma associated with syndrome. I do not want a syndrome, nor do I want to live my life under the umbrella of a man's name. But whatever my reason in choosing to refer to myself as an aspie, I never meant for it to imply anyone in my Asperger Syndrome community was or is crazy, insignificant, separate and unequal, or anything remotely negative.

– Liane Holliday Willey

1

Asperger Syndrome
in the Adolescent Years

Richard Howlin

*Adolescents sense a secret, unique greatness in themselves
that seeks expression.*

(Joseph Chilton Pearce, *Evolutions End*)

Mark (15)

*Mark was described as a passive youth who had minimal interest in other
children. In earlier years his parents reported that he was more sociable, but
clearly preferred his own company. His vocabulary was highly developed, yet
his speech had an odd, formal quality. His interactions with other students were
awkward and he would often want to talk on his terms only with little regard
for the listener. He was fascinated by sports statistics and had an outstanding
memory for factual information. Mark had great difficulty participating in
school instruction, despite obvious abilities and would sometimes insist on
reading books of his own choice. Although Mark's interest in sports facts
flourished, he showed no interest in partaking in sports or related activities. He
loved computer games and spent most of his spare time in this pursuit. During
middle school he was frequently verbally bullied and responded to demeaning
and threatening comments with loud and unusual retorts that made others
laugh and chastise him further.*

*Mark reports currently having no friends in school. At home Mark
experiences frequent anger outbursts followed by periods of sincere remorse.
These troubling episodes are usually triggered by compliance problems
surrounding excessive computer time and his parent's requests for more
engagement and interaction with the rest of family.*

The above characteristics portray a behavioural and social pattern found in many adolescents and children diagnosed with Asperger Syndrome (AS). While adolescents diagnosed with AS can display varied symptomatic behaviours, similar underlying psychological and social difficulties are generic to the condition. For Mark, adolescence poses significant social challenges that may confront the most vulnerable aspects of his young personhood. Like all adolescents, Mark's journey through the teen years will entail finding a path through the context of a confusing social reality. In his particular case, the context is 'teenagerdom' in a large, highly social American high school.

Regardless of the particular cultural circumstance, as an emerging adult, Mark's challenge is to navigate through the relational and academic maze towards an authentic and socially rewarding personal existence. It is certainly feasible that some children with Asperger Syndrome move through the adolescent period unscathed, with meaningful peer relationships and few serious psychological scars. Based on a growing body of clinical evidence, this fortunate group is most likely the exception. The majority of adolescents with AS experience significant social and emotional turmoil and often regard themselves as outsiders within the school environment. This chapter discusses the more vulnerable scenarios that are ultimately referred for psychological care. Many of these adolescents have been diagnosed in early childhood and have received some level of school support for several years. Others are referred as adolescents, with a high proportion experiencing serious emotional distress.

Principle consideration will be placed on the support needs of adolescents with AS and their families. In terms of therapeutic innovation, I have found this a particularly neglected clinical population. Psychological support strategies will be discussed with a particular emphasis on the self-process of the student. Emphasis in Asperger Syndrome continues to remain predominantly directed towards pre-adolescence and early childhood. The intent of this chapter is to stimulate and promote discussion towards the needs of adolescents, young adults and their families.

Asperger Syndrome as a social learning disorder

> An encounter is typically initiated with a glance. First, the person who is initiating the encounter catches the eye of the person whom he wishes to encounter, then after a slight pause, he begins

to speak. If the other answers back with a glance and responds to the verbal overture, the encounter begins…or if unsuccessful the techniques of rejection are several.

(C.H. Swenson)

I am often reminded of the complexity of social engagement in my work with Asperger Syndrome. The social world of adolescence emerges with a plethora of rapidly changing customs and practices. These increased social expectations and organizational demands can seriously tax the social processing vulnerabilities of the AS student. There is also no evidence to suggest that the symptoms and deficits in Asperger Syndrome ameliorate during the adolescent years. In the absence of objective epidemiological data, available case studies indicate marked increases in stress and emotional instability. (Palombo 2001)

In many ways the difficulties faced by children with Asperger Syndrome are analogous to any form of learning disability. A developmental activity such as language comprehension or reading, which for the majority of children progresses relatively autonomously, is transformed into an arduous and sometimes incomprehensible subject of study. In Asperger Syndrome, the nature of the impairment is the complex neurobiological tapestry of social understanding. The use of the learning disability paradigm can prove helpful in explaining the disorder to parents and the author frequently adopts the term 'social dyslexia' when introducing the concept of AS for the first time. It has been suggested that learning disabilities as a generic term should encompass a heterogeneous group of disorders including social and other adaptive abilities. (Howlin 1998; Rourke 1989). This characterization appears reasonable given that psychological and educational development is contingent on both academic and social growth.

Furthermore, the role of central nervous dysfunction has been implicated as a primary causal factor underlying both academic learning disabilities and Asperger Syndrome (Rourke 1989). The diagnostic category of nonverbal learning disorders is one well-defined example of the neurological relationship between neuropsychology, academic disorders and social processing. Gedo (1991) asserts convincingly that psychological impairments need to be explained within neurocognitive science, as information processing deficits: 'they [chronic psychological conditions] are the consequences of developmental lags, which we may now understand as failures of certain maturational processes in the brain' (Gedo 1991, p.11). The conception of Asperger Syndrome as a social learning disorder may prove a practical option for designing school support programs and increasing awareness.

As with all areas of the autistic spectrum, the severity of social impairment and pragmatic language problems can vary greatly within the Asperger Syndrome population. Social processing impairments are typically expressed through the unique temperament qualities of the individual and thus differ from person to person (Cumine, Leach and Stevenson 1999). One student may display social processing difficulties through introverted, isolative behaviour, another in an extroverted but eccentric style. In both cases the key characteristic, as originally noted by Asperger, reflects a fundamental impairment in social interaction and reciprocity (Asperger 1944; Attwood 1999; Wing 2001).

Typical observable characteristics of Asperger Syndrome during adolescence include:

- poor communications skills – sometimes resulting in the avoidance of peer interaction

- excellent vocabulary

- intense interests and pursuits (usually isolative) that can seem obsessive

- tendency to prefer predictable events resulting in problems of social flexibility

- problems in self-organization and productivity, especially around schoolwork

- a preference and overt wish to engage in self-interest activities.

The most frequently cited psychological processing issues and conflicts underlying these behaviours are described in the following.

Impairment in social understanding

Various nonverbal foundations of social interaction, including features of imitation, social motivation and 'reading' or sensing the intentions and behaviour of others are impacted in Asperger Syndrome. It is readily apparent that the student with AS lacks a fundamental social 'sense' and is typically confused by the interactions of others. This can contribute to various social habitual coping styles, ranging from a blunt, insensitive intellectualizing style to a more withdrawn, avoidant persona. Communications are frequently directed 'at' the person, seldom with, and others may find themselves on the receiving end of lengthy monologues.

Problems in pragmatic language

Problems in pragmatic language can be observed in most adolescents with AS. Using language for social-communicative purposes involves the aforementioned nonverbal appreciation of gesture and prosody (voice melody). This feature can have a 'two-way' effect in that the student may miss important but subtle communications from others and draw negative attention to themselves through their unusual intonation and choice of words.

Preoccupations with special interests

Special interests can become overbearing and socially isolating pursuits in Asperger Syndrome. Realizing the importance of the interest for the adolescent, parents are often at a loss to help the student become less fixated and more engaging with both family members and peers. The actual content of interests can be peculiar, such as train schedules or more conventional (sports statistics). An abundance of factual information is a common feature and it is often impossible to predict when such fixations will change or be replaced.

Problems with identity and self-esteem

Aspergian teens are not immune to the turmoil of identity issues faced during adolescence. They are in many ways, however, extremely socially and emotionally restricted and thus stunted in their role explorations. Figure 1.1 describes a model of social-emotional development and maturation. Development is viewed as progressing in a predictable order. The five stages proposed in Figure 1.1 lean heavily on the work of Erikson (1977) and Wood (1996) in which development is configured as a dynamic and 'expanding arena of interplay' between the self and the social. Stages 3 to 5 directly imply social mastery, which would align itself with the frequently observed deterioration in school adjustment observed in Aspergian children beyond the later elementary period. In this model, peer relations progressively assume both a more central and demanding role. The developmental progression is toward increasing levels of competence and independence in social situations and a diminishing need and desire for direct adult supervision.

The social and emotional challenges of adolescence demand increased social sophistication. There is a dramatic shift from parent orientation towards the standards and appearances of the peer group. Difficulties in the recognition of emotional states, both in themselves and others, can exacerbate interpersonal confusion and reinforce the tendency of social withdrawal in the AS student. Consequently, it is not uncommon to observe a complete dependence of self-worth in academic or special interest areas. AS students may state, in no uncertain terms, their wish for the social to 'just go away.'

The nonverbal social processing deficits found in Asperger Syndrome have both interpersonal and personal consequences. By adolescence, the child has likely experienced years of social confusion, formed negative self-attributions and become highly sensitive or indifferent to peer relationships. Children with social learning disorders are thus significantly handicapped in their efforts to achieve a generalized sense of personal mastery and self-confidence. Several authors have stressed the importance of autobiographical continuity, an awareness of an unfolding personal narrative that has evolved from past experiences. Given that interpersonal experiences are an important factor in whether a youngster develops a sense of belonging or alienation, these experiences significantly impact the early adolescent's self-perception. The emerging self system of the adolescent with Asperger Syndrome can present as defensive, vulnerable and emotionally brittle in response to repeated social failure. Many AS teens are intellectually above average. However there is often an unrealistic appraisal and inflation of their own competence and potential in this regard. In some cases adolescents can form overly narcissistic and idealistic intellectual worlds that are, in reality, frail and desperately defended.

For educators and therapists alike, it is fundamentally important to acknowledge this vulnerability, and provide safe and consistent relational anchoring in conjunction with directive interventions and strategies.

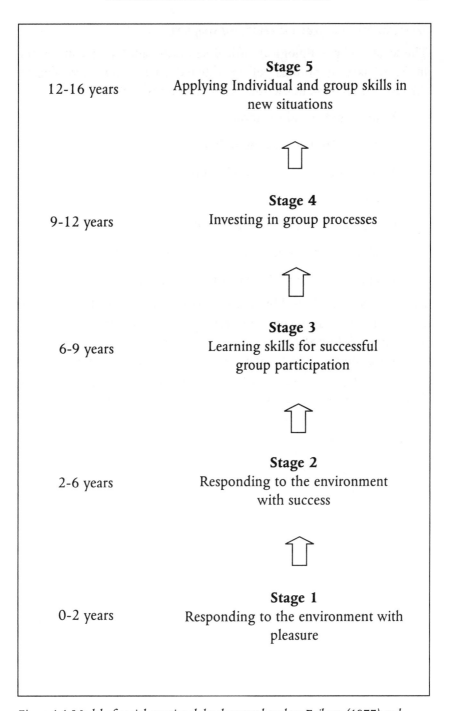

Figure 1.1 Model of social-emotional development based on Erikson (1977) and Woods (1996)

Increased psychological and emotional symptoms

The social and psychological difficulties during adolescence may result in 'secondary symptoms' of heightened social and psychological distress. An increase in the following symptoms can be observed:

- increased social isolation
- anxiety and anxious agitation
- poor organization and school performance
- depression
- increased rigidity and inflexibility
- increased preoccupations with isolating hobbies
- episodes of oppositional behaviour and anger.

Based on current clinical literature, it would be reasonable to describe these features as fairly common occurrences in AS during adolescence and young adulthood (Attwood 1998; Tantum 1992; Wing 1999). It is certainly understandable why many AS children find this period particularly daunting. Anxiety is perhaps the greatest obstacle in the process. The rift between sociocultural expectations and the social processing impairment creates a continued source of confusion and compounds the scope of anxiety.

In the specific context of social adjustment, at no other time is the social curriculum more challenging than during adolescence. For most children, adolescence presents as a time of upheaval and increased social drama. For those with social impairments, it can further reinforce confusion and withdrawal from the social world.

Asperger Syndrome and the social context of adolescent development

Within the framework of normal development, adolescence is viewed as a particularly unstable period of intense social change and intrapsychological growth. Although adolescence does not in itself represent a psychological crisis, the period typically presents some significant challenges including a heightened vulnerability to emotional symptoms. The characteristic psychological hallmarks of adolescence include:

- reduced dependence on parents – increasing autonomy
- increased influence of peers
- beginning of sexual relationships
- increasing educational demands/tests and examinations
- gradual entry into work or higher education
- eventual achievement of legal adult status.

Almost without exception, developmental scholars accentuate the profound importance of the social relationships within which each adolescent negotiates their journey. Given the characteristic social processing problems faced by AS children, the horizon of adolescence must seem overwhelming and ominous. The growing number of insightful biographical accounts and clinical case studies from high functioning autistic and Aspergian individuals (Grandin 1995; Willey 1999) bears witness to this. More than most, the AS adolescent lives within his or her own world, often maintaining a fragmented and tenuous relationship with social customs. This can have far more challenging implications than the simple avoidance or frustration with aspects of social discourse. Many young people with AS suffer extreme emotional stress due to the reality of self-confusion and conflicts generated by their struggle with social understanding. Often, these struggles are effused with fundamental issues of dependency and trust with parents, exacerbated by a seemingly illogical social world that will not relent in its intrusive demands.

It is, after all, social interactions that provide the essential ground for how we define ourselves. Thus, for many children with AS, adolescence represents a particularly fragile struggle for identity. As Mead (1934, p.164) so clearly states: 'Selves can only exist in definite relationships to other selves. No hard and fast line can be drawn between our own selves and the selves of others.' The task of education and self-development, one could argue, is to understand and adaptively express our own voice within this ubiquitous social arena.

School and peer relations

Given the growing importance of social identity, adolescents with AS typically experience a heightened sense of 'differentness' during the middle and high school years. Open social environments (i.e. school) are particularly challenging as they continually confront the AS student's vulnerabilities with respect to social processing and need for consistency and predictability. Neurotypical students are often alerted to the differences or unusual behaviour of AS students through peculiarities in speech quality and use of language and their apparent tendency to avoid social gatherings. An estimated 10 per cent to 20 per cent of typical school-aged children suffer social rejection by their classmates (Burleson 1985). We can assume that for children with AS this statistic will be significantly higher. In researching the specific issue of social rejection, Frankel (2001) describes two distinct socially outcast groups: the rejected (disliked) and the neglected (ignored). Over the past ten years I have experienced evidence for both these negative scenarios in virtually all of the school sociograms or 'social maps' of adolescents with Asperger Syndrome. The lack of best friendships in the early adolescent period has shown to be a significant factor in chronic loneliness in later adulthood (Bagwell, Newcomb and Bukowski 1995). Authors cite specific behaviours in 'critical' social situations as keys for establishing acceptance. An example of such a critical situation is the transition into a common-ground activity, such as a group decision to study in the library. Such seemingly trivial scenarios can be important opportunities for peer success or rejection and, apparently, opinions are formed quickly. Furthermore, an ever-increasing mass media culture is promoting a pseudomaturity in children that emphasizes adult image and 'fitting in' on ever-changing, superficial terms. This undoubtedly adds to the social confusion and alienation of many children, including those with Asperger Syndrome.

The particular quality and features of the social environment play an important role in either promoting or inhibiting social comfort. This is an important aspect, as many children with AS demonstrate varying degrees of empathy, motivation and social tolerance depending on the familiarity of the situation and people involved. In general, for the neuroatypical AS student, everyday school life is often perceived as a challenging and frustrating obligation. The social climates of schools often show little hospitality towards students who appear intelligent, articulate and yet not necessarily socially astute or interested in social agendas.

Thus, in approaching adolescence, the social maps of AS children may already reflect a history of confusion and struggle in conventional ways of interacting. If meaningful social integration is a key to adolescent adjustment, then facilitating healthier school integration surfaces as an important treatment consideration in Asperger Syndrome. While the meaning of social success will vary from child to child, it appears that some form of friendship or group identity is essential to the maintenance of adolescent self-esteem.

Fostering personal navigation through the teen years

Perhaps the most unexplored area of supportive treatment in Asperger Syndrome remains the individual psychological dimension. To what degree a neuroatypical condition such as AS will respond to one of the various forms of psychotherapy is unclear. Within the realm of neurobiological conditions, therapeutic considerations typically encompass an eclectic approach utilizing various modes of interventions. Methods can range from purely supportive (lifespace management) alternatives to more formal cognitive, behavioural and pharmacological options.

Objectives of therapeutic support in Asperger Syndrome

The overriding goal of individual therapeutic support for the adolescent with Asperger Syndrome is to improve functioning in several key areas of self-management. First, improving insight and awareness regarding their psychological strengths and weaknesses builds a central foundation for subsequent discussions. Understanding and openness towards Aspergian traits and how these traits directly impact their lives and lives of those around them is central to this process.

Second, providing support in the management of mood and anxiety is critical and typically involves direct coaching in the recognition of emotions and emotional crisis. It is often helpful to discuss the aspects of central nervous functioning involved in regulating anxiety and the role of fight or flight mechanisms in situations of distress. Simultaneously, strategies of emotional management are reviewed and suggested for everyday occurrences and conflicts.

Third, improving social competence is addressed through discussion and study segments. The student reviews films and the typicalities of social engagement are explored. Discussions of actual experiences are encouraged and often applicable to constructive dialogues regarding parent–adolescent and peer conflicts.

Finally, these discussions are encompassed within a framework aimed at facilitating a more positive and self-directed journey, a process summarized under the term personal navigation (PN). The term 'personal navigation' has been utilized to describe an individual's awareness and control over his or her life's circumstances and direction. Ferrari and Sternberg (1998) describe further:

> One's personal navigation is enhanced to the extent that one is self aware with respect to needs, desires and goals…we believe that navigation is an apt metaphor for what people actually do in order to gain, maintain and at times, reestablish control over their lives. (Ferrari and Sternberg 1998, p.221)

From the reported experiences of individuals with AS, it would appear that the repeated experiences of social failure impact many central aspects of self-development and navigation. Poor self-esteem is often the most notable manifestation, especially in the social arena. Basch (1988, pp.24-25) describes self-esteem as: 'A genuine sense of one's self as worthy of nurture and protection…which stems from the experience of competence, the experience of functioning appropriately.'

Social efficacy, the sense and belief that one has an impact and can achieve success in social situations, is perhaps the greatest challenge facing the student with AS. Adolescents with AS are often confused regarding their own feelings and struggle to identify and express needs and feelings in effective ways. Furthermore, they are frequently unable to verbalize their fears and may resort to ineffective coping mechanisms such as projection and denial regarding social conflicts. Thus an important and ongoing foundation of therapeutic support surrounds the management of anxiety. The recognition and identification of affective states emerges as a foundation for developing coping skills and improved social empathy. Labeling feelings, recognizing feelings in others, responding to one's own feelings and the feelings of others are all key items on the therapeutic agenda.

How, then, can we build and foster personal navigation in adolescents with Asperger Syndrome? Following a discussion of PN, one young man who was in the midst of significant school difficulties forwarded an email entitled 'Lost at Sea!' As is often the case, his words contained both sentiments of humor and truth.

In my work with AS, the current author has found the above generic goals useful as guiding principles of treatment. In the implementation of a treatment plan, these principles are formulated in specific detailed objectives in response to the needs of the particular client and situation. The following client-centered therapeutic model will include those treatment segments that in the author's experience are especially relevant in supporting the needs of the adolescent with Asperger Syndrome. The development of insight through constructive dialogue forms the underlying mechanism of this component. Within this context, personal beliefs, emotional responses and aspirations are explored and examined from considerations of rationality and social adaptation.

Implementing a treatment plan

In individual therapy, I have found the following five components to be important considerations toward implementing a therapeutic plan for adolescents with AS.

1. Evaluation and review of cognitive, emotional regulation and personality.

2. Establishing rapport, motivation for change and the formulation of goals.

3. Providing a theoretical foundation for discussing individual learning differences and the meaning of Asperger Syndrome.

4. Development of self-reflective thinking and management skills in mood regulation and interpersonal skills.

5. Involvement of school and parents in supporting objectives.

These elements interact selectively and dynamically during the course of therapeutic work. Other options can be introduced, based on the psychological needs and orientation of the therapist. One common and often utilized adjunct is the use of medication in supporting psychotherapeutic goals.

*Evaluation and review of cognitive skills, emotional regulation
and personality*

A complete psychological and educational evaluation during the early
adolescent period can serve as an important basis for planning the
student's subsequent school years and the anticipated programmatic
needs. A central goal in the psychological assessment of Asperger
Syndrome lies in the mapping of differential abilities and weaknesses
within the context of the social learning disorder. In conjunction with
the primary focus of social processing issues, the assessment and subsequent management of AS requires a fundamental developmental
platform. Child and adolescent abilities seldom evenly follow chronological age and typically manifest themselves in a varied pattern of developmental trajectories. In Asperger Syndrome, we can expect a
delayed and uneven social and emotional adjustment profile with a
varied pattern across other cognitive and adaptive abilities. In attempting to gain an accurate clinical picture of AS, clinicians are required to
delve beyond diagnosis and negotiate the individual variation and
meaning of social impairment. For example, a significant number of
children diagnosed with AS appear to have highly developed
visual–spatial analytic skills. Identifying such skills in conjunction with
other symptom configurations may lead to advances in our understanding regarding the underlying nature of social impairments. In what way
does highly developed analytic reasoning correlate with social processing? Although new research findings and hypotheses rarely provide
explicit guidelines for diagnosis, they can offer important insights and
clues for the assessing clinician. In conjunction with clinical experience,
they aid in the establishment of a more complete developmental appreciation of the complexity of Asperger Syndrome.

Thus, psychologists are attempting to more fully define the psychological processes that impact social understanding and interest in social
processing has led to cognitive theories including 'theory of mind' and
'frame of reference theory.' Standardized measures of these concepts are
not yet available. However it is feasible that reliable developmental
measures will be developed to assess these important domains of social
intelligence.

Providing a theoretical foundation for discussing individual learning differences and the meaning of Asperger Syndrome

One primary goal of psychological support is aimed at helping the student organize experiences more effectively. Discussing the reality of learning disorders is viewed as positive and necessary step in organizing the inner world of the adolescent with AS. A frank and honest dialogue regarding the student's strengths and weaknesses and a review of Asperger Syndrome is an important therapeutic step. All therapeutic endeavors benefit from a clearly formulated conceptual framework or philosophy. In my work with Asperger Syndrome, the general axiom or theory of treatment leans on the concepts of multiple intelligence and directly references the 'social thinking or social intelligence' model of social and interaction and learning. I have found that the introduction of a theoretical framework can be established as a foundation of the therapeutic work. In a positive model of learning competence (Seagal and Horne 1997) the student is provided with an illuminating perspective on strengths (i.e. analytic reasoning) and inherent struggles (social intelligence), with the fundamental argument that social competence can be improved and can lead to greater satisfaction in all areas of life. The work of psychologists such as Sandra Seagal and Dawna Markova (1992) provide empowering maps of learning and processing differences. In such meta formats, social reasoning is introduced as one of several important components in human processing. Some adolescents with AS are initially skeptical and critical of this idea. Introducing the 'logic' of the social can often remain a relevant and ongoing theme of therapy.

Establishing rapport, motivation for change and the formulation of goals

A key differentiating feature in the therapeutic programming needs of adolescents is the role of motivation. In contrast to childhood, adolescence is a time of separation and independence. Both therapeutic and educational interventions must take this critical transition into account. The adolescent is typically reluctant or even doggedly unwilling to passively accept adult 'training' methods, regardless of how well intentioned. Adolescents with AS often find themselves in a precarious dilemma, one that necessitates some level of adult support while seeking independence, especially from parental figures. The establishment of alternative supportive adult relationships, either in school or clinic, can function as important intermediaries in furthering the student's independence and self-process. Seeking and maintaining the adolescent's cooperation in this process is perhaps the most central therapeutic issue. Understandably, interventions for Asperger Syndrome have remained largely dependent on the educational paradigm, i.e. teaching and remediating social skills. As the child enters adolescence, there is a typical and healthy shift of self-assertion that seeks and demands more imput and negotiation. Like many challenging adolescents, the young adolescent with Aspergers Syndrome may need help but does not necessarily want it! The student begins to demand explanations for the interventions of others. Thus, a fundamental consideration in treatment must involve some degree of cooperation of the student and a gradual exploration of the student's implicit assumptions with the aim of improving reflective social thinking. Therapists, educators and parents alike are challenged to open a supportive dialogue, paying close attention to both the needs and perspective of the student. This requires close attention to the student's own perspective, which is often key to effecting motivation for change.

The initial meetings should encompass the clarification of needs and formulation of goals. This process is informed by the psychological assessment findings and can help the student identify problems and help in formulating the basis for a working agreement. What situations are creating the most stress and tension? How does the student respond when under stress? What coping skills are utilized? What are the student's personal goals and interests? How realistic are these goals? What system supports are needed to achieve the student's goal?

As is generic to most therapeutic approaches, the therapist must attempt during the first sessions to align with the student. The development of mutual understanding and relational ease is an essential foundation for all future work. In my work with AS, I have found the recognition and appreciation of the student's strengths are fundamental at this stage and generally essential in the treatment of the Aspergian student. The experience of social rejection often serves to create a fundamental vulnerability within the individual that can scarcely tolerate more critical analysis. An authentic appreciation and appraisal of the style and abilities of the student bears frequent reiteration.

Perhaps one of the most challenging tasks of any psychological assessment or intervention is the avoidance of problem-saturated thinking. This refers to an unbalanced emphasis on dysfunction at the expense of more a complete and imaginative view of individual potential. Adolescents with AS are often troubled and have numerous social difficulties as a result of their poor social understanding, and yet there is always more. I am alluding to the fascinating complexity and mystery of psychological identity. Beyond the problem-focused history, failures and successes, there are also new stories waiting to unfold. As mentors we cannot and should not ignore immediate conflicts. Yet as instruments of change, therapists are also called to look beyond presenting pathologies toward the potential and the possible. This aspect is reinforced if we consider the developing self-narrative of the adolescent, how they view themselves and how this view is impacted by the views and opinions of others.

The acceptance of the young client's uniqueness and affirming his or her experience without judgement provides a fundament that can often become obscured behind the pathocentric blinders of the therapeutic field. This does not minimize the need for confrontation surrounding conflicts and behavioural difficulties. This authentic affirmation, however, provides a necessary balance and actually facilitates the ongoing problem-oriented dialogues between the adolescent, parents and therapist (Wachtel 1993).

Finally, in negotiating Asperger Syndrome, the therapist should try and avail himself with particular scrutiny of the interests, personal style and idiosyncrasies of the student. This can be a slow process and it is typical for Aspergian clients to be guarded and reserved. Self-disclosure can be a particularly helpful characteristic on behalf of the therapist is such situations. I have often witnessed the extreme vulnerability of these students and how the use of autobiographical vignettes of the therapist can provide a welcome relief and reduction of anxious tension.

Development of reflective thinking and self-management skills in areas of mood regulation and interpersonal functioning

Adolescents with AS typically resort to extremes in judging social experiences. A goal is to provide students with more realistic and effective cognitive perspectives in judging their own behaviour and the behaviour of others.

Organizing and regulating inner experience in response to the social demands of the adult and peer world is key to the adaptive success of any individual. This requires accurate recognition of inner emotional states in relationship to external demands. This central task of the reflective self is to recognize, encode and respond to inner and external signals effectively. Attunement with one's own emotive states and needs in context of social demands requires continuous attention and represents a distinct aspect of intelligence. David Wexler describes this foundation of emotional intelligence thus:

> When feelings are recognized and labeled, when the ways in which others respond are based on some predictability and familiarity, when there is some of perception of confidence that the current stresses or challenges can somehow be met, then the immediate world makes sense. (Wexler 1991, p.18)

A cornerstone of developmental therapy in the adolescent period is directed at increasing this capacity for reflective thinking. A central characteristic of reflective thinking is the increased capacity to consider new perspectives regarding self and others. This capacity may be potentially utilized to support fundamental deficits such as reading social behaviour and intention. Directing therapeutic intervention towards perspective taking, discussing the meanings of emotional responses and the social reactions of others is a fundamental therapeutic goal. Maintaining a therapeutic theme or focus is often challenging, given the 'storm and stress' of school and social adjustment. A balance is required that allows for crisis management and, ideally, integration of the general therapeutic goals. For example, a crisis situation involving a social altercation can be behaviourally managed and then (in a subsequent session) be used to address the problem of inflexible, rigid thinking. The Aspergian adolescent may become overly fixated on the moral issue of 'right and wrong' in social altercations, hindering the social reality and need for forgiveness, closure and resolution.

Improving reflective functioning is typically enhanced by the therapist's elaboration around social conflicts. New ideas and perspectives are introduced, sometimes verbally, or with the use of video scenes. Assumptions around objective events are discussed and reviewed from the vantage of expected social behaviour. Care must be taken to acknowledge the subjective position of the student, meanwhile providing various alternative options that may prove more adaptive. Thus, more opportunities are provided by the therapist with sensitivity to the young client's pace and reflective capabilities. An important perspective on this therapeutic approach is found in the developmental theory of Vygotsky (1986). In this context, therapy would be viewed as an active learning experience. The therapist or facilitator engages the student in cooperative learning tasks that minimally outstrip current levels of competence. This 'zone of proximal development' can be applied to most therapeutic tasks, such as improving reflective competence and narrative flexibility in relation to conflicts. One typical problem found in Asperger Syndrome is a thinking rigidity, which often results in a blunt, all or nothing polarized thinking style. The therapist can assume an inquisitive stance, gradually opening a dialogue toward expanding the boundaries of the student's thought process. This may involve many sessions and include readings, etc. The key is to allow space for exploration, planting ideational seeds whilst monitoring the emotional regulation of the young client.

Management of AS should also address direct social skill teaching aimed at improving the appreciation of the interpersonal and the feelings of others. The majority of adolescents with AS do not know how to engage and maintain conversations with others. They often require direct behavioural modeling and role-play situations. Clinical rationale would suggest that supporting both interpersonal skills while helping the child grasp the meaning of internal emotional experiences is the preferable therapeutic premise.

Finally, individual therapy should encompass potential pharmacological treatments. As stated, the unique neurobiological constitution of each student may present with specific emotional vulnerabilities, including predisposition toward depression and anxiety. Although no single medical regimen is indicated in Asperger Syndrome, symptom management may necessitate psychiatric intervention as a key component of treatment.

Parent relations

As discussed, adolescence signals intense physical changes involving developmental acceleration and ending in the completion of physical growth and achievement of sexual maturity. But, more than anything, psychological and social changes define this period. These developments are symptoms of a fundamental new voice of self-identity that emerges and changes everything, especially the relationship with the parents. Adolescence primarily mandates a turning away from childhood toward a new, and inevitably, less secure future. Before adolescence, children are free to act and feel as children. Parental love and care was received with openness and innocent acceptance. With the dawning of adolescence, a new force within dictates that the teenagers must experience him-/herself as independent, and they turn to peers for confirmation and validation.

The emerging adolescent must strive for a new, redefined and objective view of the social world. Thus, adults, including parents, are recognized in their flaws and shortcomings. This serves an important function, and the now fallible parents are faced with having to tolerate frequent critique and judgement.

Within the Asperger Syndrome, such changes must seem overwhelming and all-together frightening for the adolescent self. One can only scarcely comprehend the potential anxieties and conflicts that Aspergian youngsters experience during these years of change and challenge. Anticipating and understanding the needs of parents and students directly affected by Asperger Syndrome remains a vital objective for both school and clinical psychology.

Parents are faced with the daunting task of encouraging independence in a child that may have a fragile and conflicted social life. This vulnerability can exacerbate the dependency conflicts inherent in the parent–child relationship and ultimately stymie the developmental direction towards separation and self-reliance. These situations can intensify emotional tension and increase symptomatic behaviours such as negativity and rigidity. The parents of AS teens, due to the persistent issues of social management, need frequent feedback. Weekly or, when necessary, daily reports are helpful. Encouragement for both the teen and the parent in recognizing each small step in social progress is an essential component of this journey. This may involve ongoing conjoint counseling.

In response to the stresses of Asperger Syndrome, subtle maladaptive patterns may establish in relations between adolescent and parent. These difficulties have the potential of creating added distress by frustrating developmental progress. In a broader systems perspective, parents and adults are challenged to avoid allowing the conflicts and symptoms of the disorder from obscuring or consuming the relationship with the teen. Such a symptomatic 'cycle' is one of the most common forms of problematic family adaptation when faced with ongoing crisis. The symptomatic cycle describes the process by which symptoms can exert profound influence over the interpersonal relationships in family members, particularly parents. Thus, a reactive parenting style can emerge that may prevent new experiences from being recognized and necessary challenges from being productively mastered. A typical example of a symptomatic pattern is 'enmeshment' (Minuchin 1974).

Symptoms of enmeshment can often be observed in parents who experience normal transitions and changes as threatening. Thus, for the adolescent with AS, an exaggerated emphasis may be placed on the student's problematic behaviours and distract the family from making needed developmental transitions. Given the severity and scope of the difficulties faced in Asperger Syndrome, this dynamic can present as a common theme in therapeutic intervention. Parents are often faced with the daunting dilemma of being their child's most important advocate and simultaneously maintaining a developmentally adaptive position that reinforces individuation.

The role of school support

Providing for the most effective psychological management of Asperger Syndrome during the adolescent period typically involves a combination of individual, educational and family supports. A multi-level approach is viewed as the most promising foundation in the treatment of the majority of child and adolescent psychological conditions, and Asperger Syndrome is no exception. In general, studies suggest that the coordination of support services between school, clinic and home serves to improve both student adjustment and family communication (Erikson 1998).

Typically, the school situations require monitoring, and direct intervention during the middle and high school years may be necessary. Programs ranging from crisis management strategies to the availability of 'safe' places and adults, options for intellectual pursuits such as chess clubs and favored interests such as drama clubs are typical considerations for school support.

School recognition of Asperger Syndrome has been gradual. The development of support programming both in the US and Europe is an encouraging sign. Public school services have been hampered by existing special education criteria which essentially limit eligibility for special education services to infantile autism, learning disabled or physically impaired. Thus special educational support staff are placed in a quandary which may often involve flexing the existing guidelines to meet the needs of the individual student. Support in the school environment is usually necessary for students with AS to be successful. An individualized program that provides opportunity for crisis counseling and support in peer interactions is desirable. Essentially, the school district support systems for AS require a core of knowledgeable and specialized staff. It would be clearly efficient if staff already trained and familiar with autism receive further and ongoing training regarding this aspect of the autistic spectrum. Once recognition increases, more children will be identified and service will improve. Mainstreamed supports can include a variety of options:

- specialized staff for IEP implementation and individual treatment plans

- pragmatic language/social therapy groups

- opportunities for supervised high interest AS activities (chess clubs, computer clubs, art clubs, animal husbandry clubs, etc.)

- alternatives to lunchroom and other unstructured social situations

- individualized programming (this may include a range of options ranging from modified assignments to a reduced program, alternative credit options)

- possibilities for off-campus credit

- the availability of 'safe adults,' possibly the most important component; the safe person is a staff member who is aware of the student's situation and able to support the student in time of crisis.

In general, I have found the following diagnostic questions useful for guiding student assessment and school programming.

STUDENT

1. How is the student's emotional regulation and well-being?

2. What are the student's cognitive processing deficiencies/strengths?

3. How do peers generally respond to the student?

4. Does the student have any friends or close relationships in school?

5. Is academic performance reflective of the student's abilities?

6. What are the students perceptions regarding school?

SCHOOL

1. What high interest activities are available for the student?

2. What crisis supports are available in the school?

3. How valued are the student's abilities and contributions?

4. What can be changed to improve the student's school life?

In terms of accommodations, a case manager(CM) is one of the most important components of high school support. The CM could be an assigned special education support staff or counselor. This role can provide vital support for day-to-day functioning. The CM can also provide facilitate a designated 'cool off' room in times of stress. The use of such supports should be mapped out with the student in advance in the form of a simple, graduated self-management program. A well-structured behavioural contract should be employed which anticipates identified problem areas. This contract or plan should contain clear and concrete expectations regarding teacher and peer respect. Some AS teens are compliant and extremely passive, while others may verbally attack teachers in times of stress in areas of perceived intellectual weakness. Irrespective of the specific nature of behavioural difficulties faced by the AS child, an anxious and rigid inability to cope with interpersonal interactions is the dominant underlying feature.

The goal of school support is aimed at anticipating and reducing emotional duress and thereby increasing possibilities for learning and social engagement. Schools vary considerably in their flexibility and openness to children with social processing needs.

A school that is willing to creatively work with parents toward making school life safe and stimulating for the student is an ideal partner for progress. Integrating school accommodations with the student's individual therapeutic goals should serve to maximize learning and sense of social competence. For example, teaching rule-based behavioural strategies for reading emotions in stressful social situations is one example of a therapeutic goal that can be readily integrated in an individualized student plan.

The discovery of Asperger Syndrome has provided a great opportunity for a renewed understanding of what it means to be a fully functioning being. With proper intervention strategies, psychological and emotional supports, and openness to accept and appreciate individual differences, adolescents affected with Asperger Syndrome stand a much improved chance of living fully productive and happy lives.

References

Asperger, H. (1944) 'Die autischen Psychopathen in Kindesalter.' *Archive für Psychiatrie und Nervenkrankheiten 117*, 76–136.

Attwood, T. (1999) *Asperger's Syndrome: Diagnosis and Support.* London: Jessica Kingsley Publishers.

Bagwell, C.L., Newcomb, A.F. and Bukowski, W.M. (1995) 'Preadolescent friendship and peer rejection as predictors of adult adjustment.' *Child Development 69*, 140–153.

Basch, M.F. (1988) *Understanding Psychotherapy.* New York: Basic Books.

Burleson, B.R. (1985) 'Communication skills and childhood peer relations: an overview.' In M. McLaughlan (ed) *Communication Yearbook*, Vol. 9. London: Sage.

Cumine, V., Leach, J. and Stevenson, G. (1998) *Asperger Syndrome.* London: Fulton.

Erikson, E.H. (1977) *Toys and Reasons.* New York: Norton.

Erikson, M.T. (1998) *Behaviour Disorders of Children and Adolescents.* New Jersey: Prentice-Hall.

Ferrari, M. and Sternberg, R. (1998) 'Personal navigation.' In M. Ferrari and R. Sternberg (eds) *Self Awareness.* New York: Guilford Press.

Frankel, F.D. (2001) 'Common peer relationship problems in childhood.' *Primary Psychiatry 8*, 12, 25–30.

Gedo, J.E. (1991) *The Biology of Clinical Encounters.* New Jersey: Analytic Press.

Grandin, T. (1995) *Thinking in Pictures: And Other Reports on my Life with Autism.* New York: Doubleday.

Hillman, J. (1996) *The Soul's Cade.* New York: Random House.

Holliday Willey, L. (1999) *Pretending to be Normal: Living with Asperger's Syndrome.* London: Jessica Kingsley Publishers.

Howlin, R. (1998) 'Non verbal learning disabilities.' In *Symposium on Psychological Testing.* Ann Arbor: University of Michigan. Unpublished manuscript.

Markova, D. (1992) *How Your Child is Smart.* Berkeley, CA: Conari.

Mead, G.H. (1934) *Mind, Self and Society.* Chicago: University of Chicago Press.

Minuchin, S. (1974) *Families and Family Therapy.* Cambridge, MA: Harvard University Press.

Palombo, J. (2001) *Learning Disorders and Disorders of Self.* New York: Norton.

Rourke, B.P. (1989) *Nonverbal Learning Disabilities.* New York: Guilford Press.

Seagal S. and Horne, D. (1997) *Human Dynamics.* Cambridge, MA: Pegasus.

Tantum, D. (1992) 'Characterizing the fundamental social handicap in autism.' *Acta Paedopsyciatrica 55*, 83–91.

Vygotsky, L. (1986) *Thought and Language.* Cambridge, MA: MIT Press.

Wachtel, P.L. (1993) *Therapeutic Communication.* New York: Guilford Press.

Wexler, D. B. (1991) *The Adolescent Self.* New York: Norton.

Wing, L. (1999) *The Autistic Spectrum.* London: Constable.

Woods, M.M. (1996) *Developmental Therapy.* Austin, TX: Pro-Ed Publications.

2

Cognitive Behaviour Therapy (CBT)

Tony Attwood

The person with Asperger Syndrome has no distinguishing physical features but is primarily viewed by other people as different because of their unusual quality of social interaction, conversation skills and cognitive abilities. One of the unusual aspects of their social abilities is a conspicuous difficulty with the understanding and expression of emotions.

The diagnostic criteria for Asperger Syndrome, as outlined in *DSMIVTR* (American Psychiatric Association 2000) includes in criterion A a description of some of the qualitative impairments in social interaction. The list of characteristics includes impairments in the nonverbal communication of facial expression, body posture and gestures and a lack of social or emotional reciprocity. Clinical experience and autobiographies confirms that such individuals have considerable difficulty with the understanding and expression of emotions. Research studies have also identified a high incidence of comorbid mood disorders and the current theoretical models of Asperger Syndrome provide an explanation of the qualitative impairments. However, while we have increasing knowledge of the distinct profile of social abilities, we are only just beginning to develop effective remedial programs for children and adults with Asperger Syndrome to improve their understanding of emotional states and to modify psychological treatments to accommodate their unusual profile of cognitive abilities.

When one considers the diagnostic criteria for Asperger Syndrome and the effects of the disorder on the person's adaptive functioning in a social context, one would expect such individuals to be vulnerable to the development of secondary mood disorders. The current research indicates that around 65 per cent of adolescent's with Asperger Syndrome have an affective disorder that includes anxiety disorders (Kim *et al.* 2000; Ghaziuddin, Weider-Mikhail and Ghaziuddin 1998; Gillot, Furniss and Walter 2001; Green *et al.* 2000; Tantam 2000; Tonge *et al.* 1999) and depression (Green *et al.* 2000). There is also evidence to suggest an association with delusional disorders (Kurita 1999), paranoia (Blackshaw *et al.* 2001) and conduct disorders (Tantam 2000). We know that co-morbid affective disorders in adolescents with Asperger Syndrome are the rule rather than the exception, but why should this population be more prone to affective disorders?

Research has been conducted on the family histories of children with autism and Asperger Syndrome and identified a higher than expected incidence of mood disorders (Bolton *et al.* 1998; De Long 1994; DeLong and Dwyer 1988; Ghaziuddin and Greden 1998; Lainhart and Folstein 1994; Piven and Palmer 1999). Individuals with Asperger Syndrome could be vulnerable to a genetic predisposition to mood disorders. However, when one also considers their difficulties with regard to social reasoning, empathy, verbal communication, profile of cognitive skills and sensory perception, they are clearly prone to considerable stress as a result of their attempts at social inclusion. Chronic levels of stress can precipitate a mood disorder. Thus there may be constitutional and circumstantial factors that explain the higher incidence of affective disorders.

The theoretical models of autism developed within cognitive psychology and research in neuro-psychology also provide some explanation as to why such individuals are prone to secondary mood disorders. The extensive research on Theory of Mind skills confirms that individuals with Asperger Syndrome have considerable difficulty identifying and conceptualizing the thoughts and feelings of other people and themselves (Baron-Cohen and Jolliffe 1997; Baron-Cohen *et al.* 1999a, Heavey *et al.* 2000; Kleinman, Marciano and Ault 2001; Muris *et al.* 1999). The interpersonal and inner world of emotions appears to be uncharted territory for people with Asperger Syndrome.

Research on Executive Function in subjects with Asperger Syndrome suggests characteristics of being disinhibited and impulsive with a relative lack of insight that affects general functioning (Eisenmajer *et al.* 1996; Nyden *et al.* 1999; Ozonoff, South and Miller

2000; Pennington and Ozonoff 1996). Impaired Executive Function can also affect the cognitive control of emotions. Clinical experience indicates there is a tendency to react to emotional cues without cognitive reflection. Research using new neuro-imaging technology has also identified structural and functional abnormalities of the amygdala of subjects with autism (Adolphs, Sears and Piven 2001; Baron-Cohen *et al.* 1999b, 2000; Critchley *et al.* 2000; Fine, Lumsden and Blair, 2001). The amygdala is known to regulate a range of emotions, including anger, fear and sadness. Thus we also have neuro-anatomical evidence that suggests there will be problems with the perception and regulation of the emotions.

Modifications to conventional psychotherapy

When clinicians diagnose a secondary mood disorder, they need to know how to modify standard psychological treatments in order to ac-commodate the unusual cognitive profile of people with Asperger Syndrome. As the primary psychological treatment for mood disorders is Cognitive Behaviour Therapy (CBT), this chapter examines such modifications based on our knowledge of the disorder and preliminary clinical experience.

CBT has been designed and refined over several decades and proven to be effective in changing the way a person thinks about and responds to feelings such as anxiety, sadness and anger (Graham 1998; Kendall 2000). CBT focuses on aspects of cognitive deficiency in terms of the maturity, complexity and efficacy of thinking and cognitive distortion in terms of dysfunctional thinking and incorrect assumptions. Thus it has direct applicability to clients with Asperger Syndrome who are known to have deficits and distortions in thinking.

The therapy has several components, the first being an assessment of the nature and degree of mood disorder using self-report scales and a clinical interview. The subsequent stage is affective education with dis-cussion and exercises on the connection between cognition, affect and behaviour and the way in which individuals conceptualize emotions and construe various situations. Subsequent stages are cognitive restruc-turing, stress management, self-reflection and a schedule of activities to practise new cognitive skills. Cognitive restructuring corrects distorted conceptualizations and dysfunctional beliefs. The person is encouraged to establish and examine the evidence for or against their thoughts and build a new perception of specific events. Stress management and cue-controlled relaxation programs are used to promote responses incompatible with anxiety or anger. Self-reflection activities help the person to recognize their internal state, to monitor and reflect on their thoughts and construct a new self-image. A graded schedule of activities is also developed to allow the person to practise new abilities, which are monitored by the therapist.

Assessment of the nature and degree of the mood disorder

The initial component of CBT is an assessment of:

- the nature and degree of the mood disorder
- the cognitive abilities of the client
- evaluation of their circumstances.

There are several self-rating scales that have been designed for children and adults with specific mood disorders that can be administered to clients with Asperger Syndrome. However, there are specific modifications that can be used with this clinical group, as they may be more able to accurately quantify their response using a numerical or pictorial representation of the gradation in experience and expression of mood. Examples include an emotion 'thermometer', bar graphs or a 'volume' scale. These analogue measures are used to establish a baseline assessment as well as being incorporated in the affective education component. To minimize word retrieval problems, multiple choice questions can be used in preference to open-ended sentence completion tasks. A pictorial dictionary of feelings can also be used as additional cues for a diary or logbook completed during the therapy by the client.

The assessment includes the construction of a list of behavioural indicators of mood changes. The indicators can include changes in the characteristics associated with Asperger Syndrome such as an increase in time spent engaged in solitude or their special interest, rigidity or incoherence in their thought processes, or behaviour intended to impose control in their daily lives and over others. This is in addition to conventional indicators such as a panic attack, comments indicating low self-worth and episodes of anger. It is essential to collect information from a wide variety of sources as children and adults with Asperger Syndrome can display quite different characteristics according to their circumstances. For example, there may be little evidence of a mood disorder at school but clear evidence at home. Parents and teachers can complete a daily mood diary to determine whether there is any cyclical nature to or specific triggers for mood changes.

The clinician will also need to assess their vocabulary of emotional expression and coping mechanisms. While there are no standardized tests to measure such abilities, some characteristics have been identified by clinical experience. For example, discussion with parents can indicate that the child displays affection but the depth and range of expression is usually limited and immature for their chronological age. Their reaction to pleasure and pain can be atypical, with idiosyncratic mannerisms that express feeling excited such as hand flapping and a stoic response to pain and punishments. Examples of characteristics that parents may be concerned about are a lack of apparent gratitude and remorse and para-   ⨯ doxical and atypical responses to particular situations. For example, the child may giggle when expected to show remorse (Berthier 1995) and be remarkably quick in resolving grief. They may also misinterpret gestures of affection such as a hug with the comment that the squeeze was perceived as uncomfortable and not comforting. Their emotional reactions can also be delayed, perhaps with an expression of anger some days or weeks after the event.

The impaired comprehension of the signals that indicate emotional states can include the perception and recognition changes in facial expression, tone of voice, body language and context. There can also be an impaired perception and recognition of their own internal and behavioural cues. Clinical experience indicates that they appear to be less aware of their mood state and of early warning signals of increasing emotional arousal. The impaired expression can include a lack of subtlety and paucity in the range of expressions. Parents have described how the child can have an emotional on/off switch set at maximum volume.

Their coping or emotional recovery mechanisms need to be assessed and can include characteristics such as retreating into solitude, increasing time spent engaged in a special interest, reading fantasy literature and computer games. Some individuals internalize their reaction with self-blame and low self-esteem while others externalize their reaction and may be critical of others and develop an arrogant and intolerant per- ⨯ sonality. The former may show signs of depression and anxiety while the latter are often referred for problems with anger management. However, different emotions can prevail at particular times of the day, for example being anxious before school and angry when returning home. It is also valuable to assess not only how the children repair their own feelings but also how they repair the feelings of others. Research suggests that subjects with Asperger Syndrome use fewer of the available cues in facial expression, body language, etc. to infer emotional states (Koning and Magill-Evans 2001). The clinician needs to assess the client's ability to identify the cues of emotional states in others and to know when specific words and actions are anticipated; for example, providing gestures and words of affection when a family member or friend is sad or reassurance when they are anxious. Questions can be asked such as 'How would you know when your mother is feeling sad?' and 'What would you do if she were crying?' Another area of assessment is their awareness of the impact of their own mood state and associated behaviour on the thoughts and feelings of others, namely an assessment of empathy. Unfortunately we do not have any standardized tests to measure empathy so the majority of information is obtained from discussion with the person with Asperger Syndrome and their family for examples of a relative lack of empathic response.

An assessment is also conducted of the client's cognitive abilities using standardized intelligence scales to determine their level of intellectual reasoning and profile of cognitive abilities. Some individuals with high functioning autism and Asperger Syndrome have asymmetrical abilities with regard to verbal and visual reasoning and this can be valuable information in determining whether the client's comprehension is enhanced by strategies emphasizing verbal skills such as discussion and reading or visual skills such as drawing and role play. At present we do not have a range of standardized tests to measure social reasoning skills or the understanding and expression of emotions, but the research literature includes tests that can be incorporated in the client's initial assessment. Examples are tests of advanced Theory of Mind skills, the conceptualization of friendship (Rubin 2002) and ability to read the facial cues of particular feeling states.

Other important areas to assess are the circumstances and triggers that influence or precipitate mood states such as:

- the person's ability to cope with change and surprises

- the number of people in a situation
- sensory perception such as acute sensitivity to specific sounds, noise level, tactile experiences, aromas and temperature   ✗
- unfamiliar situations
- the ability to cope with mistakes
- the comprehension and expression of emotions
- experiencing humiliation, social rejection, teasing and bullying
- a perceived sense of injustice.

Medical factors can be important such as the child's response to illness and pain and whether conditions such as seizure disorders and diabetes are relevant. It is also important to know the parents' and child's attitude to taking medication. Some young adults with Asperger Syndrome are concerned about the sedative effects of their medication, which can affect compliance. One client said, 'It was as though I was locked out of my own home'. Finally, an assessment is made of whether key people in their life understand and accommodate their profile of abilities and whether their mood is modeled upon or reinforced by certain individuals.

Affective education

Affective education is the next stage in a course of Cognitive Behaviour Therapy and an essential component for those with Asperger Syndrome. The main goal is to learn why we have emotions, their use and misuse and the identification of different levels of expression. A basic principle is to explore one emotion at a time as a theme for a project. The choice of which emotion to start with is decided by the therapist, but a useful starting point is happiness or pleasure. A scrapbook can be created that illustrates the emotion. For young children this can include pictures of people expressing the different degrees of happiness or pleasure but can be extended to pictures of objects and situations that have a personal association with the feeling, for example, a photograph of a rare lizard for a person with a special interest in reptiles. For adults the book can illustrate the pleasures in their life, with a list based on the song 'My favorite things.' The content can also include the sensations associated with the feeling such as aromas, tastes and textures. The scrapbook can be used as a diary to include compliments, records of achievement such as a certificate and memorabilia. At a later stage in therapy the scrapbook can be used to change a particular mood, but it can also be used to illustrate different perceptions of a situation.

If the therapy is conducted in a group, the books can be compared and contrasted. Talking about trains may be an enjoyable experience for one participant but perceived as remarkably boring or dominating for another. Part of the education is to explain that while this topic may create a feeling of well-being in the one participant, their attempt to cheer up another person by talking about trains may not be a successful strategy, perhaps producing a response that they did not expect. One of the interesting aspects that the author has noticed is that clients with Asperger Syndrome tend to achieve enjoyment primarily from knowledge, interests and solitary pursuits and less from social experiences in comparison to other client groups. They are often at their happiest when alone.

The affective education stage includes the therapist describing and the client discovering the salient cues that indicate a particular level of emotional expression in facial expression, tone of voice, body language and context. The face is described as an information centre for emotions. The typical errors include not identifying which cues are relevant or redundant, and misinterpreting cues. The therapist uses a range of games and resources to 'spot the message' and explain the multiple meanings, for example, a furrowed brow can mean anger or bewilderment, or may be a sign of aging skin. A loud voice does not automatically mean that a person is angry.

The author has noted that when young clients with Asperger Syndrome are asked to express a particular emotion using facial expression, they sometimes only express one facial element, for example the mouth shape when sad, or changing the position of their eyebrows to express being angry. This appears to indicate that they only look at one element when examining the face of another person to determine their mood. Activities are undertaken comparing the range and pattern of facial elements in the expression of a specific emotion in pictures and noting the pattern of the eyes and mouth. Other educational activities include listening to audiotapes of someone's speech and noting the changes in prosody and emphasis that identify mood. Another activity is for the same sentence to be repeated using a different tone of voice to indicate the person's mood. An activity to identify the 'hidden message' in speech is to explain how the change in emphasis or tone can indicate mood state, for example 'Come here', whispered, shouted, accompanied with a sigh or said quickly has very different meanings (Pyles 2001). Tuition in gestural communication can be provided using a modified version of the game Charades that requires both the expression and comprehension of actions, e.g. playing tennis, and also the expression of the mood of the person performing the mime.

Another activity is to watch a video of a drama and comedy program with the volume control set at mute and using the actors' body language to determine their emotions. The pause and replay buttons can be used while the significant gestures and facial expressions are identified. Activities used in drama classes can be modified to provide tuition in posture and voice. The client can also be encouraged to acquire and practice a new 'role,' perhaps based on a fictional character or someone they know who is clearly consistent in expressing and managing their emotions. There are also a number of publications that are written for the general public which explain how to read body language.

Once the key elements that indicate a particular emotion have been identified, it is important to use an 'instrument' to measure the degree of intensity. The therapist can construct a model 'thermometer', 'gauge', or volume control and use a range of activities to define the level of expression; for example, using a selection of pictures of happy faces and placing each picture at the appropriate point on the instrument. During the therapy it is important to ensure the client shares the same definition or interpretation of words and gestures and to clarify any semantic confusion. Clinical experience has indicated that some clients with Asperger Syndrome can use extreme statements such as 'I am going to kill myself' to express a level of emotion that would be more moderately expressed by another client. During a program of affective education the therapist often has to increase the client's vocabulary of emotional expression to ensure precision and accuracy.

The education program includes activities to detect specific degrees of emotion in others but also in oneself using internal physiological cues, cognitive cues and behaviour. Technology can be used to identify internal cues in the form of biofeedback instruments such as auditory

EMG and GSR machines. The client and those who know them well can create a list of their physiological, cognitive and behavioural cues that indicate their increase in emotional arousal. The degree of expression can be measured using one of the program's special instruments such as the emotion thermometer. One of the aspects of the therapy is to help the client perceive their 'early warning signals' that indicate emotional arousal which may need cognitive control. A metaphor can be the warning lights and instruments on a car dashboard.

Once the concept of a measuring instrument is established, it can also be used to determine the client's perception of the degree of emotional response in particular situations. When exploring the dimension of happiness or pleasure, questions can be asked such as 'How happy would you feel if...?' requiring both a numerical rating on the 'instrument' and the associated words, facial expression, tone of voice and body language that represent the degree of expression. This activity is particularly useful to determine the client's emotional response to specific situations that elicit anxiety, sadness or anger. This activity initially explores how the words and actions of others affect the feelings of the client. However, people with Asperger Syndrome have considerable difficulty recognizing how their own words and actions affect the feelings of others, a consequence of impaired theory of mind and empathy skills. Questions can be asked such as 'How happy would your mother feel if you said that you love her?' Or 'How sad does she feel when you say...?' This can be quite an important discovery for both parties.

When a particular emotion and the levels of expression are understood, the next component of affective education is to use the same procedures for a contrasting emotion. After exploring happiness, the next topic explored would be sadness. Feeling relaxed would be explored before a project on feeling anxious. The next stage of Cognitive Behaviour Therapy is cognitive restructuring. This includes knowing which thoughts or emotions are an 'antidote' to a feeling, for example, which strategies or activities associated with feeling happy that could be used to counteract feeling sad.

When exploring positive emotions such as happiness and affection, clinical experience suggests that some clients with Asperger Syndrome have difficulty coping with and responding to moderate levels of expression of these feelings in other people. When family members express physical signs of delight or affection and consolation, the client can report feeling uncomfortable and not know how to respond. They may need guidance in the appropriate response and in how to inform others of their discomfort. In particular, affection from others may not be as effective a means of emotional repair or recovery as one would expect. If the person is generally confused about why other people express affection physically and unsure how to show affection themselves, they can develop a fear of what they do not understand.

When exploring negative emotions such as anxiety and anger, conventional activities to explain the concept of fight or flight are included in the affective education program. The client discovers how such emotions affect their bodies and thinking, such as increasing heart rate, changes in biochemistry, perspiration, muscle tone and perception and problem-solving ability. Over many thousands of years, these changes have been an advantage in threatening situations. However, in our modern society we can have the same intensity of fight or flight reaction to what we imagine or misperceive as a threat. An aphorism is 'Being angry is OK, the problem is what we do or say.' It is also important to explain that when we are emotional we can be less logical and rational and this affects our problem-solving abilities and decision making. To be calm and 'cool' will help the client in both interpersonal and practical situations.

Some individuals with Asperger Syndrome can have considerable difficulty translating their feelings into conversational words. There can be a greater eloquence, insight and accuracy using other forms of expression. The therapist can use prose in the form of a 'conversation' by typing questions and answers on a computer screen or techniques such as Comic Strip Conversations which uses figures with speech and thought bubbles (Gray 1996, 1998). When designing activities to consolidate the new knowledge on emotions, one can use a diary, e-mail, art or music as means of emotional expression that provides a greater degree of insight for both client and therapist.

Other activities to be considered in affective education are the creation of a photograph album that includes pictures of the client and family members expressing particular emotions, or video recordings of the client expressing their feelings in real-life situations. This can be particularly valuable to demonstrate their behaviour when expressing anger. Another activity entitled 'Guess the Message' can include the presentation of specific cues such as a cough as a warning sign or a raised eyebrow to indicate doubt. It is also important to incorporate the person's special interest in the program. For example, the author has worked with individuals whose special interest has been the weather and has suggested that their emotions are expressed as a weather report. There are several children's reading books that have a particular emotion as a theme and self-help books for adolescents with specific mood disorders that can be used as a form of bibliotherapy. We also now have books and computer programs that provide a social and emotional curriculum which includes activities for affective education for children with Asperger Syndrome (McAfee 2002; Moyes 2001; Silver and Oakes 2001).

When considering therapy programs for clients with Asperger Syndrome, one also needs to consider education in social reasoning skills. This involves tuition in the codes of social conduct, conflict resolution and friendship skills. The anticipation and experience of breaking the social codes can be one of the causes of their anxiety, depression and anger. Social Stories, developed by Carol Gray specifically for this clinical population, provides tuition in the rationale for social codes, the cues that indicate a specific social rule and the rationale and script for what to do (1996, 1998). However it is important that the text and style of the Social Story is appropriate for an adolescent or young adult; for example, they can be written in the style of an article in a teenage magazine. As many clients with this diagnosis are relatively less proficient with Theory of Mind skills, they fail to recognize the perspective, beliefs and thoughts of the other person, which results in a propensity for disagreement and conflict. They may need a program to specifically teach Theory of Mind skills (Howlin, Baron-Cohen and Hadwin 1999). They are also often less skilled in the art of compromise and use of strategies to repair the conversation or interaction. Such situations can be the trigger for inappropriate emotional responses, particularly anger. Instruction may be required in conflict resolution.

As one of the causes of depression in people with Asperger Syndrome is the strong desire to have friends, while recognizing their considerable difficulties with achieving and maintaining genuine friendships, education programs can be used that assist the client to improve their abilities in this area. The programs are based on conventional activities designed for ordinary children and adults with adaptations to incorporate the client's level of social maturity. Finally, the education component of CBT includes informing significant individuals in the client's life about the nature of Asperger Syndrome and how it affects their recognition and management of emotions. This knowledge can lead to a change in their attitude towards the client and subsequent changes in expectations and circumstances that has a beneficial effect on their mood.

Cognitive restructuring

Cognitive restructuring enables the client to correct distorted conceptualizations and dysfunctional beliefs. The process involves challenging their current thinking with logical evidence and ensuring the rationalization and cognitive control of their emotions. The first stage is to establish the evidence for a particular belief. People with Asperger Syndrome can make false assumptions of their circumstances and the intentions of others. They have a tendency to make a literal interpretation, and a casual comment may be taken out of context or to the extreme. For example, a young teenage boy with Asperger Syndrome was once told his voice was breaking. He became extremely anxious that his voice was becoming faulty and decided to consciously alter the pitch of his voice to repair it. The result was an artificial falsetto voice, which was quite incongruous in a young man. A teenage girl with Asperger Syndrome overheard a conversation at school that implied that a girl must be slim to be popular. She then achieved a dramatic weight loss in an attempt to be accepted by her peers. We are all vulnerable to distorted conceptualizations, but people with Asperger Syndrome are less able to put things in perspective, seek clarification and to consider alternative explanations or responses. The therapist encourages the client to be more flexible in their thinking and to seek clarification using questions or comments such as 'Are you joking? or 'I'm confused about what you just said'. Such comments can also be used when misinterpreting someone's intentions such as 'Did you do that deliberately?' and to rescue the situation after the client has made an inappropriate response with a comment such as 'I'm sorry I offended you' or 'Oh dear, what should I have done?'

To explain a new perspective or to correct errors or assumptions, Comic Strip Conversations can help the client determine the thoughts, beliefs, knowledge and intentions of the participants in a given situation (Gray 1996, 1998). This technique involves drawing an event or sequence of events in storyboard form with stick figures to represent each participant and speech and thought bubbles to represent their words and thoughts. The client and therapist use an assortment of fibro-tipped colored pens, with each color representing an emotion. As they write in the speech or thought bubbles, the person's choice of color indicates their perception of the emotion conveyed or intended. This can clarify the client's interpretation of events and the rationale for their thoughts and response. This technique can help the client to identify and correct any misperception and to determine how alternative responses will affect the participants' thoughts and feelings.

One common effect of misinterpretation is the development of paranoia. Our knowledge of impaired Theory of Mind skills in the cognitive profile of children with Asperger Syndrome suggests a simple explanation. The child can have difficulty distinguishing between accidental or deliberate intent. Other children will know from the context, body language and character of the person involved that the intent was not to cause distress or injury. However, individuals with Asperger Syndrome can focus primarily on the act and the consequences – 'He hit me and it hurt so it was deliberate' – while other children would consider the circumstances, 'He was running, tripped and accidentally knocked my arm.' There may need to be training in checking the evidence before responding and developing more accurate 'mind reading' skills.

Cognitive Restructuring also includes a process known as 'attribution retraining'. The client may exclusively blame others and not consider their own contribution or they can excessively blame themselves for events. One aspect of Asperger Syndrome is a tendency for some clients to adopt an attitude of arrogance or omnipotence where the perceived focus of control is external. Specific individuals are held responsible and become the target for retribution or punishment. These clients have considerable difficulty in accepting that they themselves have contributed to the event. However, the opposite can occur when the client has extremely low self-esteem and feels personally responsible, which results in feelings of anxiety and guilt. There can also be a strong sense of what is right and wrong and conspicuous reaction if others violate the social 'laws' (Church, Alisanski and Amanullah 2000).

The child may be notorious as the class 'policeman', dispensing justice but not realizing what is within their authority. Attribution retraining involves establishing the reality of the situation, the various participants' contribution to an incident and determining how the client can change their perception and persona.

The client with Asperger Syndrome may have a limited repertoire of responses to situations that elicit specific emotions. The therapist and client create a list of appropriate and inappropriate responses and the consequences of each option. Various options can be drawn as a flow diagram that enables the client to determine the most appropriate response in the long term. Another part of cognitive restructuring is to actually challenge certain beliefs with facts and logic. Information can be provided that establishes that the statistical risk of a particular event is highly unlikely and not necessarily fatal, for example, being struck by lightning.

Another technique is to use the client's special interest as a metaphor to help conceptualize the treatment program and to generate new strategies. For example, a client had a special interest in the science fiction character, Dr Who. A scenario was constructed where the client imagined they were Dr Who stranded on a planet where there was an invisible monster that created and fed upon people's anxiety. The therapist was considered as a scientist who had studied this monster. The two experts were then able to devise a way for the hero to escape.

Cognitive restructuring also includes activities that are designed to improve the client's range of emotional repair mechanisms. The author has extended the use of metaphor to design programs that include the concept of an emotional toolbox to 'fix the feeling'. Clients know that a toolbox usually includes a variety of tools to repair a machine and discussion and activities are employed to identify different types of 'tool' for specific problems associated with emotions.

One type of emotional repair tool can be represented by a hammer that signifies physical 'tools' such as going for a walk or run, bouncing on a trampoline or crushing empty cans for recycling. The intention is to repair emotions constructively by a safe physical act that increases the heart rate. One client explained how a game of tennis 'takes the fight out of me'. A paintbrush can be used to represent relaxation 'tools' that lower the heart rate such as drawing, reading or listening to calming music. A two-handle saw can be used to represent social activities or individuals who can help repair feelings. This can include communication with someone who is known to be empathic and able to dispel negative feelings. This can be by spoken conversation or typed communication, enabling the client to gain a new perspective on the problem and providing some practical advice. A picture of a manual can be used to represent 'thinking' tools that are designed to improve cognitive processes. This includes phrases that encourage reflection before reaction.

Evan, a young man with Asperger Syndrome, developed his 'antidote to poisonous thoughts'. The procedure is to provide a comment that counteracts negative thoughts, for example, 'I can't cope' (negative or poisonous thought) 'but I can fix it with help' (positive thought or antidote). The client is also taught that becoming emotional can inhibit their intellectual abilities in a particular situation which requires good problem-solving skills. When frustrated, one needs to become 'cool' and less rigid in one's thinking in order to solve the problem, especially if the solution requires social cognition.

There is a discussion of inappropriate tools (with the comment that one would not use a hammer to fix a computer) in order to explain how some actions such as violence and thoughts such as suicide are not appropriate emotional repair mechanisms. For example, one client would slap himself to stop negative thoughts and feelings. Another tool that could become inappropriate is the retreat into a fantasy world (perhaps imagining they are a super hero), or to plan retaliation. The use of escape into fantasy literature and games can be a typical tool for ordinary adolescents but is of concern when this becomes the exclusive coping mechanism; the border between fantasy and reality may be unclear and the thinking becomes delusional. Cognitive restructuring can be used to return to concrete thinking. Also of concern is when daydreams of retaliation to teasing and bullying are expressed in drawings, writing and threats. While this is a conventional means of emotional expression, there is a concern that the expression is misinterpreted as an intention to carry out the fantasy or indeed a precursor to retaliation using weapons. Unusual tools are also discussed. For example, during a group CBT session on sadness, a teenage girl explained that 'crying doesn't work for me, so I get angry'. Clinical experience suggests that tears may be rare as a response to feeling sad and a common response to sadness is anger. The program includes the development of a range of conventional means of emotional expression and repair mechanisms and an explanation as to why some of their reactions are misinterpreted by others.

Clinical experience with the concept of an emotional toolbox has provided some interesting comparisons between clients with Asperger Syndrome and their peers. Other children use a wider range of tools, the most popular and effective being social tools. Clients without Asperger Syndrome often need to be encouraged to consider and use other people, especially parents and specific friends to repair their mood. Unfortunately individuals with Asperger Syndrome are more likely to be confused by gestures and words of affection and often choose solitude to repair their mood.

Physical acts are often the first 'tool' to be employed, to quickly and effectively 'discharge' the emotion. Emotion management is achieved by actions rather than reflection and relaxation. In the diagnostic assessment, the author asks children what they would do if they walked into the kitchen and saw that their mother was crying. While other children would almost immediately use words or gestures of affection to repair her feelings, the comments of those with Asperger Syndrome are more practical acts and deeds than compassionate words and gestures. Suggestions include making her a cup of tea, giving her a tissue for her tears and helping with the chores. This indicates that a more effective repair mechanism for their own mood is a physical or practical act. Indeed, many parents have indicated that the expression of love is not as effective a repair mechanism as with their other children and can sometimes be counter-productive. One teenager said, 'I get angry when someone tries to cheer me up'.

Their preferred 'toolbox' can include their special interest as an effective relaxant. The clinical problem arises when the pleasurable interest is virtually the only repair tool and becomes an irresistible activity when they are severely anxious, such that the interest becomes part of an obsessive-compulsive disorder. If access is denied, the reaction can be panic or anger.

Clinical experience has also indicated that humor and imagination can be used as 'thinking tools'. Those with Asperger Syndrome are not immune to the benefits of laughter and can enjoy jokes typical of their developmental level and be remarkably creative with puns and jokes (Werth, Perkins and Boucher 2001). One 'tool' or mechanism that appears to be unusual is that of being quick at resolving grief and serious tragedies. This characteristic can be of concern to the person's family who expect the classic signs of prolonged and intense grieving. They consider the person as uncaring, yet the rapid recovery is simply a feature of Asperger Syndrome. Other interesting characteristics are the inclusion of talking to pets as a 'social tool', sometimes in preference to talking to friends, and the positive effects on mood by helping someone. This strategy can be effective for clients with Asperger Syndrome who also need to be needed and can improve their mood by being of practical assistance. Finally, the concept of a toolbox can be extremely helpful in enabling the person with Asperger Syndrome to not only repair their own feelings, but also to repair the feelings of others. They often benefit from guidance in learning what tools to use to help friends and family and which tools are used by others, so that they may 'borrow' tools to add to their own emotional repair kit.

Stress management

Individuals with Asperger Syndrome will be prone to greater stress in their daily lives than their peers. Social interaction, especially with more than one person, where they have to identify, translate and respond to social and emotional cues, and cope with unexpected noise levels, inevitably increases stress to a point where the person's coping mechanisms collapse. A stress assessment based on our knowledge of Asperger Syndrome will help the clinician determine what are the natural and idiosyncratic stressors for the client (Groden *et al.* 2001). An effective stress management program is an essential component of Cognitive Behaviour Therapy as increasing stress can be explanation or trigger for mood disturbance.

A major cause of stress for adolescents with Asperger Syndrome is the satisfactory completion of homework. Why would this group of children have such an emotional reaction to the mere thought of having to start their homework, and such difficulty completing assigned tasks? There may be two explanations. The first is based on their degree of mental exhaustion during their day at school and the second is due to their profile of cognitive skills.

A child with Asperger Syndrome has to learn, in addition to the traditional educational curriculum, the social curriculum, which may be a source of stress. They have to use their intellectual reasoning to determine the social rules of the classroom and the playground. Other children do not have to consciously learn social integration skills, but these children have to decipher the social cues and codes of conduct and cognitively rather than intuitively determine what to do and say in social situations. Recess is an enjoyable and relaxing time for their peers as it is an opportunity for unstructured and unsupervised social interactions. For the same reasons, it is a stressful time for the child with Asperger Syndrome. Another particularly stressful time is the journey to and from school and measures may need to be taken to ensure they are safe from being tormented or bullied when in unavoidable proximity to their peers with limited adult supervision. Thus they have few opportunities during the long school day to relax and often return home exhausted and irritable, to the distress of parents and siblings. The author has discussed the issue of school and stress with adolescents with Asperger Syndrome and the general consensus is that they want a clear division between home and school. Their comments can be summarized as: 'School is for learning, home is for fun or relaxation.' The prospect of interrupting their much needed and deserved fun and relaxation with homework is more than they can cope with.

Their unusual profile of cognitive skills must also be recognized and accommodated when they are undertaking academic work at school and home. One aspect of the profile is impaired Executive Function. The profile is similar to that of children with Attention Deficit disorder in that they can have difficulty planning, organizing and prioritizing, a tendency to be impulsive and inflexible when problem solving and poor working memory. Other features include a difficulty generating new ideas, a need for supervision and guidance, determining what is relevant and redundant, as well as poor time perception and time management. Thus they are notorious for not completing their schoolwork and homework within the time expected. Academic tasks can be a significant source of stress unless teachers accommodate the child's impaired executive functioning and need for emotional restoration after school.

Traditional relaxation procedures using activities to encourage muscle relaxation and breathing exercises can be taught to clients with Asperger Syndrome as a counter-conditioning procedure, but one must also consider the circumstances in which they are particularly prone to stress. Environmental modification can significantly reduce stress. This can include reducing noise levels, having a safe area for periods of solitude to relax or concentrate on schoolwork and minimizing distractions. If the clinician recognizes that a particular event is a major cause of stress then it would be wise to consider whether the source of stress could be avoided, for example, recommending the temporary suspension of homework. At school, one option for the child who becomes stressed in the playground is to be able to withdraw to the school library or for the worker who is anxious about socializing during the lunch break to complete a crossword puzzle or go for a walk. Another source of stress for children and adults is unexpected changes in work demands or circumstances. They may need advance preparation and time to adjust their work schedule.

Cue-controlled relaxation is also a useful component of a stress management plan. One strategy is for the client to have an object in their pocket that symbolizes or has been classically conditioned to elicit feelings of relaxation. For example, a teenage girl with Asperger Syndrome was an avid reader of fiction, her favorite book being *The Secret Garden*. She kept a key in her pocket to metaphorically open the door to the secret garden, an imaginary world where she felt relaxed and happy. A few moments touching or looking at the key helped her to contemplate a scene described in the book and to relax and achieve a more positive state of mind. Adults can have a special picture in their wallet such as a photograph of a woodland scene to remind them of the solitude and tranquility of nature.

Self-reflection

In conventional Cognitive Behaviour Therapy programs, the client is encouraged to self-reflect to improve insight into their thoughts and feelings, promoting a realistic and positive self-image as well as enhancing the ability to self-talk for greater self-control. However, the concept of self-consciousness may be different for individuals with Asperger Syndrome. Frith and Happe (1999) have extended our conceptualization of impaired Theory of Mind and Autism to suggest there may be a qualitative impairment in the ability to engage in introspection. Research evidence, autobiographies and clinical experience have confirmed that some clients with Asperger Syndrome and high functioning autism can lack an 'inner voice' and think in pictures rather than words. (Grandin 1995; Hurlburt, Happé and Frith 1994). They also have difficulty translating their visual thoughts into words. As an adolescent with Asperger Syndrome explained in relation to how visualization improves his learning (a picture is worth a thousand words) 'I have the picture in my mind but not the thousand words to describe it.' Some have an 'inner voice' but have difficulty disengaging mind and mouth and vocalize their thoughts to the confusion or annoyance of those near them. Obviously, the therapy needs to accommodate such unusual characteristics.

The modifications include a greater application of visual material and resources using drawings, role play and metaphor and less reliance on spoken responses. It is interesting that many clients have a greater ability to develop and explain their thoughts and emotions using other expressive media, especially typed communication in the form of an e-mail or diary as well as music and art and a pictorial dictionary of feelings (Attwood 1998).

An interesting study by Lee and Hobson (1998) indicates that, when talking about themselves, young adults with autism and Asperger Syndrome do not anchor their self-attributes in social activities and relationships or employ as wide a range of emotions in their descriptions as their peers. They are less likely to describe themselves in the context of their relationships and interactions with other people. The self-reflection component of CBT may have to be modified to accommodate a concept of self primarily in terms of physical, intellectual and psychological attributes.

One of the contributory factors to mood disorders is the person's self-image and self-esteem. Those with Asperger Syndrome can be vulnerable to distortions of self-image in terms of severe self-doubt and criticism which can be associated with depression and anxiety or the opposite, arrogance and omnipotence that can be associated with problems with anger management. When the author asks adults with Asperger Syndrome when they first recognized they were different from their peers, many reply that they felt different when they first started school. Their subsequent reactions were either to develop extremely low self-esteem and become anxious when with their peers and worried that they would not know what to do in social play; or alternatively to develop compensatory mechanisms that implied they did not make social errors and were smarter than their peers who were stupid and illogical. The options are to internalize with self-blame or externalize with grandiose delusions.

The therapy includes programs adjusting the client's self-image to be an accurate reflection of their abilities and the neurological origins of their disorder. Some time needs to be allocated to explaining the nature of Asperger Syndrome and how the characteristics account for their differences. The author recommends that as soon as the child or adult has the diagnosis of Asperger Syndrome, the clinician needs to carefully and authoritatively explain the nature of the disorder to the family but the child must also receive a personal explanation. This is to reduce the likelihood of inappropriate compensatory mechanisms to their recognition of being different and concern as to why they have to see psychologists and psychiatrists. They may also be concerned as to why they have to take medication and receive tuition at school that is not given to their peers. Over the last few years, there have been several publications and programs developed specifically to introduce the child or adolescent to their diagnosis. The choice of which book or program to use is determined by the clinician, but it is important that the descriptions are accurate and positive. The client will perceive the diagnosis as it is presented. If the approach is pessimistic, the reaction can be to trigger a depression or to reject the diagnosis and treatment. The clinician can also recommend the client read some of the new autobiographies written by children (Hall 2001), adolescents (Jackson 2002) and adults (Holliday Willey 2001; Lawson 2000) and refer to renowned individuals such as Thomas Jefferson (Ledgin 1998) or Einstein and Wittgenstein who may have had the characteristics associated with Asperger Syndrome. The subsequent discussion is whether and how to tell other people of the diagnosis, especially extended family, neighbors, friends and colleagues. Chapter 12 by Stephen Shore provides further information on this topic.

When an accurate perception of self has been achieved, it is possible to explore cognitive mechanisms to accommodate their unusual profile of abilities, which the author describes as their talents and vulnerabilities, and to consider the directions for change in self-image. One approach is using the metaphor of a road map with alternative directions and destinations developed for children by Tammie Ronen (1997). A Personal Construct Assessment uses logical and visual techniques and can be particularly effective with adults with Asperger Syndrome (Hare, Jones and Paine 1999). Personal Construct Theory was developed by George Kelly who considered individuals as 'scientists' in the way they interact with the world. His study of mathematics led him to design a method of assessment called a repertory grid.

Other strategies that can be used in the self-reflection component of Cognitive Behaviour Therapy are encouraging the client to be more perceptive at a conscious level of their internal mood signals, and training in the use of mental self-talk to remain in cognitive control of the emotion. The Affective Education component will have included activities to identify and measure the internal signals such as breathing, heart rate and specific thoughts and external signals such as body language and actions. The client can use their recognition of their body's signals as an early warning system, use their intellectual 'strength' to control their mood, and use self-talk or antidote strategies such as such as 'I am doing well', 'I can control my feelings', or if the concern is the management of anger, 'I can stay calm' described in the Cognitive Restructuring component.

Another activity is to create a self-affirmation pledge to encourage self-esteem. For example, Liane Holliday Willey (2001) has Asperger Syndrome and uses the following statements that could be suggested to a client who is depressed:

- I am different.
- I will not sacrifice my self-worth for peer acceptance.
- I am capable of getting along with society.
- I will ask for help when I need it.
- I will be patient with those who need time to understand me.
- I will accept myself for who I am.

The client with Asperger Syndrome can be encouraged to write their own pledge.

Practice

Once the client has improved their cognitive strategies to understand and manage their moods at an intellectual level, it is necessary to start practising the strategies in a graduated sequence of assignments. The first stage is for the therapist to model the appropriate thinking and actions in role play with the client, who then practises with the therapist or other group members, vocalizing thinking to monitor their cognitive processes. A form of graduated practice is used, starting with situations associated with a relatively mild level of distress or agitation. A list of situations or 'triggers' is created from the assessment conducted at the start of the therapy, with each situation written on a yellow 'Post-It'. The client uses the thermometer or measuring instrument originally used in the Affective Education activities to determine the hierarchy or rank order of situations. The most distressing are placed at the upper level of the 'instrument'. As the therapy progresses, the client and therapist work through the hierarchy using fading (Luiselli 2000) or systematic desensitization using a schedule of graduated exposure to encourage the client to be less emotionally reactive.

After practice during the therapy session, the client has a project to apply their new knowledge and abilities in real situations. The therapist will obviously need to communicate and coordinate with those who will be supporting the client in real-life circumstances. After each practical experience, therapist and client consider the degree of success, using activities such as Comic Strip Conversations to debrief, reinforcement for achievements and a 'boasting book' or certificate of achievement. It will also help to have a training manual for the client that includes suggestions and explanations. The manual becomes a resource for the client during the therapy but the information can be easily accessible when the therapy program is complete. One of the issues during the practice will be generalization. People with Asperger Syndrome tend to be quite rigid in terms of recognizing when the new strategies are applicable in a situation that does not obviously resemble the practice sessions with the psychologist. It will be necessary to ensure that strategies are used in a wide range of circumstances and no assumption made that once an appropriate emotion management strategy has proved successful, it will continue to be used in all settings.

The duration of the practice stage is dependent upon the degree of success and list of situations. Gradually the therapist provides less direct guidance and support to encourage confidence in independently using the new strategies. The goal is to provide a template for current and future problems, but it will probably be necessary to maintain contact with the client for some time to prevent relapse.

Other modifications to Cognitive Behaviour Therapy

When conducting Cognitive Behaviour Therapy, the therapist will encounter some of the anticipated issues associated with individuals with a mood disorder but there are some aspects that are more apparent in this clinical population. The development of a rapport between client and therapist is essential but clients with Asperger Syndrome can take an instant and lasting like or dislike of other people, especially professionals. It will be important that the therapist has an understanding of the nature of Asperger Syndrome and the associated linguistic and cognitive profile. The linguistic profile includes difficulties with the pragmatic aspects of language, especially conversational turn taking, when and how to interrupt, literal interpretation and being pedantic. In comparison to other clients who do not have Asperger Syndrome, they will require more time to cognitively process explanations and new strategies. They will need a clear, structured and systematic approach with shorter but more frequent therapy and practice sessions. Obviously the complexity of the educational aspects would be based on the client's level of understanding. It will help to have the main points from each session typed and made available to the client and to review those points at the start of the next session. It is also important to establish and review ground rules during each session and to explain the nature of a therapeutic relationship such as when is an appropriate time to contact the therapist by telephone, knowing what the therapist needs to know and recognizing that they are helping them in a professional capacity, not as a personal friend (Hare and Paine 1997).

The therapist will incorporate and review conventional behavioural strategies such as rewards and consequences but there are modifications when considering clients with Asperger Syndrome. Some rewards may be less effective, particularly expressions of delight and approval. Due to impaired Theory of Mind abilities, creating a pleasurable response in others may not be as much a priority or motivation as with other clients. Their rewards may need to be more tangible. Children with Asperger Syndrome may be motivated by access to preferred activities, perhaps linked to their special interest, a mercenary approach of actual payment, or by appealing to their intellectual vanity rather than altruistic desire to please the therapist or parent. An effective reward may be to comment that their response was an illustration of their intelligence, wisdom or maturity.

The approach during therapy is to focus on an attitude of equal respect and discovery, especially as advice can be perceived as criticism and an implication of stupidity. When one considers consequences, especially punishment administered by parents, clinical experience has indicated that this can be of limited effectiveness. Children with Asperger Syndrome can appear to be remarkably stoic when accepting punishments such as deprivation of access to preferred activities. While natural consequences are important, and having the diagnosis is not an excuse to avoid natural justice, such children are more likely to change their behaviour through greater understanding and change in cognition. They will need to know why a particular action was unacceptable. The approach is one of using logic employing written analysis in diary or journals, Social Stories and Comic Strip Conversations rather than expecting obedience.

One of the goals of Cognitive Behaviour Therapy that is particularly important for this client group is to increase the client's awareness of the impact of their behaviour on others. They tend to be egocentric, less aware of other people's inner thoughts and feelings and need to move from a consideration of self to others. As such they need to learn the value of aspects of repair such as an apology and restitution. The program is as much one of tuition in Theory of Mind and Affective Education as a psychological therapy.

Other issues particular to this population are their choice of responses and complementary strategies. Clinical experience and research has indicated that their solutions to situations or problems that require social reasoning can be inventive but socially inappropriate (Channis et al. 2001). There may need to be guidance in the social and criminal codes that explain why a particular response is unacceptable. Adults with Asperger Syndrome may need supplementary treatment and support that complements the Cognitive Behaviour Therapy in the form of careers guidance, and relationship and sexuality education and counseling.

Aspects of Cognitive Behaviour Therapy can be incorporated into conventional Family Therapy (Stoddart 1999) and Social Skills groups (Howlin and Yates, 1999), as well as being conducted as the primary psychological treatment. Other specialists may be consulted during the program, especially if the client has signs of Attention Deficit disorder, Tourette's Syndrome and specific learning problems. Predictors of a successful outcome may include the complexity and degree of expression of the mood disorder and diagnostic characteristics, the intellectual capacity of the client and their circumstances and support. Two predictors that have been recognized by the author from clinical experience are a sense of humor and imagination.

Finally our scientific knowledge in the area of psychological therapies and Asperger Syndrome is remarkably limited. We have case studies (Hare 1997) but at present there are no systematic and rigorous independent research studies that examine whether Cognitive Behaviour Therapy is an effective treatment with this clinical population. This is despite the known high incidence of mood disorders, especially among adolescents with Asperger Syndrome. As a matter of expediency, a clinician may decide to conduct a course of Cognitive Behaviour Therapy on the basis of the known effectiveness of this form of psychological treatment in the general population. However, we have yet to establish whether it is universally appropriate and to confirm the modifications to accommodate the unusual characteristics and profile of abilities associated with Asperger Syndrome.

References

Adolphs, R., Sears, L. and Piven, J. (2001) 'Abnormal processing of social information from faces in autism.' *Journal of Cognitive Neuroscience 13*, 2, 232–240.

American Psychiatric Association (2000) *Diagnostic and Statistical Manual of Mental Disorders, 4th edn, text revision.* Washington DC: American Psychiatric Association.

Attwood, T. (1998) *Asperger's Syndrome: A Guide for Parents and Professionals.* London: Jessica Kingsley Publishers.

Baron-Cohen, S. and Jolliffe, T. (1997) 'Another advanced test of theory of mind: evidence from very high functioning adults with autism or Asperger Syndrome.' *Journal of Child Psychology and Psychiatry 38*, 813–822.

Baron-Cohen, S., O'Riordan, M., Stone, V., Jones, R. and Plaisted, K. (1999a) 'Recognition of faux pas by normally developing children and children with Asperger Syndrome or high functioning autism.' *Journal of Autism and Developmental Disorders 29*, 407–418.

Baron-Cohen, S., Ring, H.A., Wheelwright, S., Bullmore, E.T., Brammer, M.J., Simmons, A. and William, S.C.R. (1999b) 'Social intelligence in the normal autistic brain: an fMRI study.' *European Journal of Neuroscience 11*, 1891–1898.

Baron-Cohen, S., Ring, H.A., Bullmore, E.T., Wheelwright, S., Ashwin, C. and Williams, S.C.R. (2000) 'The amygdala theory of autism.' *Neuroscience and Biobehavioural Reviews 24*, 355–364.

Berthier, M.L. (1995) 'Hypomania following bereavement in Asperger's Syndrome: a case study.' *Neuropsychiatry, Neuropsychology and Behavioural Neurology 8*, 222–228.

Blackshaw, A.J., Kinderman, P., Hare, D.J. and Hatton, C. (2001) 'Theory of mind, causal attibution and paranoia in Asperger Syndrome.' *Autism 5*, 2, 147–163.

Bolton, P., Pickles, A., Murphy, M. and Rutter, M. (1998) 'Autism, affective and other psychiatric disorders: patterns of familial aggregation.' *Psychological Medicine 28*, 385–395.

Channon, S., Charman, T., Heap, J., Crawford, S. and Rios, P. (2001) 'Real-life problem-solving in Asperger's Syndrome.' *Journal of Autism and Developmental Disorders 31*, 5, 461–469.

Church, C., Alisanski, S. and Amanullah, S. (2000) 'The social, behavioural and academic experiences of children with Asperger Syndrome.' *Focus on Autism and Other Developmental Disabilities 15*, 1, 12–20.

Critchley, H.D., Daly, E.M., Bullmore, E.T., Williams, S.C.R., Van Amelsvoort, T., Robertson, D.M., Rowe, A., Phillips, M., McAlonan, G., Howlin, P. and Murphy, D.G.M. (2000) 'The functional neuroanatomy of social behaviour.' *Brain 123*, 11, 2203–2212.

De Long, R. (1994) 'Children with autistic spectrum disorder and a family history of affective disorder.' *Developmental Medicine and Child Neurology 36*, 647–688.

De Long, G.R. and Dwyer, J.T. (1988) 'Correlation of family history with specific autistic subgroups: Asperger's Syndrome and bipolar affective disease.' *Journal of Autism and Developmental Disorders 18*, 593–600.

Eisenmajer, R., Prior, M., Leekman, S., Wing, L., Gould, J., Welham, M. and Ong, N. (1996) 'Comparison of clinical symptoms in autism and Asperger's Syndrome.' *Journal of the American Academy of Child and Adolescent Psychiatry 35*, 1523–1531.

Fine, C., Lumsden, J. and Blair, R.J.R. (2001) 'Dissociation between theory of mind and executive functions in a patient with early left amygdala damage.' *Brain Journal of Neurology 124*, 2, 287–298.

Frith, U. and Happe, F. (1999) 'Theory of mind and self-consciousness: what is it like to be autistic?' *Mind and Language 14*, 1, 1–22.

Ghaziuddin, M. and Greden, J. (1998) 'Depression in children with autism/pervasive developmental disorders: a case-control family history study.' *Journal of Autism and Developmental Disorders 28*, 111–115.

Ghaziuddin, M., Wieder-Mikhail, W. and Ghaziuddin, N. (1998) 'Comorbidity of Asperger Syndrome: a preliminary report.' *Journal of Intellectual Disability Research 42*, 279–283.

Gillot, A., Furniss, F. and Walter, A. (2001) 'Anxiety in high-functioning children with autism.' *Autism 5*, 3, 277–286.

Graham, P. (1998) *Cognitive Behaviour Therapy for Children and Families.* Cambridge: Cambridge University Press.

Grandin, T. (1995) *Thinking in Pictures: And Other Reports on my Life with Autism.* New York: Doubleday.

Gray, C. (1996) 'Social assistance in higher functioning adolescents and young adults with autism.' In A. Fullerton, J. Stratton, P. Coyne and C. Gray (eds) *Autism.* Austin, TX: Pro-Ed.

Gray, C.A. (1998) 'Social stories and comic strip conversations with students with Asperger Syndrome and high-functioning autism.' In E. Schopler, G. Mesibov and L.J. Kunce (eds) *Asperger Syndrome or High-Functioning Autism?* New York: Plenum Press.

Green, J., Gilchrist, A., Burton, D. and Cox, A. (2000) 'Social and psychiatric functioning in adolescents with Asperger Syndrome compared with conduct disorder.' *Journal of Autism and Developmental Disorders 30*, 4, 279–293.

Groden, J., Diller, A., Bausman, M., Velicer, W., Norman, G. and Cautela, J. (2001) 'The development of a stress survey schedule for persons with autism and other developmental disabilities.' *Journal of Autism and Developmental Disorders 31*, 2, 207–217.

Hall, K. (2001) *Asperger Syndrome, the Universe and Everything.* London: Jessica Kingsley Publishers.

Hare, D.J. (1997) 'The use of cognitive-behavioural therapy with people with Asperger Syndrome: a case study.' *Autism 1*, 215–225.

Hare, D.J. and Paine, C. (1997) 'Developing cognitive behavioural treatments for people with Asperger's Syndrome.' *Clinical Psychology Forum 110*, 5–8.

Hare, D.J., Jones, J.P.R. and Paine, C. (1999) 'Approaching reality: the use of personal construct assessment in working with people with Asperger Syndrome.' *Autism 3*, 165–176.

Heavey, L., Phillips, W., Baron-Cohen, S. and Rutter, M. (2000) 'The awkward moments test: a naturalistic measure of social understanding in autism.' *Journal of Autism and Developmental Disorders 30*, 3, 225–236.

Holliday Willey, L. (2001) *Asperger Syndrome in the Family: Redefining Normal.* London: Jessica Kingsley Publishers.

Howlin, P., Baron-Cohen, S. and Hadwin, J. (1999) *Teaching Children with Autism to Mind-Read: A Practical Guide for Teachers and Parents.* Chichester: Wiley.

Howlin, P. And Yates, P. (1999) 'The Potential Effectiveness of Social Skills Group for Adults with Autism.' *Autism 3*, 299–307.

Hurlburt, R.T., Happe, F. and Frith, U. (1994) 'Sampling the form of inner experience in three adults with Asperger's Syndrome.' *Psychological Medicine 24*, 385–395.

Jackson, L. (2002) *Freaks, Geeks and Asperger Syndrome: A Users Guide to Adolecence.* London: Jessica Kingsley Publishers.

Kendall, P.C. (2000) *Child and Adolescent Therapy Cognitive Behavioural Therapy Procedures.* New York: Guildford Press.

Kim, J.A., Szatmari, P., Bryson, S.E., Streiner, D.L. and Wilson, F. (2000) 'The prevalence of anxiety and mood problems among children with autism and Asperger Syndrome.' *Autism 4*, 117–132.

Kleinman, J., Marciano, P. and Ault, R. (2001) 'Advanced theory of mind in high-functioning adults with autism.' *Journal of Autism and Developmental Disorders 31*, 29–36.

Koning, C. and Magill-Evans, J. (2001) 'Social and language skills in adolescent boys with Asperger's Syndrome.' *Autism 5*, 1, 23–36.

Kurita, H. (1999) 'Brief report: delusional disorder in a male adolescent with high-functioning PDDNOS.' *Journal of Autism and Developmental Disorders 29*, 5, 419–423.

Lainhart, J. and Folstein, S. (1994) 'Affective disorders in people with autism: a review of published cases.' *Journal of Autism and Developmental Disorders 24*, 587–601.

Lawson, W. (2000) *Life Behind Glass: A Personal Account of Autism Spectrum Disorder.* London: Jessica Kingsley Publishers.

Ledgin, N. (1998) *Diagnosing Jefferson. Evidence of a Condition that Guided his Beliefs, Behaviour and Personal Associations.* Arlington TX: Future Horizons.

Lee, A. and Hobson, R.P. (1998) 'On developing self-concepts: a controlled study of children and adolescents with autism.' *Journal of Child Psychology and Psychiatry 39*, 1131–1144.

Luiselli, J.K. (2000) 'Case demonstration of fading procedure to promote school attendance of a child with Asperger's Syndrome.' *Journal of Positive Behaviour Interventions 2*, 1, 47–53.

McAfee, J. (2001) *Navigating the Social World: A Curriculum for Individuals with Asperger's Syndrome, High-functioning Autism and Asperger Syndrome*. London: Jessica Kingsley Publishers.

Moyes, R.A. (2001) *Incorporating Social Goals in the Classroom: A Guide for Teachers and Parents of Children with High-functioning Autism and Asperger* Syndrome. London: Jessica Kingsley Publishers.

Muris, P., Steerneman, P., Meesters, C., Merckelbach, H., Horselenberg, R., Van Den Hogan, T. and Van Den Hogan, L. 'The TOM test: a new instrument for assessing theory of mind in normal children and children with pervasive developmental disorders.' *Autism and Developmental Disorders 29*, 67–80.

Nyden, A., Gillberg, C., Hjelmquist, E. and Heiman, M. (1999) 'Executive function/attention deficits in boys with Asperger Syndrome, attention disorder and reading/writing disorder.' *Autism 3*, 213–228.

Ozonoff, S., South, M. and Miller, J. (2000) 'DSM-IV defined Asperger Syndrome: cognitive behavioural and early history differentiation from high-functioning autism.' *Autism 4*, 29–46.

Pennington, B.F and Ozonoff, S. (1996) 'Executive functions and developmental psychopathology.' *Journal of Child Psychology and Psychiatry Annual Research Review 37*, 51–87.

Piven, J. and Palmer, R. (1999) 'Psychological disorder and the broad autism phenotype: evidence from a family study of multiple-incidence autism families.' *American Journal of Psychiatry 156*, 557–563.

Pyles, L. (2001) *Hitchhiking through Asperger Syndrome*. London: Jessica Kingsley Publishers.

Ronen, T. (1997) *Cognitive Developmental Therapy with Children*. Chichester: Wiley.

Rubin, K. (2002) *The Friendship Factor*. New York: Viking.

Silver, M. and Oakes, P. (2001) 'Evolution of a new computer intervention to teach people with autism or Asperger Syndrome to recognize and predict emotions in others.' *Autism 5*, 299–316.

Stoddart, K. (1999) 'Adolescents with Asperger Syndrome: three case studies of individual and family therapy.' *Autism 3*, 255–271.

Tantam, D. (2000) 'Psychological disorder in adolescents and adults with Asperger Syndrome.' *Autism 4*, 47–62.

Tonge, B., Brereton, A., Gray, K. and Einfeld, S. (1999) 'Behavioural and emotional disturbance in high-functioning autism and Asperger Syndrome.' *Autism 3*, 117–130.

Werth, A., Perkins, M. and Boucher, J. (2001) 'Here's the weavery looming up.' *Autism 5*, 2, 111–125.

3

The Sexuality of Adolescents with Asperger Syndrome

Isabelle Hénault

Understanding sexuality

A basic introduction to the working definition of sexuality

Up to now, remarkably little research and clinical attention has been directed to the sexuality of adolescents with Asperger Syndrome (AS), both in terms of their sexual profiles and their knowledge of sexuality. In addition, several parents and professionals feel uncomfortable talking about sexuality. Nonetheless, sexuality is an integral part of the normal development of adolescents and we have recently begun to recognize that Aspies have the right to experience and fulfill this important part of their life. Adolescents with AS have a genuine need to learn about sexuality; they are curious and seeking information and opportunities to experiment with sexuality. Clearly, this is an opportune and appropriate time at which to provide them with sexual education. In addition to going through the same stages of sexual development (increase in hormones, body hair, genital maturation, etc.) as other adolescents, Aspies have similar sexual interests and needs. They differ in that they experience major difficulties with communication and social interaction, which directly impair their ability to interact sexually as well as re-inforcing the emergence of inappropriate sexual behaviours.

There are numerous solutions to dealing with inappropriate sexual behaviours. Concrete and practical strategies are often the most practical and pragmatic. Since each case is unique, specific techniques may differ from one individual to the next. The choice of technique used should be based upon the level of functioning and development of the adolescent with AS. In some cases, concrete learning methods such as pictures, simple educational material and a variety of software may be used initially. For individuals with higher levels of functioning, the use of games, thematic discussions and social skills activities may be more appropriate.

When the topic of sexuality has been addressed in the literature, it has usually been restricted to a discussion of problem behaviours (i.e., compulsive masturbation, inappropriate sexual interactions). Such a perspective is limited in that it fails to consider the complexity of sexuality in general. As in any other context, sexuality in AS consists of intimacy, friendship, pleasure, communication, love, masturbation, intercourse, dating, desire, identity and belonging in addition to problematic behaviours.

For the majority of Aspies, sexual behaviours are perceived as any other behaviour, free of social rules and convention. In contrast, parents and professionals often view sexuality in a very different manner. For them, sexuality may be taboo, value laden and a source of malaise. The need to protect the adolescent may be so strong that the subject of sexuality is avoided or banned altogether. There is also a tendency to define everything with respect to AS. This perspective fails to consider that adolescence, as a developmental period, brings about a variety of changes, new behaviours, and a need for discovery.

The topic of sexuality is often ignored and parents may wait until it emerges by itself. They frequently express fears that their teens will engage in more sexual experiences if their knowledge about sexuality increases. In fact, having a solid sexual knowledge base contributes to better decision-making skills.

The five senses related to sexuality

To the author's knowledge no studies to date have examined the link between sensory states and sexuality in AS. Given the intimate link between sexuality and the senses, this lacuna is certainly puzzling, especially in light of the fact that individuals with AS can experience sensory hyper- or hyposensitivity. The former can be defined as extreme sensitivity experienced by one or several of the five senses. Auditory and tactile hypersensitivity are common in AS and may be associated with neurological disorders. For example, light background music, played at a low volume, can be perceived as loud and shrill. Similarly, a slight brushing up against the skin can provoke the same intensity of pain as that caused by a sharp object. Various forms of sexual stimulation can therefore cause discomfort or even pain for individuals with AS, reinforcing avoidance behaviours and hindering the development of intimate relationships.

In contrast, hyposensitivity can be defined as weak sensory responses to modest forms of stimulation. In this case, multiple exposures to stimuli are necessary to experience the sensation as a whole. This condition increases the probability that inappropriate sexual conduct will occur. An individual with AS may resort to masturbatory behaviour because pleasure is otherwise barely perceived. Thus, genital self-stimulation can be more intense and more frequent, carrying the potential for compulsive masturbation.

The five senses activity (Figure 3.1) was devised to explore sensory responses to various experiences. As such, the adolescent with AS will be better equipped to identify and avoid situations that could lead to sensory confusion. The goal of the exercise is to test each of the five senses and to check the appropriate box to determine the level of sensitivity experienced. For example, what is the adolescent's reaction to soft music? To a loud noise? This can be tested by placing headphones over the adolescent's ears and playing soft and loud music through them (i.e., classical music and hard rock, or whispering in his ear and slamming a door). The sensory reaction is usually quite marked. In order to test the sense of touch, the forearm can be caressed with a plush fabric or fur. The exercise should then be repeated using sandpaper. This concrete experiment will allow the adolescent to express what he feels and to realize that what is perceived by his senses has an impact on his behaviour. The second part of the activity examines the impact of the sensory response on sexuality. This question can be a useful starting point to addressing the subject of sexual behaviours.

FIGURE 3.1 THE FIVE SENSES ACTIVITY

	− Hyposensitivity Under-sensitive	Sensitive Acceptable	+ Hypersensitive Over-sensitive
1. Hearing			
2. Smell			
3. Touch			
4. Sight			
5. Taste			

Experiences: Try each of these experiences and check out your reaction

1. Soft music/loud noise 2. Perfume/alcohol 3. Plush/sand paper 4. Bright colors/blurry image 5. Lemon/honey or chocolate

What impact does this have on your sexuality?

_____

_____

_____

_____

Possible ways, means and behaviours you could use this knowledge to understand your sexuality?

_____

_____

_____

_____

©Isabelle Hénault

Figure 3.1 The five senses activity

Issues of development

Below are some general data regarding the sexuality of individuals with AS:

- frustrations expressed as inappropriate or aggressive behaviours

- gender identity as a source of conflict

- social limitation

- difficulty interpreting emotions

- complex interpersonal relationships misunderstood

- sexual drive is part of normal development.

Frustrations expressed as inappropriate or aggressive behaviours

Adolescents with AS commonly misunderstand requests that are made of them. It is also difficult for them to detect or express their own internal processes (hormonal variation, conflicting emotions, mood changes, etc.). Such situations may bring about confusion and frustration that are often expressed as inappropriate behaviour. These impulsive reactions frequently become the only vehicle by which internal tensions are released. The functional analysis of aggressive or inappropriate behaviours consists of observing what happened before, during, and after the behaviour occurred. Conducting such a descriptive analysis provides clues that help to recreate the sequence of behaviours, which could help to understand the contingencies under which the behaviour took place. The aggressive behaviour can usually be traced back to and identified as a 'symptom' of a frustration.

Gender identity of autistic adolescents can be a source of conflict

Adolescents with AS do not have the natural tendency to question their identity. Adolescence is commonly viewed as a developmental stage where identity in general is questioned. Belonging to the male or female sex determines several of our behaviours. As such, adolescents will usually have the desire to belong to the subgroup with which they identify. This sets into motion a whole series of protocols and changes related to dress code, musical preferences, interests, and behavioural repertoire. Adolescents with AS are less attuned to social rules and do not feel the same pressures to belong to or affiliate with any particular group. Their tendency to isolate themselves can become a source of conflict if the Aspie has no bearings with respect to a sense of belonging. Sexual preference does not seem to obey the strict social rules typically associated with adolescence. The general categories are more flexible and more movement between categories is observed in individuals with AS. It therefore appears that Aspies respect their own sense of identity over socially determined norms.

Clinical observations seem to reveal the presence of high levels of homosexual fantasy and behaviour. To date, these findings have not been supported in the scientific literature, but the author and Dr Anthony Attwood will soon present the results of an international (Canada, USA, Australia) study aimed at establishing the sexual profile of individuals with AS. The results are interesting and show that, in general, the AS sexual profile differs in several respects from that of the general population. Body image, sense of belonging to one's sex, and the erotic imagery of individuals with AS seem to be less influenced by social norms. Aspies would appear to act according to their internal desires, regardless of whether they are directed to a person of the same or the opposite sex. The author has recently been in contact with a discussion group composed of transgendered individuals with AS. Could there be a high comorbidity rate between Pervasive Disorders of Development and Gender Identity Disorders? This hypothesis requires empirical attention.

Social imitation is frequent

A behavioural repertoire consists of the rituals and routines that provide adolescents with a sense of security. In AS social behaviours are poorly developed, which renders interpersonal relationships difficult. Adolescents tend to imitate their peers' behaviour without necessarily decoding the inherent complexity. As such, they can reproduce an observed behaviour without considering the context in which it took place. For example, an Aspie who has seen a couple kissing in the street could attempt to kiss the first girl he meets. An adolescent could also repeat a form of touch that he experienced. Failing to consider the context in which these behaviours take place can increase the likelihood that an inappropriate sexual behaviour will occur.

Difficulties regarding interpretation of emotions

Youth with AS present with numerous difficulties regarding the decoding of their own emotions in addition to interpreting those of others. Emotions are typically reduced to the most basic such as joy, anger, or sadness. The full range of emotions needs to be explored in order to allow adolescents to express more clearly what they are feeling. Sexuality entails a variety of emotions which surpass two or three basic ones. It is within these subtle nuances that relationships with others are enriched. Therefore, adolescents with AS would benefit from a more elaborate repertoire of emotions.

Consider the following: in the midst of a conversation with a classmate, an Aspie detects joy from his smile. The classmate had to explain to her that he was more than simply happy. In fact, he desired her. According to him, this desire could also have been detected in his eyes and in his general attitude towards her. Learning about and being able to decode emotions are important aspects of sexuality. Having a better developed ability to express one's emotions and to interpret those of others can decrease frustration and any possible subsequent impulsive reactions displayed by adolescents with AS.

Complex interpersonal relationships are misunderstood

Aspies have difficulty decoding the messages that are simultaneously emitted during interactions with several individuals or in conversational dyads. Words and phrases with double meanings lead to confusion. Non-verbal communication (which acts as a parallel language) is also difficult to detect. As such, a simple conversation can easily turn into a nightmarish experience. Sexuality is filled with subtleties and small gestures and intentions that must be decoded on a second level. Adolescents with AS report that their interactions feel as though they were in the presence of someone who was talking an unknown dialect. 'It is like learning a new language each time.' Some Aspies learn to detect and decode specific cues (key words, precise gestures, intonations of voice). Nonetheless when they are too rigid, conflicts are likely to occur. Human interactions take place on a variety of levels: emotional, non-verbal, cognitive, etc. which render them complex for individuals with AS.

One method of learning to decode complex messages is to begin by exploring one's own levels of communication. Using case vignettes and simple role-playing situations, we ask the adolescent to explore all the different messages transmitted. For example, what can be decoded from the following: 'I like you, would you like to go out tonight?' The first interpretation is the invitation to go out (factual level), the second is the interest that the other has for me (emotional level), the third is related to the other's intent (interpersonal level), and the fourth is the other's non-verbal communication (the language parallel to the gestures, the smile, proximity, tone of voice, etc.). Simple examples can be used to explore all possible interpretations and meanings. The exercise continues by dealing with situations that are progressively more complex in terms of the number of messages conveyed and the number of interactions involved. Learning therefore takes place in a safe manner where the focus is on the desire to interact with others and not on performance. The more adolescents feel competent in their social interactions, the less they will isolate themselves.

Sexual drive is part of normal development

During adolescence, sexual desire is in constant flux. Sex hormones, particularly testosterone in men, cause numerous changes. These include the development of the secondary sexual characteristics, physiological changes, the need to explore, and sexual desire. This stage of development is normal and explains why adolescents display much curiosity with regards to sexuality. The levels of sexual desire experienced by Aspies are comparable to those of the general population, but they experience fewer actual experiences.

Factors influencing sexual development

According to Griffiths, Quinsey and Hingsburger (1989), six factors must be considered in order to understand the complexity of the sexual development of individuals with autism or AS. These include deficits in socio-sexual information, gender segregation, limitations in the environment, intimacy, medication, and rights and attitudes.

Deficits in socio-sexual information

Aspies do not have the same number of experiences as other teenagers. Young individuals with AS are viewed as asexual, as if their condition prevented them from having a sexual life. This is even more painful when their families and friends deny their sexual development and needs. Furthermore, they often have a limited social support network. This poses another problem: with whom can they discuss their experiences and feelings? Their peers and parents can feel awkward about the topic of sexuality which may influence the teenager to withdraw from subsequent social contacts. Emotions affiliated with sexuality are equally ambivalent. Many warnings are sent to them for their own protection against abusive situations or behaviours. These warnings may create a high level of irrational angst, the result of which serves to extinguish the teenager's desire and willingness to understand his sexuality.

Gender segregation

Several people with AS have lived through gender segregation in group homes or institutions. In such situations we often find that homosexual and masturbatory behaviours emerge as a result of unsatisfactory (or lack of) contacts with people of the opposite sex. If sexual segregation disappears in favor of inclusion, then the sexual behaviours of people with autism will be more likely to resemble those of the general population.

Limitations in the environment

Limitations in the environment to people with AS are often frequent in establishments and enforced by staff members, especially with regards to sexuality. They may constitute formal or informal rules. If there are no predetermined rules, who determines if a behaviour is acceptable or not? Does a person with autism receive a variety of different and inconsistent messages? Do the rules apply everywhere and do they stay the same? There appear to be no norms regarding sexual conduct in institutions or group homes. Punishment of behaviour is frequent, which diminishes the opportunity for more responsible behaviour to develop. Teams working with teenagers should create an atmosphere that promotes responsibility by preventing sexual abuse, by sexual education and by recognizing the possibility of sexual contacts between them (Griffiths 1998). It is of utmost importance to educate personnel, workers and parents since they can transmit erroneous information concerning sexuality.

Intimacy

Intimacy can be defined as the possibility of being alone or with a partner whether it is for emotional or sexual reasons. This opportunity is rare for teenagers with AS (Griffiths 1998). Furthermore, intimate moments are not solely opportunities for sexual contacts, but may also serve to expand interpersonal experiences for people with AS. One objective would be to provide them with time and opportunities to develop intimate relationships with others. Intimacy is the foundation upon which relationships are built. It can be experienced at several levels: relational, emotional, and physical. Adolescents should have the possibility to explore these different aspects of intimacy while being guided by a responsible adult. Here too, the tendency to overprotect becomes quickly manifested. Limiting experiences will in no way be helpful as this only serves to place the youth in vulnerable situations.

Medication

Medication can directly affect sexual functioning or have secondary negative effects. Teens with AS can have health problems. Furthermore, they commonly take more than one medication, which can create synergistic effects. The drug interaction effects can then lead to other problems. For example, antidepressants (e.g. Luvox) can lead to low sexual drive, erectile dysfunction or retarded ejaculation. Antipsychotics (e.g. Neuroleptics) can also have negative effects on sexual drive, erection and ejaculation. Risperdal can also accentuate agitation and anxiety and dyskinetic involuntary movements (tics) if taken over the long term or in combination with another antipsychotic drug.

Unfortunately, medications are often prescribed without any specifications as to their side effects on sexuality. You should always ask your physician or psychiatrist if the doses prescribed cause side effects.

Rights and attitudes

Stereotypes are often found concerning the rights and attitudes of people with AS. It is important to state that these individuals have the same right to a sexual life as do individuals in the general population. This means that each individual's needs and sexual desires must be considered. Education and intervention programs dealing with sexuality can only come into play when this right is respected.

What can parents do to support their adolescent as they experience their sexual awakening?

Parents play a critical role in the social and sexual development of their adolescents. Parents are the first educators and transmit values and mores with respect to sexuality. Positive parental attitudes contribute to the development of an Aspie's sense of responsibility regarding sexuality. Open communication is advantageous on many levels in that it ensures that sexuality is acknowledged (sexuality exists since we can talk about it) and it allows the adolescents to ask their parents questions in their quest for knowledge and information.

Adolescence is also the period in which self-esteem is built. Sexuality is intimately linked to self-esteem, which is another reason why adolescents with AS require parental support. Their role is to provide a space in which their teenagers can express their conflicting emotions, experiences, worries, and states of mind. They can welcome and help them to accept their 'differences,' and encourage them to develop their strengths, special abilities, and their potential. Adolescents are extremely sensitive and they need to develop an image of themselves that is affirming and not 'deficient.'

Here are some tips on how to address sexuality with your adolescent:

- Start with simple explanations of themes you feel confident about, e.g. gender issues (what does it mean to be a boy or a girl), general knowledge (hygiene, anatomy) and sexual characteristics (physical, emotional, etc.).

- Be concrete in your explanations: they must be simple and effective (concrete facts, examples, games, etc.).

- Talk about sexuality in a positive way; avoid stereotypes and prejudices.

- Value the differences, particularities, special capacities of the adolescent: what makes him/her unique?

- Integrate these discussions with family members, groups or classes to create continuity.

- Avoid being overprotective. This leads to misinformation and ambivalence regarding sexuality.

- Use reinforcement when they ask for information (only when you feel they are ready to integrate it).

- Open communication is a process that needs to be worked on over the long term.

It is also important to establish safe limits to exploration. Parents can guide their adolescents by explaining to them consequences as related to sexuality. Information should be transmitted in a realistic and positive manner such that they can form their own impressions and judgments. As such, issues such as reproduction, contraception, marriage and different kinds of unions, and the different contexts in which sexuality can be experienced need to be addressed. One simple way to address these is to provide them with books on adolescence and sexuality. It is better to provide them with accurate and valuable information since that conveyed in magazines and on television is often biased and stereotyped.

In popular media, sexuality is often unnatural and performance oriented. Values and emotions are often excluded to capitalize on unrealistic images. On this subject, a 21-year-old Aspie recently described to me his reaction upon seeing his girlfriend nude for the first time. In the habit of reading erotic magazines, he expected all women to look like those in the magazines. To his dismay he had to adjust to reality! This event demonstrates the importance of offering accurate and diverse information so as to avoid rigidity.

Establishing and maintaining an open line of communication between the parents (or another trusted adult) and the Aspie is important. As such, they will have access to information and comfort in a warm and welcoming environment.

Sex education

Considering the diagnostic criteria of Asperger Syndrome, sex education should include three main themes that are directly linked to the difficulties of adolescents: social skills, relationships and problem behaviours. The author is currently examining the efficacy of a socio-sexual skills program in an Aspie population. The themes are addressed in the ten-week group program, delivered in 90-minute sessions. For more information on this program, please write the author at: ihenault@internet.uqam.ca.

Sexual health education programs must consider the intellectual capacities and learning capabilities of adolescents with AS. Overly complex or abstract explanations are likely to lead to confusion and must therefore be avoided at all costs. A pragmatic and varied learning experience should be favored over one imparting value judgments and philosophical viewpoints.

A number of factors must be considered before addressing the topic of sex education:

- How could the adolescent's particular history and personality affect his/her social and sexual development?

- How could these affect his/her ability to learn information about sexual issues?

- What extra information or materials could be provided to address these specific individual characteristics?

Several topics need to be addressed during adolescence. These are the basis of sexual education and examples include:

- sex organs: names, functions and concrete descriptions
- self-esteem and body changes
- information regarding nocturnal emissions
- values and steps involved in decision making
- intimacy: private and public settings
- sexual health: behaviours and initial examination of sex organs
- communicating about dating, love, intimacy and friendship
- how alcohol and drug use influence decision making
- intercourse and other sexual behaviours
- masturbation
- sexual orientation and identity
- menstruation and the responsibilities of childbearing
- condoms, contraception and disease prevention
- emotions related to sexuality need discussion since they are powerful motivators (National Information Center for Children and Youth with Disabilities, 1992).

When dealing with these different themes and topics, it is important to teach both the scientific terms and their popular counterparts. Aspies likely know several scientific terms as they relate to sexuality (especially if they have a particular interest in trivia). It is also important to use the more common names and labels to allow them to associate more than one term to a given concept. A rigid learning experience is likely to be more harmful than anything else and should therefore be avoided. Popular jargon used by other teens must be made accessible so that they can interact with their peers on a more equal basis. This does not imply that vulgar language be used with regards to sexuality but rather that an open-minded attitude towards popular culture be displayed. As such, the probability of stigmatization and rejection by peer group decreases.

There are several goals to the proposed interventions, namely:

- to learn adaptive and positive behaviours

- to replace inappropriate behaviours with new behaviours that serve the same function

- to create new opportunities to learn, experience, and share with others

- to increase self-esteem

- to foster harmonious development

- to encourage independence in choices made, decision making, and judgments

- to maximize social integration rather than segregation.

Social skills

Sexual education is accompanied by social learning because, aside from self-stimulation, sexual behaviours are of a mutual nature. Social skills can therefore be viewed as precursors to sexual education. Adopting such a strategy allows appropriate social behaviours to emerge within the context of interpersonal relationships. Over the long term, the individual with AS will develop a better understanding of what constitutes social relationships, will demonstrate adequate behaviours in different contexts (school, community centers, family), and will enlarge his/her social network. The goal of social skills training is to refine and increase the individual's repertoire of appropriate behaviours. However, certain basic skills are required prior to this taking place. For example, how does one enter into contact with another person? How does one initiate a conversation? How is interest manifested? The interventions emphasize the specific characteristics of individuals with AS. It will be much easier to maintain their interest and motivation if their strengths and special capabilities are valued (refer to Anthony Attwood and Carol Gray's ASPIE diagnostic criteria based on the abilities, strengths or talents of the person instead of his/her deficits. Ex. qualitative advantage in social interaction, fluent in language such as a determination to seek truth and an advance use of pictorial metaphor.). All instructions and learning segments must be concise and concrete. If sex education is provided in a group's format, the behaviours and skills encouraged could include the following:

1. Demonstrating interest towards other participants by establishing eye contact and listening.

2. Waiting for others to have finished their thought before speaking.

3. Voicing opinions and defending points of view.

4. Providing constructive criticism and suggestions.

5. Learning to decode the intentions of others.

These skills foster individual participation and allow certain favorable social skills to be maintained during group activities.

A behaviour can only be judged as effective in the social context in which it is emitted. Discrimination and discernment allow for adjustments to take place. There are several positive consequences to developing appropriate social skills, which include:

- improvement in overall functioning

- decrease in psychological distress due to incomprehension

- increase in the quality of interactions with others

- possibility of creating friendships and acquaintances based on shared interests (hobbies, sports, outings, etc.)

- sense of accomplishment

- reinforce social autonomy and initiation of social contacts.

Studies examining the effectiveness of intervention programs report significant positive results. The group intervention approach differs considerably in the learning possibilities that it can offer: role-play scenarios, retroaction, modeling, peer reactions, group discussions, and teamwork. Such an approach leaves much room for creativity and innovation.

Exploration and relationships

Teaching adolescents to understand the difference between harmless self-exploration and harmful sexual encounters can be a major issue.

The Making Waves program: what is a good relationship anyways? (available on the Internet at www.mwaves.org) is an indispensable resource. In a simple and effective manner that requires active participation, adolescents are made to think about the different types of relationships that can take place between two individuals. An initial questionnaire assesses the teen's knowledge of a variety of themes such as friendship in general, affection, intimacy issues, and standard sexuality topics. Based upon the obtained results, the limits to love are explored in order to evaluate what is healthy, unhealthy and abusive. Finally, sexual abuse is addressed. Ample examples, resources, and suggestions are provided.

Problem behaviours

Inappropriate sexual behaviours (aggressive behaviours, excessive self-stimulation, sexual compulsions, etc.) are observed in the Aspie population. Griffiths, Hingsburger and Quinsey (1989) suggest five explanations of problem sexual behaviours:

- behavioural history
- modeling and imitation
- partner selection
- sexual history
- medical history.

BEHAVIOURAL HISTORY

The individual's behavioural history can contribute to the development of inappropriate sexual conduct. Griffiths (1998) reports the case of a young man who was punished every time he tried to establish contact with a woman, despite the fact that his behaviour was appropriate. He then forced himself sexually onto a non-consenting woman. He acted rapidly, thinking that this would decrease the likelihood that he would be reprimanded. Conducting a functional analysis of his behaviour allows us to understand the sequence and the meaning of his actions. This young man's strategy was adequate if we take into consideration the circumstances in which it was performed. When an individual is constantly socially repressed, inappropriate conduct can become the only alternative. If no sexual contact is allowed, problem behaviours may emerge.

MODELING AND IMITATION

Modeling and imitation can also contribute to inappropriate forms of conduct. Imitating a routine or rituals outside of their context can certainly be inappropriate and can demonstrate an Aspie's difficulty in choosing the adequate moment for performing certain behaviours. The following helps illustrate this point: a young woman with autism leaves her door open when she goes to the bathroom. Once finished, she dresses in the corridor on her way to class. What is taking place? According to Griffiths (1998) it is important to analyze the inappropriate behaviour in order to understand it. It seems that in this case the young woman can't discriminate between what is public and what is private. Teens with AS frequently present with problems related to privacy. They are so used to receiving services and help from many different people that they can't discern when, where and in front of whom they can do certain things.

RESTRICTED PARTNER SELECTION

Individuals with AS often have restricted choices regarding their selection of a partner. They can become attached to their counselors and the personnel with whom they spend the majority of their time. According to Griffiths (1998) this confusion is normal since these are the people who take care of them. They have special and close relationships with them, which encourage attachment and intimacy to develop. From this point of view, it is preferable to encourage the development of relationships with other people in order to expand their social networks.

SEXUAL HISTORY

The individual's sexual history can have an influence on inappropriate behaviour. Children with autism are frequently sexually abused. The American Academy of Pediatrics (1996) sponsored a study for the National Center on Child Abuse and Neglect and found a reported sexual abuse rate of 36 per 1000 cases in children with pervasive developmental disorders. This rate is 1.7 times higher than that found in the general population. The limited social skills of people with autism can cause them to lack experience and judgment. Their lack of sexual knowledge can also have a negative influence on how they choose to respond to sexual demands (Griffiths 1998; Hingsburger 1993). A history of abuse can lead to the development of inadequate behaviours since the abused child or teenager can reproduce the behaviours of which he was the victim. In this way, a teenager who has been touched on his genitals can repeat this behaviour with another person since he is unable to discriminate the intimate nature of this behaviour; he is basically reproducing the same behaviour that he experienced.

MEDICAL HISTORY

The individual's medical history is an important source of information regarding inappropriate sexual conduct. For example, a genital or urinary tract infection can create a tickling sensation and an inflammation of the pelvic area. The teenager may be continuously touching his genitals due to the sensations caused by an infection. One must be careful to differentiate sexual stimulation from self-soothing behaviours. Side effects of medication must also be taken into consideration.

Frequently asked questions

WHAT IF SEX BECOMES AN OBSESSIVE INTEREST?

Since individuals with AS have a propensity towards repetitive and ritualized activities, it is possible that sexuality could become one of their special interests. In such a case, it would be difficult to curb the interest, especially if it brings about satisfaction and pleasure. While it is important to provide the adolescent with a framework for understanding sexuality, it is not recommended that it be forbidden, especially if the sexual interest does not harm the Aspie or anyone else. To forbid sexuality would only serve to increase interest in it. It is important to remember that, in general, there is an upsurge of interest in sexuality during adolescence. The combination of curiosity and excitement renders sexuality attractive. The desire to explore (within reasonable limits) must be respected, especially since it also represents interest towards others. This stage of sexual development is perfectly normal and, in fact, desirable. It brings about socialization and the development of friendships. Adolescents with AS may or may not have the need for affiliation, but in the event that they do, they should have the right to experience it.

However, sexuality could take another turn and become a genuine obsession. It is important to qualify this phenomenon since it is by no means present in all adolescents with AS. To date we have no scientific data on this subject, but sexual obsessions have been detected in a minority of cases through clinical observation. Sexual obsessions can be characterized as uncontrollable and disproportionate sexual desire. As such, sexuality becomes the sole source of interest and stimulation, to the detriment of all other activities. The obsession can take on several forms: use of pornographic materials (magazines, Internet, etc.), voyeurism, compulsive masturbation, seeking out sexual contacts, desire for closeness, repetitive fantasies, etc. If the obsessions are not satisfied (which is quite likely), frustration, isolation, and depressed mood can ensue. Each case is unique, but a few general recommendations can be made. First, it is best not to punish or neglect the situation since this would only serve to increase the underling anxiety. Despite being a difficult subject to broach, the Aspie should have the opportunity to express what he is experiencing and the way in which it is preoccupying him.

For example, a 21-year-old Aspie consulted me for 'sexual difficulties.' I immediately asked him to clarify what he meant by 'difficulties' (it is important to be clear and concrete). He confided that he was completely obsessed with the idea of having sex. The previous year, he had experienced an intimate contact with a 25-year-old woman and since then had found himself unable to stop thinking about it and, in fact, trying all possible means to meet a woman. His desire was fueled by a very rich fantasy life and erotic magazines that he consulted on a daily basis. He described himself as obsessed. His psychiatrist had prescribed medication that was supposed to calm his obsession, but to no avail.

I encouraged him to talk about his obsessions and to describe them in detail so as to decrease his anxiety. After four to five one-hour sessions, he reported being less distressed and that talking about his obsessions had enabled him to dedramatize the situation. The first reaction of most would be to avoid talking about the obsession for fear of feeding into it. On the contrary, talking about the sexual urges decreases the tension that they generate. I then encouraged him to join a group of young adults taking part in activities at a day center. Since he was less anxious, his desire was less pressing, albeit equally present. He behaved more appropriately with women and was less direct in his requests.

He made friends with one of the young women in the group and they became a couple after one month. He told me that she too desired to have a sexual relationship with him. After having assured myself that he knew about proper condom use, I asked him to explain how he intended to experience his first sexual contact with his 20-year-old girl-friend. He had planned everything out: dinner at a restaurant, movie, and rental of a hotel room, which is in fact what happened. His only disappointment was that he judged his girlfriend's body to be quite different from that of models in magazines. The shock was so great that he could not refrain from telling her. They talked about it and he decided to adapt to the situation, given that there were a number of advantages to being with her (outings, activities, sexual contact, etc.).

Adolescents need to have sexual experiences in order to get to know their own sexual functioning. It is important to remember that, since each individual is unique, sexuality can take on a variety of forms. As is the case with adolescents in general, they need our support and advice. Overprotection will only serve to increase unwanted behaviours since desire for what is forbidden usually increases.

If sexuality takes on the form of an obsession, here are some questions and suggestions to help guide you:

- What is the sexual behaviour?

- When did the obsession begin?

- In what specific circumstances is the obsession expressed (time of day, before or after what activity, which individuals are involved)?

- What is the functional value of the obsession?

- How does the adolescent behave when talking about the obsession?

- What emotions accompany the repetitive behaviour(s) (anxiety, anger, sadness, fear, joy, excitement, etc.)?

With the preceding information, it becomes possible to establish the context and function of the obsession. Below are some possible interpretations regarding the meaning of the obsessions:

1. Sexuality becomes the only source of satisfaction, pleasure, excitement, or gratification.

2. The sexual behaviour serves to decrease the adolescent's anxiety (more specifically, in situations where a lot is expected of him).

3.   Sexuality becomes a means by which to defy authority or what is forbidden.

4.   Engaging in sexual activities allows the youth to accede to adulthood (the adolescent no longer wishes to be viewed as a child).

5.   Sexual contacts stimulate the sensory systems (tactile, visual, olfactory). If the Aspie is hyposensitive, it is possible that over-stimulation be required to attain a given threshold of sensation.

6.   Sexuality becomes the symptom of an underlying conflict (quest for identity, frustration related to their differences, peer rejection, failure in romantic relationships, social isolation, etc.).

7.   For Aspies, sexual behaviour can have the same value as any ordinary behaviour. It is important to explain to them the ways in which any given sexual behaviour can be different (social context, emotions involved, respect for certain norms, etc.).

8.   A sexual obsession can, like the majority of obsessions, allow the adolescent to find security in a controlled routine.

WHAT IF SEX BECOMES A SELF-STIMULATORY BEHAVIOUR PERFORMED IN PUBLIC OR AT THE EXPENSE OF REGULAR LIFE?

Masturbation is a very important issue. Self-stimulation is the most common source of sexual satisfaction during adolescence. In the general population, rates of masturbation range from 75 percent to 93 percent (Masters and Johnson 1988). As such, masturbation can be viewed as a healthy and normal behaviour which allows for a release of sexual tension and which 'can be a way of becoming more comfortable with and/or enjoying one's sexuality by getting to know and like one's body' (NICHCY 1992). This behaviour can become a problem if it is performed in an inappropriate place or accompanied by strong feelings of guilt or anxiety. Should this be the case, it is essential to discuss the situation.

Adolescents need to be taught the difference between public (school, stores, friend's house, library, community center, bathrooms, playgrounds, etc.) and private (bathroom at home, bedroom) spaces. Emphasis must be placed on conditions that are acceptable in which masturbation can take place, namely when the adolescent is alone in his bedroom with the door closed. The message must be clear and precise (the use of pictograms or key words summarizing the situation can be helpful) in order to avoid misunderstandings that could result in inappropriate behaviours.

In the event that masturbation was to become the adolescent's main activity, it would be important to assess whether the behaviour is new (perhaps linked to anxiety, a change in routine, hormones, dating, etc.) or if takes on the form of a sexual compulsion. In the case of the latter, the adolescent should be allowed to engage, on a daily basis, in a few episodes of self-stimulation. It is perfectly normal for an Aspie of this age to masturbate a couple of times per day. Should the behaviour be performed at the expense of other activities, it would be desirable to broaden the teen's repertoire of stimulating and interesting activities.

Another solution would be to encourage social interactions and the development of friendships. Diverse activities and a larger social network could then become a source of pleasure that would decrease the need for self-stimulation. Another strategy, in the case of a sexual compulsion, is to keep the adolescent's hands busy, be it by drawing, painting, sculpture, writing, typing on a computer keyboard, photography, calculations, tennis, or any other activity that requires concentration. The goal is not to sublimate sexual impulses, but rather to expand and diversify the individual's repertoire of stimulating activities. The frequency of masturbation generally decreases on its own after adolescence. It is therefore important to respect the individual's sexual development and interventions should be aimed at helping the Aspie meet his needs in a manner that is both acceptable and rewarding.

WHAT IF AN UNLAWFUL OR HARMFUL ACT IS COMMITTED AGAINST THE ASPIE, OR IF THE ASPIE COMMITS ONE OF THE SAME ON SOMEONE ELSE?

Several behaviours are judged harmful or unlawful: exhibitionism, voyeurism, frotteurism, sexual abuse, pedophilia, and many other deviant sexual behaviours. An Aspie can be victim or victimizer. Below are some suggestions on how to address the issue:

1.   Sensitize the Aspie to the different forms of sexual abuse to which they may be exposed, be it in their family, outside of

the family, or within their romantic relationship. The goal is to encourage adolescents to express themselves when faced with abusive situations and to develop means to protect themselves and others.

2.   Discuss privacy and its boundaries, including personal examples.

3.   Sexuality and the law: ask the Aspie to judge various situations and to say what is acceptable or unacceptable.

4.   What about notions of when and where to exchange intimacy?

5.   The limits of love (healthy, unhealthy and abusive situations).

6.   What is dating violence? And how do you recognize the cycle of violence?

7.   How to react to sexual assault?

8.   Watch for warning signs: when someone is excessively jealous, has an explosive temper, becomes withdrawn, depressed, is extremely agitated, or acts strangely, etc.

(Making Waves Program).

Some activities which may be helpful to address the topic include:

- identifying the different forms of sexual abuse that can be experienced by boys and girls in our society

- allowing the youth to identify their own boundaries with respect to privacy, legal and societal norms, and to clarify their notions of consent

- reflecting upon the different forms of sexual abuse that can exist within the context of dating

- sensitizing the youth to the importance of confiding in someone if they are victims of sexual abuse and inform them of the resources and laws that can help them

- providing them with information about the resources and help that individuals who commit acts of sexual abuse can receive (Durocher and Fortier 1999, pp.4–27).

The topic of sexual abuse is a delicate one. You will find a list of suggested resources, aimed at facilitating discussion and learning, at the end of the chapter.

WHAT ABOUT BIRTH CONTROL AND INITIAL EXAMINATIONS
OF SEXUAL ORGANS?

With the arrival of adolescence, a major learning objective for Aspies is to develop a sense of responsibility. For this to take place, they must receive a maximum amount of information concerning their sexual development so as to avoid general misconceptions. One concrete manner in which this can be achieved is to have an initial examination of their sexual organs conducted by a physician. It will then be possible for the physician to explain the changes that take place during puberty (hormones, secondary sexual characteristics, STD and HIV prevention, reproduction, etc.). Make sure that the Aspie is referred to a physician who is comfortable and competent in dealing with the topic of sexuality. It would be helpful to explain the situation when you make the appointment and you can ask the physician to prepare pamphlets of additional information. You can explain that this medical consultation is also an opportunity for the adolescent to ask questions. There may be less shyness or discomfort if the teen is comfortable attending the appointment alone rather than in the presence of parents. This may also be an opportunity to address the issue of birth control. The efficacy and simplicity of the different forms of contraception can therefore be presented in an appropriate context.

If the Aspie refuses to consult a physician, a sex educator can provide the same information without conducting the physical exam. Ask the teen what he is most comfortable with and encourage him in his process. If there is much resistance, it is possible to present this type of routine exam in the context of the school nurse. It is possible that anxiety will decrease in a known context such as school. Such an examination can be very positive experience but it is by no means mandatory. It is always possible to delay it and wait for a more opportune moment. If the exam and sexuality become associated with high levels of anxiety, it is best to drop it for now. However, the situation is quite different if the adolescent has an infection or a health problem.

It is important to note that if such an exam allows the Aspie to better understand the different aspects of his development, we should encourage him to go through the process. However, if it becomes a source of stress it is better to wait. With respect to contraception, several methods are simple and effective. The adolescent should have the opportunity to choose the method that suits him best (in terms of cost, use, simplicity, and accessibility). Condoms and birth control pills are the most common methods used by adolescents. The combination of the two, if used appropriately, is an effective form of birth control and serves to prevent STDs. Before use, it is important to ensure that the Aspie understands the different steps and that he will be apt to follow them. Several information pamphlets are available on this subject.

Conclusion

Sexual education has both short- and long-term goals. In the short term, it allows adaptive sexual behaviours to emerge with respect to communication, emotions, and interpersonal relationships.

As the topic of sexuality is related to teenagers, the focus of sexual behaviours is self-pleasure, dating, sexual understanding and avoiding sexual exploitation. The questions of when to have intercourse should be discussed within the Aspie's morals and values, when he is at a mature age. Family and group discussions are encouraged.

Aspies, just like any other individuals, need to understand that having intercourse and active sexual relationships of other kinds are not the only way to establish a solid relationship between two people. Everybody has the right to say 'no' to sexual activities. Sexuality shouldn't serve a function other than what the teenager wants, and is ready for it to be. In this light, abstinence can be viewed not only as a judicious choice but also, and ultimately, as a form of birth control.

Over the longer term, adolescents with AS will be in a better position to understand what interpersonal relationships consist of and will engage in appropriate behaviours in a variety of relationship contexts. They should also be able to explain what is meant by a sexual relationship, how it unfolds, and the circumstances (time, place, appropriate individuals) under which it is possible for one to take place, all while conducting themselves in a manner that is consistent with the situation. Finally, they will understand what is meant by informed consent in the context of a sexual relationship (Tremblay, Desjardins and Gagnon 1993). The ultimate goal is to allow Aspies to fully experience their sexuality.

Internet resources

Sexuality

www.autismuk.com/index9sub.htm

www.amug.org/~a203/sex.html

www.nichcy.org

Facial expression

Gaining Face software:
www.ccoder.com/GainingFace

Prevention of sexual abuse

Relationships: Making Waves Program
www.mwaves.org/1.html#top

Further reading

Aston, M.C. (2001) *The Other Half of Asperger Syndrome.* London: National Autistic Society.

Cornelius, D.A. *et al.* (1982) *Who Cares? A Handbook on Sex Education and Counseling Services for Disabled People.* Baltimore, MD: University Park Press.

Ford, A. (1987) 'Sex education for individuals with autism: Structuring information and opportunities.' In D.J. Cohen, A.M. Donnellan and R. Paul (eds) *Handbook of Autism and Pervasive Developmental Disorders.* Maryland, MD: Winston. pp.430–439.

Gillberg, C. (1983) *Eveil de la conscience sexuelle chez l'adolescent autistique. L'avenir des autistes et psychotiques à travers différentes approches.* Paris: Actes du Congrès de Paris.

Gray, S., Ruble, L. and Dalrymple, N. (1996) *Autism and sexuality: A Guide for Instruction.* Bloomington, IN: Autism Society of Indiana.

Haracopos, D. and Pedersen, L. (1999) *The Danish Report.* (SFTAH, UK): Society for the Autistically Handicapped. www.autismuk.com/index9sub.htm

Hellemans, H. (1996) 'L'éducation sexuelle des adolescents autistes.' Paper presented to conference, Brussels.

Hingsburger, D. (1993) *Parents Ask Questions about Sexuality and Children with Developmental Disabilities.* Vancouver: Family Support Institute Press.

Howes, N. (1982) *Fully Human: A Program in Human Sexuality for the Developmentally Disabled.* Cambridge: Sun-Rose Associates, Black & White Publishing.

Howlin, P., Baron-Cohen, S. and Hadwin, J. (1999) *Teaching Children with Autism to Mind-read.* Chichester: Wiley.

Kempton, W. (1993) *Socialization and Sexuality: A Comprehensive Training Guide.* California: W. Kempton.

Konstantareas, M.M. and Lunsky, Y.J. (1997) 'Sociosexual knowledge, experience, attitudes, and interests of individuals with autistic disorder and developmental delay.' *Journal of Autism and Developmental Disorders 27,* 113–125.

Lieberman, A. and Melone, M.B. (1979) *Sexuality and Social Awareness.* Connecticut: Benhaven Press.

Luiselli, J.K., Helfen, C.S., Pemberton, B.W. and Reisman, J. (1977) 'The elimination of a child's in-class masturbation by overcorrection and reinforcement.' *Journal of Behavioural Therapy and Experimental Psychiatry 8,* 201–204.

Masters, W.H., Johnson, V.E. And Kolodny, R.C. (1988) *Sexuality.* Denmark: Gyldendal.

McCarthy, M. and Phil, B. (1996) 'The sexual support needs of people with learning disabilities: a profile of those referred for sex education.' *Sexuality and Disability 14,* 265–279.

McKee, L. and Blacklidge, V. (1986) *An Easy Guide for Caring Parents: Sexuality and Socialization.* California: Planned Parenthood.

Melone, M.B. and Lettick, A.L. (1979) *Sex Education at Benhaven. Benhaven Then and Now.* Connecticut: Benhaven Press.

Ousley, O.Y. and Mesibov, G.B. (1991) 'Sexual attitudes and knowledge of high-functioning adolescents and adults with autism.' *Journal of Autism and Developmental Disorders 21,* 471–481.

Robison, P.C., Conahan, F. and Brady, W. (1992) 'Reducing self-injurious masturbation using a least intrusive model and adaptative equipment.' *Sexuality and Disability 10,* 1, 43–55.

Ruble, L.A. and Dalrymple, J. (1993) 'Social/sexual awareness of persons with autism: a parental perspective.' *Archives of Sexual Behaviour 22,* 229–240.

Stavis, P. and Walker-Hirsch, L.W. (1999) 'Consent to sexual activity.' In R.D. Dinerstein, S.S. Herr and J.L. O'Sullivan (eds) *A Guide to Consent.* Washington, DC: American Association on Mental Retardation.

Team Asperger (2000) *Gaining Face.* Wisconsin: Team Asperger.

Timmers, R.L., DuCharme, P. and Jacob, G. (1981) 'Sexual knowledge, attitudes and behaviours of developmentally disabled adults living in a normalized apartment setting.' *Sexuality and Disability 4,* 27–39.

Torisky, D. and Torisky, C. (1985) 'Sex education and sexual awareness building for autistic children and youth: some viewpoints and consideration.' *Journal of Autism and Developmental Disorders 15,* 213–227.

Tremblay, R. *et al.* (1998) *Guide d'education sexuelle à l'usage des professionnels,* Vol. 1. Paris: Editions Eres.

Van Bourgondien, M., Reichle, N.C. and Palmer, A. (1997) 'Sexual behaviour in adults with autism.' *Journal of Autism and Developmental Disorders 27,* 2, 113–125.

References

American Academy of Pediatrics (1996) 'Sexuality education of children and adolescents with developmental disabilities.' *Pediatrics 97,* 2, 275–278.

Durocher, L. and Fortier, M. (1999) *Programme d'éducation sexuelle.* Montreal: Les Centres jeunesse de Montréal et la Régie Régionale de la Santé et des Services Sociaux, Direction de la santé publique.

Griffiths, D. (1998) 'La sexualité des personnes présentant un trouble envahissant du développement. Paper presented to conference, Monteal.

Griffiths, D., Quinsey, V.L. and Hingsburger, D. (1989) *Changing Inappropriate Sexual Behaviour.* Baltimore: Paul H. Brookes.

Hingsburger, D. (1993) *Parents Ask Questions about Sexuality and Children with Developmental Disabilities.* Vancouver: Family Support Institute Press.

National Information Center for Children and Youth with Disabilities (NICHCY) (1992). 'Sexuality education for children and youth with disabilities.' *NICHCY News Digest 17,* 1–37.

Tremblay, R. *et al.* (2001) *Guide d'education sexuelle à l'usage des professionnels,* Vol. 2. Paris: Editions Eres.

Tremblay, G., Desjardins, J. and Gagnon, J.P. (1993) *Programme de développement psychosexual.* Eastman: Éditions Behavioura.

4

Can my Baby Learn to Dance?
Exploring the Friendships
of Asperger Teens

Steven E. Gutstein

Friendship is unnecessary, like philosophy, like art... It has no survival value; rather it is one of those things that give value to survival.

(C.S. Lewis)

Introduction

Jack's almost perpetual scowl was evident from the moment he entered The Connections Center's waiting room. Jack is a tall, unkempt, overweight 14-year-old with Asperger Syndrome (AS) brought by his mother for help with social skills. Jack was clearly unhappy about coming to see me. He repeatedly told me that the visit was pointless. He already knew everything he needed to know about having friends. In fact he claimed he had many friends. Not surprisingly, a radically different picture emerged when I talked with Elva, Jack's mother. With one exception, Jack spent no time with his reported 'friends' away from the structured activities of his classroom. Elva felt that generally the children at school tolerated Jack but did not take any interest in him. Jack never called any of his classmates, nor did they ever call him or invite him to any activity. In fact Jack almost never went out of his house when he was not forced to, except for frequent trips to the store to purchase a new videogame. Videogames were Jack's life. He had all of the different game consoles and scores of games.

Elva told me that Jack had found one friend, David, in his special education class. David was as big a videogame fanatic as Jack. They frequently sat together at lunch, deep in discussion of game characters and scenes. David came over to Jack's house about once a week. Elva was very excited that Jack had finally made a friend. In fact this friendship was the primary reason she was bringing Jack for help. She worried that without learning better social skills Jack would soon lose his first friend. Elva became worried when she observed that often Jack would get tired of playing or more likely waiting and suddenly get up and leave the room to watch a video, oblivious to the whereabouts of his friend. While Jack was always excited prior to David's arrival, after about an hour or two he would act like he was tired of David's presence and would abruptly tell him it was time to leave.

Daniel, a very bright 19-year-old, came to see me after spending several weeks in a psychiatric hospital following what he described as a 'nervous breakdown.' It was in the hospital that Daniel was first diagnosed with AS. When I first met Daniel, he told me, much like Jack, that he had a number of friends. Unlike Jack, Daniel knew quite a bit about his friends. Daniel communicated with his friends on a daily basis. However, he had never seen any of them face to face. His friendships were all 'Internet relationships.' During his daily 10 to 12 hours on the Internet he would correspond with many people. He wrote long essays and sent them off, with no regard for whether anyone was interested in receiving them or not. Aside from his time on the Internet, Daniel was taking a couple of classes each semester at a local community college. He would attend the class and then leave and take the bus home as quickly as possible. He did not know the name of a single student in any of his classes. Other than his twice-weekly trips to college, Daniel did not leave his home unless forced to by his parents. He spent almost all of his time in the tiny garage apartment his parent's had set up for him at the back of their small home.

Adam is an extremely polite, soft-spoken 16-year-old with a great sense of humor. Adam was mercilessly teased at the private school he attended during his elementary years. Despite this, Adam recalls that he was able to make several friendships. But when he left his school, he lost contact with these friends. Adam is very close to his parents and older sister. He knows he can trust them. But Adam wonders whether he can find a friend that will not leave or hurt him. He tells me, 'It is too hard to find the right person. Everyone is either too young or has different interests. The things that interest me are usually the things that friends my age are not interested in at all, or are too young to be involved with. I feel that many friends have 'bailed' on me. They are going to different schools or things like that. For example, my best friend Tommy used to be in my class. Then in August or September 1998 he started going to a new school.'

Adam now attends a small school where he is accepted and protected from cruelty. However, he has become more fearful of leaving familiar environments and has recently stopped attending his weekly church youth group, despite being able to recount a number of memories of good times.

I have known Matthew, who is now 16, since he was 3 years old. After enduring years of cruelty and torment from other public school children, Matthew realized that kids would stop picking on him if he found allies who would join with him in targeting others. Matthew quickly went from victim to aggressor and became adept at finding other outcasts to partner with. Together they would tease children who were even less accepted. Matthew knew that this behaviour was wrong. But, he could not bring himself to stop. For Matthew, the choice was between being accepted through shared cruelty, or being the outcast and subject of teasing and beatings.

Forming friendships based around cruelty to another child is not only true in Matthew's case. Polite, rule-following Adam talked about his friend Tommy in a similar manner. 'The best thing we did? We used to pick on Cliff because he was always being annoying. We used to make up a song that made fun of him. Of course it would sound a bit vulgar. It would make us laugh. Tommy and I always played guitar in my room and he would sing silly songs to make fun of somebody. That was a secret between me and Tommy.'

Fredrick, now in college, came to me several years ago, wondering if he should take his own life. Prior to working with me, Fredrick had practiced very hard to fit in and be considered normal. He succeeded well and by his junior year in high school only a specialist in AS would recognize his condition. But the price he paid for this 'success' was enormous. He felt that he could never relax, never let his guard down. Social interaction consisted of constantly figuring out what others expected him to say or do and then providing it for them. It was a constant, terrifying ordeal, where the only reward was to avoid embarrassment or ridicule. Fredrick had memorized countless rules and scripts for social behaviour. He had used his extremely high intelligence to develop even more sophisticated scripts that had seen him through some difficult situations. But, Fredrick wondered, what was the point of all this? Why continue to perform this horrible play with no end in sight?

The friendships of AS adolescents

These brief vignettes offer only a tiny glimpse into the struggles faced by AS teens in their efforts to develop friendships. Experts agree that friendships, especially in adolescence, are critical to healthy development. Researchers and theorists studying AS believe that the ability to form real, reciprocal friendships is a critical marker of successful intervention. But what do we know about the friendships of teenagers with AS? And what methods are available to help AS teens understand and value close relationships? Surprisingly we know very little about either. When I did an extensive review of the research literature, I could find only two studies of AS teens that even indirectly studied their social functioning. The results were not hopeful. A research group (Green *et al.* 2000) recently compared AS adolescents with a matched group of non-autistic teenagers diagnosed with Conduct Disorder. Teens with a Conduct Disordered diagnosis are noted for their extremely poor social adjustment. The researchers found that teenagers with AS were significantly more socially impaired than their Conduct Disordered peers. Additionally, similarly high levels of anxiety, obsessional disorders, depression, suicidal ideation, rage and defiance were found in both groups.

Some people believe that persons with Asperger Syndrome do not need friends, allies and lovers. They talk about the disorder as if those who suffer from it were aliens from another planet, but people with Asperger Syndrome are human beings with the same needs as others. To demonstrate this, Bauminger and Kasari (2000) studied loneliness and understanding of friendship in a sample of teens with high functioning autism and Asperger Syndrome. On a loneliness rating scale, the autistic sample reported greater feelings of loneliness than did the typical teens.

However, the researchers found some striking differences in the understanding of loneliness and friendship expressed by the autistic teens. They found that adolescents with autism lacked an understanding of the emotional aspects both of loneliness and of friendship, not related to either their intelligence or language development. The researchers concluded that the teenagers did not understand that they could derive security or companionship from a friendship. Rather, they typically saw friends as playmates. They were missing out on the qualities of friendship that can reduce feelings of loneliness.

When we try to understand the social life of adults with AS, we find even less information. One recent study conducted under the auspices of the National Autistic Society of Great Britain did attempt to examine the social functioning of AS adults and the results were alarming. The authors found that 37 percent of AS adults reported no participation at all in social activities, while 50 percent reported going out no more than one or two times per month.

The six levels of friendship

We often use the term friendship without defining what kind of relationship we are talking about. We refer to friendships as if they were all alike – as if the relationship of two 4-year-olds is no different than two 16-year-olds. In reality friendship changes dramatically from the initial bonds formed in pre-school years to the close friendships of the older adolescent. For typical children, friendship is a progressively complex array of skills. Friendships gradually become more sophisticated. They reach their zenith by the close of adolescence. A number of psychologists have constructed models for the stages of friendship development. In summarizing their work I have developed a six-level model of friendship development, which we use at The Connections Center.

Level I

An important point to realize is that typically developing children are not ready for peer friendships until they have had extensive training and practice being partners with adults. Research psychologist Carollee Howes, the world's foremost expert on the development of early friendships, has conducted research showing that in typical development children are not interested in playing with peers, with the exception of brief interactions, until some time during their third year (Howes and Matheson 1992). In this initial pre-friendship level, adults function both as the principal social partners as well as guides. They prepare the child to participate as an equal partner in the less predictable but more exciting interactions with peers. This is a critical step that cannot be bypassed, as it lays the foundation for all future friendship development.

Level II

Children at Level II are mainly concerned with finding an equal partner with whom they can share and coordinate activities. Friends are considered those peers who consistently act as enjoyable playmates and who communicate their desire to interact with their friend by showing excitement and consistently choosing their friend when opportunities present themselves. Even at this beginning friendship stage, a peer friend is expected to take equal responsibility for coordinating the pair's actions.

Level III

In Level III the elements of collaboration and mutual support come into play. Friends experience the strength of acting together as a unit to solve problems and overcome obstacles. Friends help each other in simple ways. They also show concern if their friend is hurting or scared. Level III friends develop co-creative activities by combining their ideas and developing new activity variations, which become their own versions of games. These collaborative creations serve to cement the bond between friends. Children involved in Level III friendships know that friends will not tolerate a cheater or sore loser. Nor will they want to be with someone who does not find ways of compromising and collaborating with them. By the close of this level, friendships become the main arena for social comparison, as children examine similarities and differences between themselves and friends as part of their initial identity development.

Level IV

Children ready for a Level IV friendship have begun to perceive of their relationships in a more self-conscious manner. They recognize the importance of considering others' thoughts and feelings as distinct from theirs. They become aware of the need to act in a manner that will be attractive to a friend. They become interested in how they are perceived by their peers and purposefully seek to create a good impression. They also know that to keep a friend you must provide something in your interaction that is meaningful to them, not just what you find interesting. Friends begin to become highly valued as collaborators in the world of ideas and imagination.

Level V

As typically developing children approach middle school years, there is an emerging desire for friends who will share ideas and internal emotional states. The child can now differentiate between what is really felt as opposed to what may be overtly expressed. He becomes interested in deciphering friends' intentions as well as observing their actions. The enduring preferences and opinions of friends become important. One element that clearly distinguishes the Level V friendship is the knowledge that a friend should function as a reliable ally. Children describe friends as understanding, loyal, and trustworthy. An ally is someone you can count on; someone who always takes your side (except when the two of you are having a conflict). An ally will stand up for you if someone is trying to hurt you. Friends must prove themselves as trustworthy, ready to support and stand up for their buddies whenever called upon to do so. In this stage children also learn the need for regular friendship maintenance such as frequent phone calls.

Level VI

By teenage years, typically developing teenagers report that exchanging intimacy has become the crucial defining characteristic of close friendships. Friends work hard to develop and maintain a strong bond of trust and mutual concern. They know each other's fears, dreams, strengths and weaknesses and treat their friend's vulnerabilities with acceptance and respect. Teenagers view a friendship as something that exists apart from the moment, or from the individual's current actions. They learn to examine their different friendships and determine which qualify as truly close friendships. They learn to accurately define the concept and to evaluate their friendships in relation to the level in which the friend has earned their trust. Teenagers realize that all friendships do not have the same value. There are people you can have fun with, but you may not share common interests with. The very person who can be your ally and stand up for you may not be sensitive when you talk about a fear. Not everyone can keep a secret or provide constructive feedback.

Characteristics of successful adolescents

In contrast to the paucity of research about friendships of AS teens, there is considerable data about the development of friendships in typical adolescents. We know that adolescence is the most important developmental period for friendships. Typically developing teenagers spend about 30 percent of their waking time in the company of their friends, the largest percentage of time of any age group. The elements needed for successful adolescent friendships have been extensively studied over that past 20 years. I have synthesized the research findings into eight characteristics. Adolescents who are successful at forming and maintaining friendships:

1. Act as enthusiastic, enjoyable companions.

2. Adapt their actions, feelings, perceptions and ideas to coordinate with their friends.

3. Communicate to friends that they are valuable and that their friendship is highly desirable.

4. Maintain a balance of give and take in caring for friends' needs.

5. Take regular, effective friendship maintenance and repair actions.

6. Communicate appreciation for and acceptance of differences.

7. Develop trust through consistent provision of care, support and mutual disclosure.

8. Understand the many benefits of close friendship.

Enthusiastic, enjoyable companions

While many sophisticated skills and strategies are required for successful friendships, typically developing teens still consider whether their friend is fun to be around. The child who goes out of his way to communicate joy and pleasure during shared activities will typically be valued. People of all ages enjoy being around those who are upbeat and enthusiastic. Reports of 'I just feel happier when I'm with her,' or 'Her laughter is contagious,' are common indicators of friendship selection. In a similar vein, successful friends make numerous positive approaches and invitations to their peers. They invite friends to interact in an enticing manner that communicates a commitment towards the enjoyment and fun of those being invited. The time friends spend with one another is characterized by a willingness to share, cooperate, and help.

Adapting to coordinate with friends

As early as the age of four, children spend considerable time finding commonalities with selected peers in a number of domains. Shared interests often define the friendships of late-elementary aged children. By adolescence, common beliefs, values and attitudes are a significant factor in friendship selection.

The desire for coordination with others extends to the domain of emotions as well. A child, who only engages in activities that he finds enjoyable, without observing the reactions of his peers, will typically be avoided. On the other hand, the child who bases his subsequent actions on the emotional reactions of social partners will be highly valued. Emotional coordination also involves showing interest in understanding and relating to the emotional experiences of social partners. Friends must be willing and able to communicate caring and to provide help to one another when in need, even if giving assistance requires they delay or discontinue a pleasurable or desired activity. A final, critical aspect of emotional coordination is exemplified in the concept discussed by researcher Bob Emde (1989) as the 'we-go.' Even younger children share a feeling of being allied in a common unit a type of group ego or 'we-go' that together is stronger than the sum of its parts. Older children perceive their friends as crucial allies, who will drop what they are doing and come to their aid in times of need. They operate like the Three Musketeers with their motto of 'One for all and all for one.'

Communicating value and desirability

We choose to spend time with people who make us feel valued. Good friends communicate their appreciation and admiration on a regular basis. They let their friends know that they are more important than videogames or any other objects. They make a point of noticing the talents and achievements of their buddies. They quickly stop what they are doing, even if it is something of interest, to acknowledge and interact with a friend. They express the desire to get to know their friend better.

Maintaining a balance of give and take

Equality is a hallmark of all friendships. Friends are expected to provide as much as they take from others. Friends expect that they will not have to 'carry' the relationship for both parties. They expect that each will do the calling and inviting, rather than leaving it up to one of the partners. Good friends will go to a movie that their friend wants to see, even if they would prefer a different one. They will help each other when that help is needed.

Effective relationship repair

Friendships, like other relationships, do not take place in a highly rule bound, predictable arena. They operate through more loosely structured social 'frameworks' which provide for the introduction of large amounts of variety and novelty, but also result in a high degree of potential for confusion, misunderstanding and conflict. Valued friends constantly monitor their interactions for signs that their partner is confused, unhappy or that they are not coordinated with one another. Based upon these 'referencing' observations and communications, good friends adapt their actions and attempt to 'repair' misunderstandings, conflicts and the loss of social and emotional coordination.

We choose friends who function as equal partners in maintaining and repairing the relationship. If one of the partners has to do the bulk of adjusting, clarifying, adapting and repairing, the other partner will quickly find the relationship to be a 'drag' and seek out partners who take on more of the responsibility of the relationship, so that they can equally participate in the creative, enjoyable aspects of their encounters. Furthermore, because of their greater investment in one another, friends are expected to work harder to resolve conflicts and to take actions that will prevent conflicts from ever occurring.

Appreciation and accepting differences

Maintaining coordination and feelings of relatedness are one side of the friendship coin. The other side is represented by the fact that, no matter what their similarities and mutual interests, friends will have differences with one another. Skills for productive conflict resolution are essential.

Good friends value the creative contributions of their partners, even when they are quite different from their own (Asher, Parker and Walker 1996). They prefer friends who provide the excitement of new ways of playing a game, variations on activities and new and different ideas, as long as they are presented with sensitivity to their partner's reactions and with an equally shared interest in their own contributions.

When sharing a common experience, good friends appreciate that their partner's perceptions and perspective is just as 'correct' as their own, even if different. They are excited by the new ideas and methods. Valued friends express the strong desire to learn about the different ideas and feelings of their partners. They communicate that they very much want to get to know who you really are as a person and are willing to accept you, flaws and all.

Trust

By adolescence, children value their ability to trust a friend more than any other attribute. Trust is based upon a number of factors. Can the friend keep his promises and not divulge secrets? Will a friend be a consistent ally? Will he stand up for you when others are against you? Teenagers expect their friends to listen to their feelings and to empathize. They assume that a close friend will drop what he is doing to help, when he is really needed. Finally, they view close friendships as safe places to confide their personal feelings, worries, fears and mistakes, knowing that they will receive confidentiality and support.

Appreciating the benefits of close friendship

As typically developing children get older and move to the more advanced level of friendship, they expect a great deal more from their friends. Thus, the skills required for successful friendship increase dramatically. In order to sustain the motivation to maintain friendship, teenagers must experience commensurate rewards. They must recognize the value of a friend as an ally and consistent source of support. They must have accumulated years of memories where friends served to enhance their enjoyment and decrease their pain and fear. They should have memories of friends joining together with them to accomplish and overcome things they could never have done on their own.

Absolute and relative thinking

You may have noticed that many of the skills involved in being a good friend differ from the social behaviours that are taught in skills classes and groups or that can be learned through social stories. Many of us have become used to thinking of social skills as specific behaviours, such as making eye contact, waiting your turn, smiling, shaking hands and asking polite questions. In social skills classes unfortunately AS children are often taught 'absolute' formulas that if applied properly will lead to social success.

This type of absolute, scripted approach can indeed be helpful with one aspect of social competence. Teaching formulas, stories and behavioural scripts help you to get information and basic needs met and allow you to blend into society and appear more 'normal.' Too often when we use the term 'social skills' we are only referring to these types of absolute ways of thinking. Skills like learning to dress in a 'cool' manner, wearing your hair in the latest style, maintaining proper hygiene, respecting physical boundaries and similar behaviours are very important. Without such skills, children will not be accepted by most of their peers. However, obtaining social acceptance, while a good beginning, is not the same thing as forming and maintaining a real, reciprocal friendship.

Instead of a repertoire of behaviours or specific actions to take in specific situations, a person wishing to develop real friendships must learn a new way to think about and perceive his social environment. Friendship relationships require that we learn to think in a relative manner. In a relationship things are not absolute. Actions are useful or not, depending upon how they affect our level of coordination with our partner.

To be a friend, you must learn to rapidly process emotional information coming from your friend and then rapidly apply that information as the critical reference point for determining your actions. Only then will you be able to apply the appropriate behaviour to the interaction and experience both success and pleasure. Table 4.1 provides some examples of the difference between 'Absolute' and 'Relative' thinking:

Table 4.1 Differences between 'absolute' and 'relative' thinking	
'Absolute' thinking	*'Relative' thinking*
I always go to the hair stylist and ask for a 'cool' haircut.	Am I speaking too loud?
When you ask me a question I should respond with accurate information.	Are we walking together? Should I slow down a little bit to let my friend catch up?
I must always look at someone when they are speaking to me.	Is my conversation topic interesting enough?
If I want children in my class to like me, I should always smile when I see them and try to say positive things to them.	Is this the right time to ask you to do me a favor?

Instrumental and experience sharing interactions

A second crucial difference in social behaviour involves our motivation for engaging in a social encounter. A busy housewife standing in line at the bank or checkout counter, a salesman making pleasant conversation with a potential client, or a young child pointing to a toy he wants are all engaged in what we refer to as 'Instrumental' Interactions. The term implies that in these social encounters other people are the 'instruments' we use to obtain some non-social endpoint. Our social partners are means to an end. If they cannot provide what we need from them, we will move on to someone else. For example, if a checkout line appears too long, you will simply move to another line that appears shorter. Your goal is to get out of the supermarket, not to have a relationship with the clerk.

A very different reason for interacting is referred to as 'Experience Sharing.' In Experience Sharing encounters we have no specific endpoint in mind. We interact specifically to share ideas, feelings and perceptions. Experience Sharing allows us to create and deepen emotional connections between people, share excitement and joy, collaborate for novel problem solving, reach shared goals and cooperate in joint creative efforts. Part of the payoff of Experience Sharing encounters is that we do not know what they will lead to. Therefore they cannot be pre-planned and scripted.

Both types of motivation are important for a successful life. But only the motivation for Experience Sharing will lead someone to do the hard work needed to maintain a friendship. Table 4.2 provides some examples of this distinction.

Table 4.2 Distinction between instrumental motivation and experience sharing

Instrumental Motivation	Experience Sharing
Pointing to obtain an out-of-reach object.	After losing the big football game, the entire high school team huddles together to console one another. Though they lost the game, everyone feels better knowing that they have always been there for one another.
Inviting another child to play checkers so that you can win.	You and your buddy ride your bikes side by side, just for the fun of it, going no place in particular.
Following classroom behaviour rules to obtain a reward.	When you and your pal meet, you always tell a silly joke that makes you both laugh, for no apparent reason.
Standing in line at the checkout counter of the supermarket to get your food.	You meet a new classmate and get excited when you find out you share many of the same beliefs and opinions.
Working at a job you dislike, because you need the money.	

AS: a disorder of relative information processing for Experience Sharing

In prior publications I summarized extensive research, conducted over the past 30 years, supporting my belief that the primary deficit of Asperger Syndrome is the failure to develop relative information processing for Experience Sharing (Gutstein 2000; Gutstein 2002; Gutstein and Sheely 2002a, 2002b). Researchers like Peter Mundy, and Marian Sigman (1999) refer to a lack of spontaneous seeking to share their enjoyment and interests with others as a cardinal feature of all autism spectrum conditions. Noted autism theorist Peter Hobson (1993) states: 'Autistic children do not fully understand what it means for people to share and coordinate their experiences.' Trevarthen *et al.* (1996) describe people with autism as impaired in both their emotional and collaborative responses. In a nutshell, these researchers and theorists agree that AS teenagers are born with a disorder that directly impacts their ability to understand and develop the relative thinking and perceiving skills needed for Experience Sharing.

By the time he reaches adolescence, the AS teenager may have already spent years journeying down a different pathway of social development. Their road does not include the normal child's countless thousands of hours of experimenting and practicing with relative thinking for Experience Sharing. They increasingly diverge from their typical peers in their interests, drives and social thinking. In effect, they develop their own unique brand of 'social science' that excludes the study and mastery of reciprocal, Experience Sharing relationships. The teenager with AS may continue to actively pursue social interactions throughout his life. However, by never entering the arena of Experience Sharing, he misses out on the most challenging, exciting and rewarding aspect of the social world. Without the motivation for Experience Sharing, the youngster never spends the thousands of hours and conducts the extensive personal research and self-discovery process by which typical children become such experts at relationship building and maintenance.

Teaching friendship skills to AS teens

Over the past 15 years I have struggled to develop a model – Relationship Development Intervention (RDI) – that would provide children within the autism spectrum both the motivation and skills to participate in emotionally fulfilling, reciprocal friendships. The theory and methods of RDI are available in prior publications, along with hundreds of activities that are developmentally sequenced.

What I have learned in developing the RDI is that the process of learning Experience Sharing is not a simple one for people with AS, nor can it be accomplished in a short period of time. However, by understanding the critical elements involved in relationship development, teaching them in a clear developmental sequence and establishing the appropriate goals, we can dramatically improve the quality and equality of friendships in our AS teenagers. In this chapter I can only provide a summary of the complex process of teaching AS youths to build friendships. For more comprehensive guidelines for building a program you can refer to the manuals I developed along with my wife, Rachelle Sheely (2002a; 2002b), *Relationship Developmental Intervention with Children, Adolescents and Adults.*

What does friendship mean to the adolescent?

One of the first things I do when interviewing a teenager who has come to The Connections Center for help with friendships is to determine how they understand the benefits of friendship and the actions they believe are necessary to obtain and maintain friendships. As I discussed earlier, Bauminger and Kasari (2000) studied the ways in which teenagers understood the concept of friendship. They also asked the teens' mothers about their children's friends. Interestingly enough, the mothers reported that their children frequently distorted their claims of friendship. They rated a child as a friend based more on their and the child's desire than actual mutual interest and interaction. For example, parents told the researchers, 'He says that X is his friend, but X ignores him most of the time.' Or 'He tells me they are friends, but he only comes over when my son buys a new video game.'

As prior vignettes illustrate, the adolescents in my small sample demonstrate a wide range of understanding of the meaning of friendship. For example, when I asked Jack to tell me about his friends, he proceeded to recite the name of every student in his special education class. I asked Jack what made him think that these people were friends. He looked at me with disdain and replied, 'Of course they are my friends. They are nice to me aren't they?' Jack knew little about David other than his approximate age and, of course, his favorite videogames. He did not care to know his other interests, his preferences in restaurants, vacations or Christmas gifts. He did not want to know the things that scared David or made him sad. Observing Jack and David, you would see two boys sitting side by side in physical proximity, one involved in a game with his attention fully directed towards the screen, the other impatiently awaiting his turn. From time to time one boy would disparage the efforts of the other and claim that he would do much better. Occasionally, Jack would make a positive comment about David's performance like, 'Wow, you got him!' But then he would quickly punctuate this with a put down or competitive remark like, 'I reached that level a long time ago!' Either boy might talk about a game that interested him regardless of their partner's level of interest. At times their topics coincided, so that for a period of time their conversation appeared connected, but just as suddenly one of the boys would turn towards the videogame and become lost in it.

Daniel defined friends as people who responded to his long emails. He had no idea whether they were who they claimed to be. If someone took the time to email him several times, they met his definition of a friend. Daniel knew a great deal of personal information about some of his Internet friends. In fact he became quite involved in providing advice through long-winded replies. However, he framed his replies based upon his own interests at the moment, rather than the needs of the other person.

At one point, Daniel became concerned about a female Internet companion. She had emailed him with a personal problem concerning her relationship with a boy. He spent days considering what his reply should be, then painstakingly wrote a quite lengthy reply beginning with the following:

> I tend to compare close friendships to suburban sub-divisions in the sense that they are both nice to be in, but you have to go slowly in both of them because painful consequences lie in wait for anyone who flies on through both of them. I remember a good friend of mine telling me that females unintentionally bring down their boyfriends. I'm still in the dark when it comes to determining the validity of that statement, so I'll have to gather more information on that. While I'm on the subject, I want to make known that I'm highly critical of the terms 'boyfriend' and 'girlfriend.'

Although both compound words do mean 'sweetheart' most of the time and that is the first definition in any dictionary, the same terms written as two separate words have the respective dictionary definitions of simply meaning 'a friend who is male' and 'a friend who is female,' the way these terms are interpreted most of time in my day sends the message, 'If you're not going to marry him/her at some point down the road, don't start a relationship with that person of the opposite sex.' Both terms are given more importance than they're due. In the early stages of being a teen, these terms vociferously yell out to everyone, 'He's my man!' or 'She's my woman!' and make one more likely to have sex and force out other people and their contributions. It is my firm belief that an attitude and a reputation like that can and should be done without.

When I asked Adam why anyone would want a friend, he replied with a more sophisticated response:

> To have someone who will help you when you really need them to do something for you. A friend might have the same interests as mine. For example if we were both interested in the same movie, it would make going to the movie more enjoyable. One trip I remember is when Tommy and I went on XLR-8 three times. Plus, after our ride on the Tidal Wave we were going crazy. We wanted to get wet again. It was more enjoyable to be with Tommy than to be alone because I have someone I know with me in a large crowd. (Why not go by yourself?) If there were no other customers, there would be nobody to talk to. The day over there would be too short. The ride seems more fun when you go on it with a friend.

Teaching the skills

Fredrick came in one day and told me about a social encounter that left him hurt and confused. He decided that he had a crush on a good-looking classmate. He had been taught that striking up a witty conversation was a good way to get a girl to like you. He had also learned that inquiring about a girl's interests is another way to get her to want to go out with you. One day he noticed the girl entering the ladies room. He stood right outside the door and patiently waited for her to emerge. She came out of the door and immediately he greeted her in an appropriate manner and inquired about her plans for the weekend. She looked away, didn't even bother to reply and just kept on walking away. Fredrick was very confused and had no idea what to do next. He had followed all of the social rules he had been taught. He had kept his body at the appropriate distance. He had brought up only subjects that he thought she would be interested in. He followed the right protocol. But he suffered a complete failure.

Fredrick's problem was that he was trying to apply an Instrumental formula to an Experience Sharing encounter. In Fredrick's prior understanding of the world, if he performed a series of actions in the proper way he would achieve a goal that he desired. Unfortunately, Instrumental and Experience Sharing encounters require very different ways of thinking and perceiving. This fundamental difference is the reason we developed Relationship Development Intervention. When we teach Instrumental Skills, we work with memorized scripts that are employed in a specific manner. They are used in order to reach a desired endpoint. We teach people to recognize the proper context in which to perform a particular script. The curriculum for Instrumental Skills involves learning a set of rules and scripts and expecting that everyone will follow them. The progression of learning entails the gradual accumulation of a larger repertoire of discrete scripts for as many settings as possible. The main objective is to help the person cope with the day-to-day problems and situations that he faces. Instrumental skills are best taught through direct instruction, social stories, behavioural shaping and modeling.

The critical skills needed for success in Experience Sharing are quite different from their Instrumental counterparts. In an Experience Sharing encounter you cannot rely on scripts or sequenced stories. Rather the 'right thing' to say and do is based upon the just prior actions of our social partners and our predictions of what they are likely to be doing or saying next.

Teenage encounters are much too complex to be taught through scripts or stories. Just glance at a few moments of two teenagers having a typical conversation and you will realize the impossibility of 'scripting' an adolescent friendship:

Jake: I was thinking about what would happen if I won
            the lottery.

David: I'd like to live on a tropical island.

Jake: Sometimes I just want to go live on another planet.

David:	Yeah, one with no school or parents.
Jake:	I want a pet dinosaur.
David:	That's strange.
Jake:	I'd really like to find the perfect woman.
David:	I'd really like to find the perfect ice-cream cone.
Jake:	Food is the best invention ever.
David:	While we're at it, I'd like to find the perfect book to read.

Typical adolescent conversation is like a jazz riff. Topics keep changing. Free associations predominate. And we haven't even considered all of the non-verbal innuendos that change meaning so dramatically. Relationship Skills cannot rely on pre-selected scripts. The actions we take in a relationship depend heavily upon what our partner is doing as well as what they have been doing and what they intend to do. The 'right' action is only determined by 'referencing' the actions and reactions of your social partners. When a child engages in social referencing, the ongoing actions and communication of the social partner become the primary 'reference point' in determining his subsequent actions. As typical children develop, they recognize the importance of referencing many more areas of their relationship with their partners, such as their perceptions, ideas, future plans and dreams and inner (as opposed to outer) feelings. Hand in hand with this increasing motivation to reference, the child develops more sophisticated observation and communication skills to achieve a greater ability to evaluate the reactions and potential future responses of their social partners. Referencing becomes a critical skill that we must teach in all of its complex facets.

Because teenage friendships involve the ongoing introduction of novelty, they require constant regulation and balancing. Friends have to make sure that the amount of variation they introduce is not so great that the interaction degenerates into confusion and chaos. But if there is too little novelty and creation, the encounter becomes stilted and boring. Success in friendship requires learning to continually monitor and regulate a balance between variation and creativity on the one hand and predictability and structure on the other. It is like an ongoing juggling act – we try to add as many balls as possible without dropping any of them.

Determining readiness

Jack is clearly not yet ready to learn Level II friendship skills. Jack still perceives of a friend as someone who does what he wants to do, when he wants to do it. He has no interest yet in functioning in a manner to increase his partner's enjoyment, or to observe carefully to see if his actions are coordinated with his partner. In fact he does not even stop to observe whether his partner is enjoying himself. If we try to teach Jack more sophisticated skills, he will reject them, or at best reluctantly learn and never use them.

In contrast, Adam already possesses some important skills of early level friendships. He has experienced Level II and III relationships and has fond memories of them. It is apparent that we would not want to work on the same set of objectives for our five AS teenagers. A friendship development program must be customized for each person, based upon what they already know and value about relationships. To aid in this process I developed an assessment method, the Relationship Development Assessment (RDA). The RDA, a fun interactive assessment, provides a way to pinpoint each person's appropriate starting place for intervention.

Finding the right partners to practice with

When we think of teaching friendship skills to teenagers, we usually assume that we should work in a group setting with peers. However, AS teens who are struggling with Level I friendship skills are not yet ready for successful dyadic peer interaction, let alone a teen group. We have to be careful to choose a simple enough setting for the AS teen to feel comfortable and practice being competent. Jack has not yet developed a reciprocal relationship with either of his parents or any other adult. In typical development children are never ready for successful peer relationships until after they have learned to be reciprocal partners with parents or other adults. Adults can function as guides and coaches, carefully varying the degree to which they take on the 'work' of regulating the relationship encounter. They instruct the child on methods of observing and coordinating their actions and then gradually require him to function as a co-regulating equal partner.

Daniel has no interest in actually meeting any of his Internet friends. In his words, 'It would only end in disappointment and confusion. I could only see it making matters worse. Besides, look what happened the last time I got close to a friend.' Daniel is referring to a friendship he had when he was in high school. He was befriended by a typically developing young man who allowed Daniel to sometimes hang out with him. It was clearly an unequal relationship. When his friend went off to college he left Daniel behind and wanted no more to do with him. Daniel had a nervous breakdown and was hospitalized. In such unequal relationships, the typically developing 'friend' may be doing almost all the work. When a friend who has been managing the relationship is no longer available, the AS adolescent has no resources to develop a new friendship.

When the teen is ready, the initial peer partners for Experience Sharing should be those teens that are more or less evenly matched when it comes to relationship competence. Involvement with more competent, well-intentioned peers may increase initial motivation and interaction attempts. However, intervention using more competent peers, no matter how well intentioned they are, has serious disadvantages when it comes to developing relationship competence. Friendship researcher Zick Rubin points out:

> Unlike learning to play tennis, when one can usually do best by practicing with a more skilled and experienced player, when it comes to learning to interact with others, the best method seems to be to practice with those who are as inexperienced as oneself. (1980, pp.22–23)

Interacting with more capable peers prevents the less skilled child from feeling competent as well as depriving them of the experience of being an equal partner. To paraphrase Rubin, more capable peers may make communication too easy by interpreting the child's wishes based upon unclear communication. Peers who are equally struggling to be competent do not have the 'ability' to afford such compensations to the child. Therefore Rubin concludes that it is from interactions with developmentally similar peers that children best learn how to function competently in a wide range of social situations. More capable peers will not gradually increase their demands for co-regulation. They will continue to carry the weight of the relationship, leaving the autistic child dependent on their regulatory actions and at a loss to sustain a relationship on their own. Once again, Rubin makes this point most cogently: 'By practicing with peers who share one's own lack of social skill [children] are best able to learn to coordinate behaviours and to pull their own weight in social interaction' (1980, p.23).

Overcoming learned obstacles and defense mechanisms

Almost all of the children who come to The Connections Center for the first time as teenagers arrive with a long history of social failure, humiliation, defensiveness and confusion. We cannot simply wish away these obstacles and just set about teaching skills. We must first understand and address these barriers to friendship development.

The problem of overly high expectations

Many parents come to see us hoping that we will teach their AS teen age-appropriate behaviours so that they can 'fit in' with their typical peers. We can and do teach age-appropriate Instrumental skills to help our teens not stand out. But there is no way that we can or should teach sophisticated friendship skills to teenagers who will not be able to use them. That is just setting them up for failure. Teenagers with AS have a very severe learning disability which leaves them 'blind' to the subtle information we use to manage relationships.

Teaching friendship skills to AS teens based on age, without considering their current level of competence, would be like taking a severely dyslexic teenager who had never learned to read and making him read *Moby Dick* because that is the book his age mates are reading. The most he could learn to do is pretend to read the book, to look at it intently, mouth words, etc. If we took this approach, the teenager would never learn to read. He would come to hate reading as a boring, empty task. He would learn to hate reading. Similarly, if we concentrate all of our energy on making the AS teen superficially look like everyone else his age, he will never learn to have a real friendship. Expending all your energy learning to fit in deprives the teenager of the real pleasures of relationships and instead, as in Roger's case, led to peer interactions experienced as ordeals to survive, rather than opportunities for enjoyment and sharing.

The problem of prior aversive experiences

Very often we are advised to get AS children involved in social situations whether they want to or not. Well-meaning professionals recommend a 'throw them into the pool and they will swim' approach to social relationships. Unfortunately, many of our AS adolescents have numerous memories of being 'thrown into the pool' and drowning. Or, they might be able to 'tread water' and survive but learn to hate social situations and avoid them at all costs. Most of the teens we have seen have been victims of cruelty on numerous occasions. For some it leads to withdrawal; for others, like Kevin they adapt by 'identifying with the aggressor' and practicing cruelty themselves.

The problem of 'pseudo friendships'

The teen and his parents may report that their child has several friends. We later find out that these 'friends' are children who sit next to them to play videogames, or children who do visit their house. However they know very little about these friends and there is little emotion sharing or curiosity. For example, Jack displayed no interest in learning more about David. The relationship was based on their shared interest in video-games and nothing more. If David had suggested that they just hang out together instead of playing videogames, Jack would have immediately rejected the request and ignored David. In Jack's case a friend is a means to an end to be quickly discarded if not interested in his game.

Another type of 'pseudo friendship' occurs when another teenager poses as a friend to the AS youth in order to take advantage of him or her in some manner. This 'friendship' may be a means to obtain 'gifts' from the AS teen, or to secretly subject him to ridicule and abuse. This is especially concerning when AS females are 'befriended' by neuro-typical males. We have to be careful to define friends as individuals who maintain good physical boundaries, who are reciprocal in giving and taking and who are genuinely interested in you.

The problem of motivation

What obstacles do we face when working on developing motivation for social competence with the AS population? As the child with AS gets older he misses out on more and more sources of reward from Experience Sharing and obtains more and more from other means. Remember the research I presented earlier about how high functioning children in the autism spectrum had a very limited understanding of the value of friendship? Clearly Jack and David obtain a very minimal payoff from their friends. And with such a small return, why would anyone expect them to do much work to develop and maintain a friendship?

When I first discussed his friendship history with Adam, it appeared that he was feeling demoralized after being rejected or abandoned by his friends. Yet after further discussions, I realized that Adam's problems, just like Jack and David, seemed to be more related to his lack of motivation to pursue a relationship when it became less convenient than a lack of specific skills. If you recall, Adam referred to his best friend Sammy, who moved to a different school. What Adam did not share at that time was that Sammy lived less than ten minutes away and was still very available as a potential friend. Once I learned this information I discussed Sammy with Adam:

Dr G: How often do you think about Sammy?

Adam: I guess it feels like once to three times a week.

Dr G: What do you do?

Adam: I think, those were the days, or I wish I could get in touch with him somehow.

Dr G: Why don't you?

Adam: I don't know his email address.

Dr G: How often would you want to see him?

Adam: I'm guessing moderately often, like somewhere between once a week and once a month.

Dr G: How often do you see him currently?

Adam: I haven't seen him for about six months.

Dr G: What stops you from getting together?

Adam: Circumstances beyond control like my mom being busy and my not being able to drive. Sammy lives in my area, but he might not be allowed to come to my house.

Dr G: Well if you couldn't actually get together more often, would you get any enjoyment out of talking to him on the phone?

Adam: I don't think about it that much. The main thing standing in the way of the relationship is just getting distracted by other things and not thinking about him much.

To follow up on my hunch, I asked Adam if he could construct a list of reasons why he should not bother to have friends. He was happy to accommodate me and provided the following:

Reasons why you should not bother to have a friend:

1. You first have to spend lots of time finding out if you can trust him. You have to get to know him enough and often you will invest significant time on someone, only to find out they are not good friend material. What a waste!

2. You have to call him a lot to keep him interested.

3. You have to do things he wants to do, that you are not particularly interested in.

4. Spending time with him will interfere with your favorite videogames.

5. You get close to him and then he will leave you or hurt you. Then you are alone again.

6. Anything a friend can do for you, a family member can also do with less hassle.

7. A friend might have different rules and limitations than you do.

8. It is too hard to find the right person. Everyone is either too young or has different interests.

Next, I asked Adam to produce a list of why you should bother to have friends. Here is what he came up with after considerable thought:

Reasons why you should have a friend:

1. To have someone who will help you when you really need them to do something for you.

2. A friend might have the same interests as mine. For example if we were both interested in the same movie, it would make going to the movie more enjoyable.

3. A friend might cooperate with you to study for a test or finish a job of any kind. It could be easier to work together. Two is better than one in many cases.

While these are three perfectly good reasons for friendship, weighed against the many negatives he so easily produced, you can see why Adam lacked the motivation to call Sammy more and make the effort to be with him.

Gary Mesibov and Catherine Lord have pointed to the failure of most social skills interventions to ensure that the skills being taught are meaningful to the youngster. Without teaching within the context of meaning, they believe that there is little chance for skills to 'stick' and generalize outside of the training setting. An illustration of their point comes from two studies attempting to teach Theory of Mind skills to high functioning children and teens with autism. In both studies the researchers were able to successfully teach a number of Theory of Mind skills through a targeted training group. Unfortunately, both studies clearly demonstrate that those taught the skills failed to use them in daily life, or even in a follow-up laboratory conversational setting (Lord and Magill-Evans 1995; Mesibov and Lord 1997).

Conclusion

We should never define AS teens solely by their disorder. They are unique individuals, each with his or her personality, talents and obstacles. Besides struggling with their Aspergers, these heroic teenagers must also manage the physical and emotional transition into adolescence, a period of turmoil for any child. Some AS teens enter into this period with more resources than others. After a long period of hard work, some of our patients, like Adam, Matthew and Fredrick, are already developing real, reciprocal friendships. Jack and Daniel are not as fortunate. Both of these boys must first tackle the rudiments of learning to reference the actions and reactions of the adults around them and to care enough to adapt their behaviour to be more coordinated with their social partners.

Adam has developed a friendship with a classmate, Brandt, who has Tourette's Syndrome. They have become inseparable companions. They work on school projects as teammates. Brandt is very interested in cooking and wants to be a chef. Even though Adam never showed any interest in cooking, he frequently comes to Brandt's house to cook with him. They go to movies together, go bowling together and speak almost every evening on the phone. Mostly they have fun together with absurd 'inside' jokes, the type where 'you had to be there to appreciate.' Adam is often the keeper of their shared memories and brings up the hilarious times they've had together frequently.

At the time he began preparing for his Bar Mitzvah, Matthew made the decision to join the Orthodox Jewish Community. Though his family is not religious, Matthew began to follow religious law strictly. As he immersed himself in his religion, he abandoned his reliance on cruelty. Matthew found a new way of making strong emotional connections with friends. He describes his friends as of all ages some younger, some older, some his age. What they share is a love of religious study, common dress and other elements of their culture. He seeks their advice and has a strong desire to spend time with them. Matthew describes his new friendships in this manner: 'It makes having friends so much easier. I don't have to worry about what to wear or how to act. I can truly be myself.' Matthew and his friends dance together with great joy and abandon after Sabbath services. They pray and study together and they have fun and joke together as well. Matthew is truly considered a friend by several of these children teens and even adults. He is never without social invitations and spends so little time at home that his parents complain that they do not see him enough. He has found a community where he fits in and where he is admired and valued. He is not an outcast, nor is he someone who is just faking it to fit in.

Fredrick and I worked for a long time to help him give up functioning in the social world as a non-stop, high-pressure performance. He had to learn all over again how to be playful and let his guard down. In college, Fredrick has been able to leave many of these pressures behind. He and his roommates have become best friends. Here is what Fredrick has to say about his roommate: 'We've talked about so much stuff. He's had similar experiences to me, for different reasons. When he was a kid he was a bad child. He chose not to talk to anyone. He sat in a corner and never interacted. Somewhere around middle school he got a little spiritual and started being nice to everybody no matter what, even if he felt they were doing something bad. I wonder whether that means he was taken advantage of. He listens to lots of hard-core gangsta rap. I used to do that too. I used to be one of those white kids listening to gangsta rap. He listened to it for same reasons I did. He also listens to a lot of classical music. The first time I met him this dude asked me my favorite violin concerto I said Sibelius. This guy said that was his favorite too. He likes to climb things. He's trying to get me to climb random objects like poles on east campus. He wants to somehow scale the dorm we're living in. He also does those games I told you about. He likes to take random objects and have sword fights. Over time I've talked to him about more personal things. I got a general feeling that he was a person to talk to about those things.'

References

Asher, S. R., Parker, J.G. and Walker, D. (1996) 'Distinguishing friendship from acceptance: implications for intervention and assessment.' In W. Bukowski, A. Newcomb and W. Hartup (eds) *The Company They Keep: Friendship in Childhood and Adolescence.* Cambridge: Cambridge University Press. pp.366–407.

Bauminger, N. and Kasari, C. (2000) 'Loneliness and friendship in high-functioning children with autism.' *Child Development 2*, 447–456. *Disorders 5*, 539–556.

Emde, R.N. (1989) 'The infant's relationship experience: developmental and affective patterns.' In A. Sameroff and R. Emde *Relationship Disturbances in Early Childhood: A Developmental Approach.* New York: Basic Books.

Erwin, P. (1998) *Friendship in Childhood and Adolescence.* London: Routledge.

Fogel, A. (1993) *Developing through Relationships.* Chicago, IL: University of Chicago Press.

Gottman, J.M. (1984) 'How children become friends.' *Monographs of the Society for Research in Child Development 3*, 201.

Green, J., Gilchrist, A., Burton, D. and Cox, A. (2000) 'Social and psychiatric functioning in adolescents with Asperger Syndrome compared with conduct disorder.' *Journal of Autism and Developmental Disorders 30*, 4, 279–293.

Gutstein, S.E. (2000) *Solving the Relationship Puzzle.* Arlington, TX: Future Horizons.

Gutstein, S.E. and Sheely, R.K. (2002a) *Relationship Development Intervention with Young Children: Social and Emotional Development Activities for Asperger Syndrome, Autism, PDD and NLD.* London: Jessica Kingsley Publishers.

Gutstein, S.E. and Sheely, R.K. (2002b) *Relationship Development Intervention with Children, Adolescents and Adults: Social and Emotional Development Activities for Asperger Syndrome, Autism, PDD and NLD.* London: Jessica Kingsley Publishers.

Gutstein, S.E. and Whitney, T. (2002) *The Development of Social Competence in Asperger Syndrome. Focus on Autism.* Houston: Pro-Ed Publications.

Hadwin, J., Baron-Cohen, S., Howlin, P. and Hill, K. (1997) 'Does teaching theory of mind have an effect on the ability to develop conversation in children with autism?' *Journal of Autism and Developmental Disorders 5*, 519–538.

Hobson, R.P. (1993) *Autism and the Development of Mind.* Hove/Hilldale: Laurence Erlbaum.

Howes, C. and Matheson, C. (1992) 'Sequences in the development of competent play with peers, social and social pretend play.' *Developmental Psychology 28*, 5, 961–974.

Lord, C. and Magill-Evans J. (1995) 'Peer interaction of autistic children and adolescents.' *Development and Psychopathology 17*, 611–626.

Mesibov, G. and Lord, K. (1997) 'Some thoughts on social skills training for children, adolescents and adults with autism.' Unpublished manuscript.

Newcomb, A. and Bagwell, C. (1995) 'Children's friendship relations: a meta-analytic review.' *Psychological Bulletin 2*, 306–347.

Ozonoff, S. and Miller, J. (1995) 'Teaching theory of mind: a new approach to social skills training for individuals with autism.' *Journal of Autism and Developmental Disorders 25*, 4, 415–433.

Rubin, Z. (1980) *Children's Friendships.* Cambridge, MA: Harvard University Press.

Sigman, M. and Ruskin, E. (1999) 'Continuity and change in social competence of children with autism, Down Syndrome, and developmental delays.' *Monographs of the Society for Research in Child Development 1*, v–114.

Tanguay, P.E. (2000) 'Pervasive developmental disorders: A 10-year review.' *Journal of the American Academy of Child & Adolescent Psychiatry 9*, 1079–1095.

Trevarthen, C., Aitken, K., Papoudi, D. and Robarts, J. (1996) *Children with Autism*. London: Jessica Kingsley Publishers.

Volkmar, F. and Klin, A. (1993) 'Social development in autism: historical and clinical perspectives.' In S. Baron-Cohen, H. Tager-Flusberg and D. Cohen (eds) *Understanding Other Minds*. Oxford: Oxford University Press.

5

The Importance of Occupational Therapy for Adolescents with Asperger Syndrome

Marc Willey and Liane Holliday Willey

The purpose of occupational therapy is to assist people with physical, psychological and social disabilities learn how to overcome or minimize their problems so that they may maximize their potential and more successfully meet the challenges of day-to-day living. Occupational therapists work with individuals of all ages to establish goal-directed treatment plans that address specific deficits or delays. They play a key role in providing specialized evaluations for adolescents. Many occupational therapists elect to specialize in working with individuals who have developmental delays/disorders. These occupational therapists utilize a variety of evaluations and treatment approaches to help their clients manage their challenges.

One of the most popular treatment approaches is called sensory integration. Sensory integration therapy (SIT) was first developed by A. Jean Ayres in the late 1960s and 1970s. Ayres was an occupational therapist and a leader in child development with extensive training in the field of neuroscience. Ayres developed her theory to explain the relationship between deficits in interpreting sensation from the body and the environment and difficulties with academic or motor learning (Bundy and Murray 2002). Sensation is defined by *Webster's Dictionary* (1998) as an awareness or a mental process due to stimulation of a sense organ. The term integration comes from the word integrate which is defined as the ability to form, coordinate, or blend into a functioning whole. By understanding the meaning of the words sensation and integrate you can begin to define sensory integration. Sensory integration can be defined as the coordination of sensory input to facilitate learning and behaviour. If one considers the remarkable motor coordination of a world-class gymnast, or the intricate fine motor skills of a master pianist, it is easy to see that the brain can orchestrate the human body in amazing ways.

As babies grow from infants to adolescents and on to adulthood, they are bombarded with sensory input. This flow of sensory information is considered essential for brain development. In fact, if you remove sensory input from children during the first years of life, significant developmental delays will occur. This was sadly observed in the Romanian orphanages in the 1980s after the fall of the dictator Nicolae Ceausescu. After he was overthrown in 1989, thousands of Romanian children were discovered in state-run orphanages living in dire conditions. Many children were physically constrained to cribs for the first two to three years of their lives. As a result of this environment, many children were significantly developmentally delayed for many years after being institutionalized. With improved living environments that included age-appropriate activities these children improved dramatically.

Neurologically speaking it is very difficult to understand how the human brain receives, processes and interprets sensory information from the environment and from the body simultaneously. One can study the organization of the brain in neuroanatomy books to learn about how the brain is organized with literally millions of specialized sensory receptors, but for purposes of this discussion the following summary will suffice. The sensory receptors are connected to the brain through the peripheral nervous system (PNS). The peripheral nervous system is made up of receptors and nerves, which collect and relay information to the spinal cord and brain. Lane (2002) explained this relationship is similar to a computer, with the peripheral nervous system acting as the keyboard and mouse function of the computer. The mouse and the keyboard provide input to the computer through the cables that attach them to the back of the computer. This is true of the peripheral nervous system in the body. Specialized receptors in skin, muscles and joints relay sensory inputs (primarily touch, proprioception, pain, and joint position sensations) to the brain through the nerves of the peripheral nervous system via the spinal cord nerve pathways. Proprioceptive information is defined as the perception of joint and body movements. This information is critical for smooth coordinated movement. The autonomic system is also part of the peripheral nervous system. It consists of special receptors that convey information to the brain concerning pressure, body chemistry, pain and temperature. The autonomic system also maintains physiological homeostasis which keeps all our automatic body functions regulated within normal values.

The spinal cord and brain make up the central nervous system (CNS) in the body. This system acts as the mainframe super computer. It is responsible for organizing all the information that comes in from the peripheral and autonomic nervous systems, as well as information that comes from the environment through all other sensory systems of the body, i.e. sounds, olfactory (smells), vision, taste, movement, body awareness, and the pull of gravity. In addition to these tasks the central nervous system calls upon highly refined systems of the brain to produce correct movements and reactions. Balance, equilibrium, eye–hand coordination, and large and small muscle contractions are all modulated and refined by our sensory input system to produce the desired action appropriate for the environmental challenge. The central nervous system must orchestrate all the input, and produce the correct output to match the environmental demands placed on an individual.

Bundy and Murray (2002) reported that sensory integration theory has three major components. The first one is that learning is dependent on the ability to take in and process sensation from movement and the environment and use it to plan and organize behaviour. The second component states that individuals who have a decreased ability to process sensation also may have difficulty producing appropriate actions, which in turn may interfere with learning and behaviour. The third component states that enhanced sensation, as a part of meaningful activity that yields an adaptive interaction, improves the ability to process sensation, thereby enhancing learning and behaviour.

Bundy and Murray (2002) further outlined five basic assumptions that are associated with SIT.

1. The central nervous system is plastic (the ability of brain structures to change).

2.   Sensory integration develops (behaviours present throughout the developmental sequence provide the basis for the development of more complex behaviours).

3.   The brain functions as an integrated whole (higher order function i.e. eye–hand coordination is the result of the processing and integration all lower level sensory input from multiple receptors).

4.   Adaptive interactions are critical to sensory integration (activities that elicit adaptive responses are those activities that require a give and take response of the individual to adjust to the demands placed on their sensory systems).

5.   People have an inner drive to develop sensory integration through the participation in sensorimotor activities. Ayres (1989) believed that most individuals possess a natural inner drive to master their environment through the successful acquisition of sensorimotor skills.

Sensory integration usually occurs automatically and provides a foundation for more complex learning behaviour. For some individuals, sensory integration does not develop as efficiently as it should (McMullen 2001). When this happens, problems in learning, development and behaviour may develop. In other words, sensory integration dysfunction (SID) occurs.

SID is sometimes called sensory defensiveness (SD) or sensory sensitivity. Wilbarger and Wilbarger (1993) defined this condition as a combination of symptoms resulting from aversive responses to non-harmful sensory stimuli. Some SD individuals are so sensitive to touch or sound that the stimuli are perceived as painful. Our nervous system is always on guard as a protective response to our environment. This response keeps us safe by reacting appropriately to environmental demands: i.e. when your body perceives danger it will gear up to defend itself or run away from the danger. An SD individual has difficulty tuning out environmental stimuli. McMullen (2001) described this inability to tune out certain sensory stimuli as an underactive sensory filter.

All individuals have two distinct types of sensory processing systems. One type discriminates information and the other alerts the body for protection. McMullen (2001) states that most individuals return to a normal level of arousal shortly after receiving a stimulus. This arousal is modulated as a kind of calm alertness. The SD response can be either hypersensitive – too much information comes in – or hyposensitive – where not enough information comes into the brain. This faulty information processing causes either over- or under-sensitivity in any one or more of the following sensory areas:

- tactile
- vestibular (ability to process information around balance, movements and gravity)
- proprioceptive (ability to control one's body parts and one's movements)
- oral
- visual
- olfactory (smell)
- auditory.

Though valid and reliable research studying the effects of SID on the person with AS is still in the infancy stage, personal accounts by those effected with AS point to the fact that SID makes a profound mark on their lives. Occupational therapists who work with these individuals are in agreement and they are working on the front lines to help secure sensory integration therapy for people on the autistic spectrum. It seems only proper to suggest that parents of AS teens observe the behaviours of their children to determine if they would benefit from an occupational therapy. Many behaviours indicate the need for an evaluation. The following list includes the most obvious hallmarks:

- clumsiness, frequently tripping or falling
- toe walking
- difficulty throwing or catching a ball
- unusual grasping patterns when writing
- poor fine or gross motor movement skills
- balance problems

- poor posture
- over- or under-sensitivity to sound, lights, smell or touch
- over- or under-reaction to sound, light, smell or touch
- unusually active or unusually inactive
- difficulty calming
- frequently impulsive
- difficulty with social situations
- frequent headaches or stomach aches
- specific or general learning disabilities
- tendency to obsess
- often anxious
- poor eating habits
- passive or aggressive behaviours
- developmental regression.

If a parent (or teacher) believes a teen would benefit from occupational therapy, an evaluation must be performed. The teen's functioning as measured on standardized tests and observations of behaviours involving the sensory modalities, age-appropriate performance areas and general life skill tasks will be conducted and documented. If the results of the evaluations indicate occupational therapy is needed, an individual treatment plan will be designed. Intervention with teens should be centered on activities specifically designed to encourage, strengthen and support the teen's sense of self, independent living skills, play abilities and academic success. Typically, intervention will center around a sensory diet. Sensory diet refers to sensory integration therapy.

SD is never easy for anyone affected by it, but it creates especially complicated issues for the AS teen, particularly when it comes to their social learning and social acceptance. They may not like certain sounds, oral or tactile textures or smells. They may hold their bodies in peculiar ways. They may move through personal and object spaces in unorganized or clumsy ways, and/or they may crave or reject human touch or hugging. Activities most teens take for granted, such as going to parties, assemblies and sporting events, might be nearly impossible for an AS teen with auditory SID. Fun events for most like dancing, holding hands and playing sports can be difficult to execute and master for AS teens with proprioceptive problems. Even such everyday happenings as eating at a friend's house, riding in carpool with moms who wear perfume, or trying on clothes at the mall could send an AS teen into SD mode. Add learning environment challenges to these situations and it will become very apparent that the AS teen with SD will have to walk through a mountain's worth of problems before he can concentrate on his academic needs.

Teens need to look and feel as if they fit into the normal population. AS teens with SD can find ways to do both. The strategies below are built around the sorts of things typical teens tend to engage in. If an AS teen can master just a few of these strategies, he will open the way to accomplish at least these three things:

1. He will satisfy some of his SI needs.

2. He will put himself in a better position to establish friendships with the other teens who join him in these activities.

3. He will have some new skills and information (the trendy and cool kind) to share with people he has just met but would like to be friends with.

When analyzing which kind of strategy to employ with any teen, realize that measures can be taken to feed a teen's need for a certain sensory experience, decrease the risk of having to suffer through a certain sensory experience, and desensitize the experience all together. Let the teen take a strong lead in determining which kind of experience he would like to engage in. He will often intuitively know which he needs, which to avoid, and which he might benefit from.

Take caution, however. While SI treatment will not harm neurotypical people, it can cause great pain or confusion for those with AS. Though none of the activities in this discussion are terribly unusual, we advise the entire team – the caregiver, the teen's general physician and occupational therapist – confer to be certain that no activity will have a negative impact on the teen's other sensory areas and needs, the teen's self-esteem or his general health. With that in mind, the following strategies should generate options for a sensory diet.

Note: the list of resources at the end of this chapter provides contact information for suppliers of the sensory items mentioned.

Tactile provisions

Find a teen who reaches out to touch every object in his path from the ground to the walls, eats his food with his fingers and takes virtually scalding hot showers and you will have found a teen who is probably under-sensitive to tactile experiences. Find a teen who has torn the tags from his clothing, refuses to shave, or finds it nearly impossible to offer physical affection and you will have likely discovered a teen who is overly sensitive to tactile experiences. Working with his occupational therapist, the teen might want to try any number of the activities mentioned next, but do keep in mind the fact that many people with AS have extremely high pain tolerances. Therefore, no matter which strategies are selected, all attempts to maintain and insure solid safety measures must always be taken.

- Use hot lather machines for shaving needs.

- Offer lots of tight squeeze hugs to people who you know will want a hug from you.

- Cook meals, particularly those that use recipes involving lots of mixing and chopping and washing of foods.

- Use weighted eating and drinking utensils.

- Use heavy backpacks, fill clothing with heavy items (keys and key rings, wallets, grooming supplies, etc.).

- Decorate your personal or study space with tactile rich decorations such as sisal rugs and cork board walls.

- Play with teen-approved sensory toys and gadgets such as hacki-sack balls, Koosh balls, water-filled weights, sand or salt art materials, and wire or bead jewelry making.

- Only purchase outfits, shoes, coats, etc. (trendy types if the teen likes the style) that are made of materials that will not provoke a negative reaction, and when those items are found, buy multiples of each so that acceptable spares will always be at hand.

- Consider using assisted technology to replace handwriting requirements.

- Provide a backpack on rollers.

- Reach in a backpack filled with all sorts of items and try to guess what they are before looking at them.

- Use your hands to dig in the garden, play with the worms you find, pat the dirt firm after its been watered, etc.

- Ask for deep backrubs.

- Buy a special shower wand that allows you to change the water flow from gentle to firm.

- Soak in a hot tub with the jets running.

- Take sponge baths instead of full immersion baths.

- Make sandcastles at the beach or in the park with young friends.

- Take up pottery, sculpting, wire art and/or beadwork.

- Buy a few inexpensive wigs and style them over and over again with new hairdos.

- Learn how to sew, knit, needlepoint, macramé and/or crochet.

- Help out at a pet grooming business and offer to help dry and walk the pets.

- Keep small bits of your favorite tactile object (piece of felt, tinfoil, sandpaper, feather, etc.) hidden in your pocket or purse, and feel it when you need to.

Oral provisions

All teens like pizza and Jell-O and milkshakes, right? Wrong. Teens who are under-sensitive to oral experiences will sooner spit out something slimy, wiggly or crunchy, while teens who are over-sensitive will chew and suck on most anything from pencil erasers to their hair to book bindings. Here are some more appropriate options for the AS teen who needs oral provisions in his sensory diet.

- Chew gum.

- Suck lollipops or hard candy.

- Use straws and water bottles with straw-like openings.

- Outfit the ends of your pencils and pens with tops that will not break down easily.

- Try to know ahead of time what the school cafeteria or a friend's family is serving as a meal so that you can then decide if you should bring your own foods or turn down the invitation to eat at your friend's house.

- Always bring acceptable snack foods to picnics, etc. in case you aren't able to avoid an unacceptable menu.

- When you do turn down a food, be polite and don't feel obligated to explain how horrible the texture or taste is for you.

- Because it is very possible you will not be eating a solidly balanced food diet, get into the habit of regularly taking vitamins – depending on your needs there are vitamin gumballs, vitamin gummy bears, liquid vitamins, pill vitamins and chewable vitamins.

- Learn how to whistle with your fingers.

- Make your own bubble solution and bubble wands, then share them and play with them with others.

- Play the harmonica or take up the flute, clarinet, horn, etc.

Auditory provisions

If your teen puts his hands over his ears in anticipation of an oncoming train or when he is in a crowd, his auditory system might be overly sensitive to noises of all sorts. In fact, sounds at specific levels, might cause him actual pain. If on the other hand your teen turns the TV or radio to full blast, speaks in a loud voice or sits next to speaker systems, it could be that he needs more than the average amount of auditory stimulation in his sensory diet. Because so much information comes through auditory channels (particularly in the teen world), it is imperative the AS teens learn how to rely on their auditory system and equally important that they realize what kinds of activities can harm it. These safe strategies should help the auditorily sensitive AS teen deal with his needs without making him stand out from the crowd.

- Ask movie theaters if they have individual earphones – these can be either turned up or down depending on the auditory needs.

- Wear headphones that only appear to be hooked up to music.

- Wear earplugs.

- Wear earmuffs or caps over ears during outdoor experiences.

- Do not sit too near speakers; do not turn audio equipment on full blast; do not put anything in your ear canals beyond acceptable earplugs.

- Try to appreciate and analyze the sounds of people whom your OT or parent have identified as good speakers or singers.

- Find music you enjoy and listen to it at acceptable decibel levels whenever you feel the urge.

- Do not be ashamed to ask to sit away from noises that distract your concentration.

- Try to anticipate when loud noises might be headed your way (such as a train, a parade band, a crowd of excited children, etc.) and then do what you need to get away from them as nonchalantly as possible.

- Instead of going to noisy places, arrange to meet friends at quiet spots such as the library, a quaint coffee shop, a fashionable art gallery or a peaceful park.

- Find quiet activities to engage friends in such as taking a paddleboat ride, fishing, hiking, snorkeling, etc.

- Invite friends to a concert, action-filled movie, sporting event or busy diner.

- Go to minor league sporting events if sports is your thing, but noise isn't – the crowds and therefore the noise, tend to be less.

- Set up a background noise filter that produces 'white noise,' or noise that works to cover up other environmental sounds.

Olfactory provisions

When AS adolescents flip through a teen magazine they will surely find opportunity after opportunity to turn back a small piece of a page that has been drenched with smells of all sorts. These are called perfume ads. While some teens might enjoy these pages, chances are that the sensory sensitive teen will hate them. Imagine how silly (and uncool) you would feel if you couldn't even look at magazines with the other kids. Imagine instead that you crave those smells as well as the smell of others' armpits, dirty shoes, hairspray, or anything frying in grease. How long would it take for you to look like a weirdo? Any of the suggestions mentioned next will help your teen avoid the smelly world of offensive odors or unceremoniously take pleasure in his favorites, even if they are less than popular.

- Wear a necklace holding a pendant you can fill with your favorite smell.

- Dab favorite aromatherapy oils on your wrists and other pulse points.

- Saturate a cotton ball in your favorite smell and sniff it when you are alone.

- In the event that you cannot easily get away from an smell that really upsets you, simply explain you have an allergy to that smell and if you stay near it you will surely get a migraine, then back away from it as far as you need to.

- Join the thousands of others who suffer migraines from certain smells in writing to congressmen or political representatives with a request that they work to ban perfume and other smelly ads from all public reading material.

- Learn to breath out of your mouth rather than your nose, because you are certain to find yourself in smelly situations that you cannot avoid, like the gym locker room, public transportation vehicles, crowds, lunchrooms, etc.

- Carry your favorite scent in a small spray bottle and when you feel the urge to experience it, discreetly spray it near you, on your books, your clothes, etc.

- Carry a spray bottle filled with a scent that is known to get rid of (as opposed to cover up) other smells, and spray it discreetly when horrible smells come your way or sit down beside you.

- Buy scent-free personal hygiene supplies, detergent, candles, make-up, etc. whenever possible.

Visual

Many teens have problems with their eyesight, but for the AS teen with a sensitive visual system, the problems go far beyond the need for glasses. These teens may find it difficult to settle down when their environment is filled with too many visuals or they might not budge until they have been able to take in every last detail of every single thing they see. They might find it difficult to separate the foreground from the background so that catching a ball or driving a car can only be wishes. It might appear your teen is perpetually lost and never able to find his way to the classrooms he goes to every day. They may not be able to track moving items like a puck flying down the ice or an airplane in the sky. Focusing on the board and then their paperwork may cause confusion and incorrect copying. Figuring out how far or near they are to other things could prove very difficult. Bright lights, dim lights, colored lights, strobe lights, no light, moonlight, any light, might be either too X overwhelming or too dim for comfort. Facial expressions might not be discernible, or they might be too big and distracting. Most everything within the visual field is up for debate if you are a teen with visual sensitivities and this presents no end of difficulties. Together with an ophthalmologist who understands the special issues associated with AS and sensory integration, the teen, his OT and his caregiver might elect to try strategies such as those listed below. However, teens with significant visual sensitivities really do need even more sophisticated strategies if they are to overcome the toughest issues.

- Create string art pictures of anything that interests you or things other kids might enjoy too like popular ad logos, the school mascot, or trendy sayings.

- Make collages that are visually satisfying for you, made from pictures and small objects that represent your interests and likes.

- Take beginning drawing classes but consider telling the teacher about your vision problems.

- Experiment with different colored lenses and lenses strengths – your ophthalmologist will need to help you with this, don't experiment on your own.

- Wear caps and other hats with bills that keep light directly off your eyes.

- Put together a jigsaw puzzle with friends or family members.

- See if you can learn how to draw mazes.

- Get a trusted friend who knows you well and, if you are comfortable with the idea, go through a human maze or house of mirrors.

- Set out a bunch of different sized and shaped objects on a flat surface, then try to separate the items according to their sizes, shapes, etc.

- Sit near the board and arrange to have copies of the teacher's notes provided to you.

- Find a buddy who you enjoy to help you find your way to class, your car, your home or wherever else you need to go and try to follow the same paths every time so you can increase the odds of finding your way when you are on your own.

- If you go to sporting events, try to focus on the goalposts so that you can better your chances of conceptualizing how the game is progressing for your team.

- Build model train villages, doll houses, and other three-dimensional projects.

- Toss a ball against a wall, try to catch it when it comes back to you.

- Play tennis against a special machine that tosses you the balls.

- Play street hockey with a 'puck' that is bigger than the average ball or actual puck.

- Set your interests more on activities that use big objects (radio-controlled airplanes rather than radio-controlled tiny cars, volleyball rather than golf, etc.).

- Place yourself near the outside of hallways and passageways whenever possible.

Vestibular and proprioceptive provisions

Watch your teens to see if they wobble when they walk, bang into walls, stumble over the tiniest bumps or never seem to know where their body is in relation to the environment around them. Does he often rock his body back and forth, run to the Ferris wheel or upside down rides first and foremost at amusement parks, or does he tend to walk on the edge of ledges and uneven roads? Does he find athletic activities extremely difficult to master, does he have poor eye–hand coordination, and does he find it hard to complete even simple tasks like zipping up his coat? If you notice these kinds of behaviours, chances are you have a teen who has the need for a strong vestibular/proprioceptive diet. Take note, this is an area that especially needs the supervision of the occupational therapist. Bring these kinds of ideas to your meeting with the OT.

- Do gymnastics.

- Learn how to hip hop, jitterbug, or other similar retro dances.

- Jump on a trampoline.

- Take karate or Tai Kwan Do.

- Take amusement park rides.

- Snow or water tubing.

- Horseback ride.

- Swing on a tire swing or hammock installed inside the home.

- Do aerobics or Pilate's – especially using the big balance balls popular to these exercises.

- Work out on a pogo stick.

- Ride on a skateboard or rollerblade.

- Sit on a 'T stool' (a chair that is made by putting two structures together to form the letter T) at sporting events, picnics, etc.

- Take walks or jogs on unfirm surfaces like the beach, clover fields, gravel roads, abandoned railroad tracks (have a responsible adult make certain the track is definitely abandoned and never used for any purpose).

- Learn how to ride a unicycle.

- Walk on stilts.

- Use an inversion traction unit.

- Enroll in acrobatics class.

- If a rocking chair is available, use it.

- Juggle.

- Practice your somersaulting.

- Push manual lawn mowers.

- Take classes such as diving, rappelling, rock or rope climbing.

- Play movement games like charades, tag and Twister and tag.

- Find work as a shelf stocker.

- Swim.

- Get massages.

- Play heavy musical instruments and/or instruments that encourage heavy hands such as drumming.

- Sprint, jog or run cross-country.

- Do push-ups, pull-ups and sit-ups.

- Plant trees and dig gardens.

- Fill backpacks with extra heavy items.

- Stuff heavy objects into coats, winter vests, and pockets.

- Do chin-ups and pull-ups and then hang there for a while.

- Play tug-a-war with friends or family members.

- Join a wrestling club.

- Play leapfrog with your younger friends.

It should be emphasized that SI therapy has limitations. The diagnosis of sensory dysfunction is based on deficits found in the central processing abilities of the vestibular, propprioceptive or tactile sensation that is not caused by direct damage to the CNS, PNS or cognitive deficits secondary to brain injury. Sensory Integration is not commonly utilized to address severe central nervous system dysfunction associated with conditions such as cerebral palsy, cerebral vascular assident and severe CNS dysfunction frequently observed in individuals with genetic abnormalities. A neurologist, not an occupational therapist, should first be consulted if the AS teen has neurological dysfunction related from a pathological condition.

Sensory integration treatment should focus on providing graded sensory-motor activities that are designed to challenge the brain to perform adaptive responses. Further, sensory integration should challenge the sensory system so that the entire nervous system must adapt and, through a series of adaptive responses, eventually improve. For teens with Asperger Syndrome, a sensory rich diet designed by a qualified occupational therapist could make a significant difference in the teen's ability to join in, fit in and have fun in the typical teen world.

Sensory integration product resources

OT Ideas Inc.
www.otideas.com/
124 Morris Turnpike
Randolph NJ 07869
USA
Tel: (973) 895-3622 Or call toll free 877-7-OT-Ideas
(877-768-4332)
Fax: (973) 895-4204

Rainbow Research (scent-free products)
www.rainbowresearch.com

Sensory Comfort
www.sensorycomfort.com/
Phone: 1-888-436-2622

Resources

Sensory Integration International
1603 Cabrillo Avenue
Torrance, CA 90501-2819
USA

American Occupational Therapy Association,
4720 Montgomery Lane, PO Box 31220,
Bethesda, MD 20824-1220
USA
Consumer line: 1-800-668-8255
www.aota.org/featured/area6/links/link02d.asp

References

Ayres, A.J. (1989) *Sensory Integration and Praxis Test Manual.* Los Angeles: Western Psychological Services.

Bundy, A.C. and Murray, E.A. (2002) 'Sensory integration: A. Jean Ayres' theory revisited.' In A.C. Bundy, S.J. Lane and E.A. Murray (eds) *Sensory Integration Theory and Practice* 2nd edn. Philadelphia: F.A. Davis, pp.3–12.

Lane, S. J. (2002) 'Structure and function of the sensory systems.' In A.C. Bundy, S.J. Lane, E.A. Murray (eds) *Sensory Integration Theory and Practice* 2nd edn. Philadelphia: F.A. Davis, pp.36–37.

Merriam-Webster Dictionary Home and Office Edition (1998) Springfield, MA: Merriam-Webster, pp.273, 474.

McMullen, P. (2001) 'Living with sensory dysfunction.' In R.A. Huebner (ed) *Autism: A Sensorimotor Approach to Management.* Aspen: Gaithersburg, p.469.

Wilbarger, P. and Wilbarger, J. (1993) 'Sensory defensiveness and related social/emotional and neurological problems.' Professional Development Programs workshop, Albuquerque, New Mexico.

6

Safety Issues for Adolescents with Asperger Syndrome

Dennis Debbaudt

Do we shudder in fear of the consequences every time we snap on a seatbelt, lock a back door before going to bed, or pay a health insurance premium? Of course we don't. We've learned to understand and accept these risks that are associated with everyday life and routinely deal with them, without even giving a second thought to the consequences of not doing so. Risks factor into our decision-making powers automatically. We want our curious adolescents who have Asperger Syndrome (AS) to give thought to risks too. Peer pressure is high. Protective parental monitoring wanes. Adulthood is right around the corner. Like it or not, independence and the decision-making power it carries has arrived. And we want our teens to make the best decisions that they can.

Teens are at greater risk of getting into trouble than at any other time in their lives. Without support, any teen can make the wrong decision. To make it through those short but tough years, teens who have Asperger Syndrome will need a good understanding of themselves as well as support from family, peers, school and the community.

Internationally, autism spectrum disorders (ASD) advocacy groups are making great strides in educating our law enforcement and criminal justice professionals. But these efforts are only one side of the equation if successful community experiences for our loved ones are the goal. Teens with AS are at a disadvantage when they haven't received education about how to recognize, respond to and understand the risks associated with everyday life. These perils can include personal security, sexual assault and dangerous sexual activity, peer pressure to engage in risky and criminal activities such as substance abuse, of becoming a victim of crime, and of not recognizing and responding well to the law enforcers they will interact with. They'll need to learn how to identify and appropriately report bullying, teasing and taunting. Personal safety, risk awareness and law enforcement recognition and response education are critical life skills that students with AS will need to learn and use throughout their lifetimes.

In this chapter, I'll discuss some of the risks associated with adolescents who have AS and offer some effective ways that parents and caregivers can deal with them.

Shopping

Most of us take for granted the first rule of shopping: don't take anything without paying for it. However, when shopping, those on the autism spectrum that appear as if they're not following the rule will surely get the attention of attentive clerks, shoppers, and uniformed or plainclothes store detectives. Sometimes just being unknown and in the wrong place at the wrong time puts the AS teen into the limelight of suspicion. It could be that innocent handling of merchandise – picking up and inspecting an item without any intention of buying it or worse yet carrying the item with the intent of purchasing it only to be distracted by a sensory pleasure or panic, or even temporarily forgetting about the purchase – is happening in a department store that's experiencing increased or organized shoplifting. Anyone who appears different among the crowd of shoppers will stir the suspicions of security staff.

Beyond their personal observations and store videotapes, security officials will look for additional evidence that a crime has been committed. In many cases their observations will lead to interactions with the shopper that can include accusatory questioning or detainment and interrogation. These tactics are used to obtain what store security is now looking for: a confession from the suspected shoplifter.

Techniques often used during interrogation will include the use of trickery and deceit by the interrogator. When these techniques are used with the concrete thinking person with AS – persons whose worlds are unadorned with pretext, pretense, sham and dishonesty – the results may not produce what the security worker should be looking for: the truth. Indeed, false confessions may be the result when interrogating the suspicious appearing, yet innocent person with AS.

In addition to the risk of obtaining a false confession, such questioning can leave behind lifelong trauma for the innocent, yet suspicious appearing teen with AS. Without prior knowledge of the person's condition, a passer-by or private security officer may see the teenager with Asperger Syndrome's behaviour as suspicious, as someone under the influence of drugs or as evidence of their guilt. An under-trained security worker's actions after making this faulty but understandable assumption can lead to a heightened emotional confrontation or needless and often permanent fear and trauma for the AS teen. One person with AS describes what many with the condition feel during questioning that involves the use of psychological game playing, trickery and deceit.

'Words can be more abusive to us than anything physical. For one, our pain threshold is often astounding. But words can be so confusing, so misleading, so misconstrued that, if we are talked to in sarcasm, or with word games, or with double intentions, we can crumble from the inside out. We won't understand the reverse psychology and all the other psychological intentions of interrogation. We need fair and honest language that explores consequences and the like, but we do not need to be toyed with like lab rats.'

Private sector law enforcement workers are typically not as highly trained as those in the public sector. They tend to have less stringent hiring protocols, background and training requirements, and less education than their public sector counterparts. The state of Michigan, for example, is one of ten states that do not require training for private security personnel. Currently, the only requirement is passing a criminal history check and proof of having an eighth-grade education. Legislation was passed there in 2002 to upgrade the qualifications – training and educational requirements – for workers in this industry. Basic training and a high school diploma would be required for all workers. Regardless of the educational level or aptitude for this work, even the best trained law enforcement professionals will probably not be aware of the communication dilemmas a person with AS can present during interactions that can easily downgrade into confrontations, interrogations, and misunderstandings.

Sudden encounters between police or private security officers who are unfamiliar with AS and teenagers with the condition are fraught with risk and paradox for both groups. An officer may see someone who seems to lack respect for the uniform or a plainclothes officer's badge and credentials, the officer's command presence, etc, and hear instead a rude, fidgety and belligerent kid who, through his lack of eye contact and evasive conversation, appears to have something to hide. An AS teen may have no idea of the effect their behaviour is having on the officer, may not understand the significance of the uniform, badge or credentials or recognize the officer's command body language. The teen may close into the officer's personal space without realizing it, may read the officer's name tag, badge number or credentials, or repeat the officer's words in a manner that appears to be rude. The teen may be unable to return eye contact, insist on changing the officer's topic of conversation, and be generally unaware that they are losing whatever communication and socialization skills they possess. They simply may not be able to recognize that they have lost a credibility battle in the officer's mind. The officer may respond with increased forceful questioning of the suspicious but innocent teen. What started out as standard questioning (part of everyday life for a patrol or security officer), can become an encounter punctuated with misunderstood motives, diminished communication and escalated odd behaviour.

Clearly, recognition and response training could have helped both parties during this encounter. Recognition of the unique behaviours and characteristics – for instance, lack of eye contact, invasion of officer's personal space, repeating the officer's phrases – that many with AS inherently display could have helped the officer determine that the youngster had AS and would have improved the officer's response. The AS teen would have had a better understanding of the needs of the officer and, perhaps, offered to present an AS information card at the outset of the interaction. AS advocates should proactively offer AS information to, and arrange workshops for, local store security and management personnel. Further, parents can prepare their teens for possible encounters with store security by teaching their teens the following:

1. Always carry state-issued photo ID. Consider carrying generic and/or person-specific Asperger Syndrome informational handouts or cards.

2. Understand that your loved one is entering the store's domain and that private sector store security workers may

not be bound by the same guidelines as police in the areas of questioning, Miranda warnings, and detainment. Explain these guidelines, and the possibility that they may not be followed at any given store, to your teen.

3.   Teach teens with AS to tolerate casual touch (such as a hand on the arm, shoulder or back) without overreacting to it. Create lessons to systematically desensitize individuals with AS to this type of touch when the person with AS sees the touch coming and when they don't.

4.   If questioned as a suspect in shoplifting the teen should be taught to expect the use of trickery and deceit by the questioner. The teenager or anyone with AS should be taught to ask to speak to an attorney and remain silent if questioned. This kind of scenario would go much smoother, in the event the teen did have an AS information handout or card to present to the officials.

Parents should advocate for laws that require the video and audio taping of all interactions, questioning and interrogations that occur on retail premises. Identify and encourage local law enforcement and private security agencies to develop units or persons who can become knowledgeable about AS issues and investigate with aptness when adolescents with AS are considered suspects or need to be questioned as witnesses or as victims of crimes.

Advocate to have AS education, response, recognition and risk issues included in all police and private security recruit, basic and in-service training. Lobby legislators for this training to become compulsory or mandatory, if necessary.

The best defense against misunderstandings with law enforcers in a retail setting is a proactive AS educational workshop. Retailers want shoppers to have good experiences in their stores as they seek to build customer loyalty.

Parents, caregivers and AS advocates should make AS recognition, response and awareness training a priority. But unless this is done, do not expect police or private security officers to know what AS is, even if you tell them that you have it or present them with an AS information card. They may not immediately understand what having the condition means, may believe it is a dodge being used by a crafty criminal or may not accept AS as an excuse.

All parents, caregivers and advocates for adolescents with AS must realize that, at least in the United States, interrogation techniques will include the use of trickery and deceit. Better proactive AS public awareness within those communities that employ these techniques will help guard against their unwitting use by law enforcers who are in contact with vulnerable AS teens. (See Appendix A for information to share with law enforcers regarding interrogation and AS).

When and what to report to school authorities

Unaware that their behaviours, physical posture, vocal tone, apparent aloofness and social gaffes are attracting unwanted attention, AS teens can make perfect targets for bullies. They have become victims of pranks or more serious crimes such as unarmed robbery. Parents, caregivers and educators take great pains to explain to the AS teen what constitutes bullying or threats and when to report it. More difficult to explain to the concrete-thinking teenager is when to report bullying and teasing and when not to. The gray areas of reporting are difficult concepts for the teen that may see the reporting incidents only in black or white, right and wrong.

When one AS teen was told by another student that he was going to take his girlfriend out to rape and kill her in the woods, the story-telling youth incorrectly assumed that the concrete thinker would understand that he was just making up the whole incident. The AS student didn't make the connection, took the story literally, and correctly reported his classmate to school authorities. The storyteller was reprimanded, apologized, and hopefully learned a valuable lesson about the value of telling a violent fib.

Within a few weeks the same AS teen had been approached by another student at his new high school in a bathroom with a demand to give up his money. Another student he encountered in the hallways started a false rumor that the AS student was a drug user. In each case the AS student correctly reported the offenses to authorities, and in each case the offenders said that they thought the AS teen knew they were just kidding. After being reprimanded and told to apologize, one student put out his hand to shake as a sign of his contrition and in an effort to make amends. The AS teen wouldn't return the handshake, perhaps with a once bitten twice shy attitude, perhaps without an understanding that the other student was truly sorry and wanted to be friends or perhaps because he had seen a scene like that in a movie.

Subsequently, the AS teen took to reporting to school resource police officers such seemingly obvious trivial offenses as innocent name calling, the silent stares of other students, and those students who were flicking little paper wads at him. Annoying? Of course. But were these reportable offenses? If not, how then can the teenage student with AS differentiate between seemingly innocent teasing and bullying or criminal activities and take the appropriate steps to report it?

No one wants to get labeled a snitch yet no one should be persecuted for having a disability. In today's dangerous world, important information *must* be reported to those in charge. For the AS student to come to understand the differences between bullying and innocent teasing, educators should be encouraged to teach the subtle distinctions between the two by role playing through the gray areas of reporting an incident to (a) get help, (b) stop bullying or torment and (c) recognizing when they are just being innocently teased. Classmates should be identified who are willing to be trained to help explain to the AS student what should be reported and what shouldn't and act as communication go-betweens or buffers between the AS student, other students, and school authorities.

Many schools in the US now have police officers assigned as resource officers. Parents and educators should talk to police proactively to establish guidelines for reporting bullying, taunting and torment. Ask how teasing should be reported. Involve law enforcers to develop reporting procedures, and role-playing activities that are designed to explain the differences between reporting real dangers and tattling. Clearly differentiate the differences between what should be reported such as robbery attempts, threats or planning of violent acts and trivial acts such as innocent name calling.

A school-based anti-bullying campaign is not only the right thing to do, it's the law (United States Department of Education 2000). Parents encounter the 'boys will be boys' and 'they just have to get used to it' excuse for bullying from educational system administrators who often lack awareness of anti-bullying statutes or the will to put into place anti-bullying curriculum and policies. Yet the same educational system through campaigns such as Silence Hurts engages in proactive efforts that encourage students to come forward, identify and report information about students who may be planning violent acts. Are anti-bullying campaigns any less important? At your child's next individual education plan (IEP) meeting ask school administrators what anti-bullying curriculum is in place at the school. If none exists, ask through the IEP that an anti-bullying curriculum or awareness campaign be instituted immediately.

Barbara Doyle MS, a Springfield, Illinois based special educator and clinical consultant, is a teachers' teacher who preaches the need to educate AS students early and often about life in general to ensure that they develop the necessary life skills to recognize and deal with security and risk. In her workshop Teaching Ten Important Lifetime Goals To All Children she suggests that all children need to accomplish goals that result in safe and productive lives. She presents guidelines for identifying and addressing these essential life goals, such as targeting the elimination of dangerous or potentially dangerous behaviour, who to touch and how to be touched appropriately, respectful use of other's property and knowing who to ask for help, how and when (Doyle and Iland, 2001).

To prevent bullying and to teach students with AS to report appropriately, Barbara Doyle (Doyle and Iland, 2001) writes:

> Every student with ASD needs to receive systematic instruction in understanding who and what in the environment is dangerous. This systematic instruction is *more* than just talking about it! If students with ASD could learn all about danger from hearing the topic discussed, they would know all about it by now! Here are some instructional strategies:

> 1. Make board games for individuals with AS to play with typical peers. On three by five cards, simply write a series of situations that could come up in the lives of youth. Pair a student with Asperger Syndrome with a typical partner. Using a spinner or other board game devices, a student pair selects a card, reads it aloud and then discusses if it is something that should be reported to authorities or not. The players can earn points for each logical response. Some sample cards could be:

- A boy tells a girl he wants to take her out on a date.
- A boy tells a girl to leave the school with him.
- A girl invites another girl to smoke pot in the bathroom.
- Several boys push a student and tear his jacket.
- A student says a teacher is dressed in an unfashionable way.
- A girl shows another girl some mace that she has in her purse at school.
- Some teens tell another student that they will be 'waiting for him' after school to beat him up.

2.   Make a list of the people in each environment who are the right ones to report to if bullying or dangerous behaviour is observed. Set up role-play situations in which the student with AS sees a 'pretend' dangerous situation and then reports it to a key figure on the list. Teach the student with AS to ask to speak to the authority figure in private and to speak quietly when making the report. Let the identified adults know that the individual with AS has permission to come quietly to them.

3.   Go into the community with students with AS. Sit and watch human behaviour. Discuss what should be reported and not reported. Identify authority figures in each environment. Speak with authority figures and introduce the individual with AS to them. Include the shopping mall stores, restaurants, the movies, ice cream shop, sporting events, etc.

4.   Identify students who have been previously implicated in bullying. PROVIDE SUPERVISION when known bullies are within proximity of students with AS regardless of their ages especially in large, moving groups such as lunchrooms, outdoor areas and gymnasiums. Bullies recognize the naiveté and vulnerability of students with ASD and target them without mercy, later claiming to have been teasing or 'just kidding.' It is ridiculous to think that 'all' students are kind and nice to students with Asperger Syndrome. Students with AS are mentally and physically assaulted by fellow students every year in our country.

5. Teach typical students to recognize and assist students with AS. Many high school and college students respond very well when they are taught about autism spectrum disorders and how to be of assistance. One student said, 'I had watched him be bullied before but did not know that I could do something about it. From now on, I will.'

6. Provide instruction to all adults in the environment. One physical education teacher allowed a child with AS to be hit over and over again by a ball thrown by other students. This teacher later said he mistakenly thought that the student with AS would learn to 'defend himself' if the student was left alone to handle it and not babied. This teacher was under-educated.

7. Watch videotaped movies with individuals with AS. Stop the tape periodically and check to be sure that the individuals observed and understood the meaning of what was said and done. Teach them to try to predict what might happen next to the characters in the movie. Sometimes rewind the tape to find the 'clues' that the character should have observed to be able to better predict what was going to happen next. This type of activity is a far more valuable 'social skills training' activity than learning how to say please and thank you or hold one end of a jump rope!

8. Role-play bullying situations with trusted comrades playing the part of the bully. Teach the individuals with AS to 'see it coming' and get away quickly. Teach them to seek the company of others. Teach them to use anti-bullying techniques such as speaking forcefully and drawing attention to themselves. Teach them how to seek assistance in every possible place they may find themselves in the community including public bathrooms.

9. Enroll students with AS in carefully designed self-defense classes. Many young people with AS have learned the martial arts. They have surprised many of us by NOT using these skills until and unless it is absolutely necessary. All good martial arts training include teaching how to recognize and avoid dangerous situations.

Peer pressure to commit crimes

Good parents are never perfect. My mom taught me that the only people who don't make mistakes are those who do nothing at all. When we naturally encourage our kids to make friends, we run the risk of having them find the wrong ones. We all have to realize that, if not now then some day, our loved ones will have the independence to go where they want, make their own friends, and choose what they want to do. We won't be there to do or say anything about it.

We all know how hard it is for some teens with AS to make friends. It's understandable but potentially dangerous when we overlook the backgrounds, for example, age differences, of the friends our kids' make in the neighborhood, at school or on the Internet. Those friends who are significantly older may have a more powerful influence over an impressionable teen. Those that are significantly younger, for instance, may want to discuss or experiment sexually with the older AS teenager. If reported, the younger friends' parents or police may see a sexual predator and not the behaviour of a socially immature individual. Society and the criminal justice system will expect parents and caregivers to know where their kids are going, with whom and why.

Every teen is under tremendous pressure to go along to get along. As they find their way through these difficult years, they're at risk of making bad judgments. When involved with the wrong crowd, the pressure on adolescents with AS to steal, do drugs, and commit vandalism or other criminal acts can be overwhelming. Add in friend seeking and keeping activities, and it should be no shock for anyone in the AS community to learn that their loved one was led by others into unintentional criminal involvement.

A young Pennsylvania man with few social opportunities but excellent computer skills and a computer printer to match them found this out when he was recruited by so-called friends to print up counterfeit US currency. His new friends were more than happy to distribute the bogus bills. When the ring was caught, it was a curious and responsible Assistant United States Attorney (AUSA) who read about the young man's AS in a pre-sentencing report. After learning more about AS and recognizing that the young man had been possibly duped through false friendship into making the bad paper, the AUSA recommended no jail time and probation for the AS counterfeiter.

But what about the criminal activities of those adolescents who become involved because their environment encourages that behaviour? If we are to continue to support inclusion programs for our AS teens because it provides them the opportunity to benefit from appropriate peer role modeling, then we must also acknowledge the possibility that detriment will likely occur if the teen is exposed to inappropriate peer modeling. Simply put, when a guileless and socially unaware AS teen is raised in an at-risk environment, he will be particularly vulnerable to volatile and dangerous situations.

Parents have reported their AS teens' involvement in underage drinking, pot smoking and other illegal drug use. These activities have been described by caregivers as youthful experimentation, self-medication, fascination with the colorful and unusual paraphernalia oftentimes associated with drugs, or influential, repetitive and ubiquitous alcohol advertising as reasons for their loved ones' attachment to these substances. Some in the criminal justice system and society will see these less as reasons and more as excuses by the caregiver, and will question where the parents were when their kids were out finding trouble. In reality, it won't matter if the substances were offered through acquaintances or friends or obtained on the street to satisfy a curiosity or during a quest for self-medication. These often addictive and risky activities are illegal and largely impervious to much societal or criminal justice sympathy.

Can we count on prosecutors and defense attorneys to investigate an offender's AS and make provisions for fair justice? Not yet. While there are cases when a defendant's AS was considered as a mitigating factor during the sentencing phase of a trial, there are others where defense attorneys were reluctant to present the ramifications of AS to a judge or jury during any phase of the trial. Prosecutors and investigators have been known to disregard the condition completely when they make their decision to charge an offender. A New Jersey judge and dad of an adolescent with AS recently sought AS educational materials and curriculum that he could share with other members of the judiciary there. Disappointingly, there are none. Good or bad justice for youthful or any other offenders with AS will be dependent upon the willingness of all in the criminal justice system to learn about AS, and will by and large be found only on a case-by-case basis.

It is tempting to keep our AS teens away from their environments, especially if we are concerned that the environment is a risky one. Instead, we might encourage our loved ones to turn to the World Wide Web (WWW) for friendship experiences. The WWW gives AS teens a way to communicate free of the confusing social constraints of face-to-face or spoken communications. No body language to read here. No confusing spoken words. It's a concrete way of expressing yourself. Unless, that is, you are communicating with someone who is purposely hiding their true intentions.

More and more, bad guys turn to the WWW to find their victims, and so too, it has become common to read about Internet law enforcement stings conducted by veteran male officers posing as pre-pubescent kids. Their use of trickery and deceit in these instances is applauded by the public when they root out child sex abusers who are also hiding their true intentions while searching for victims, their pawns in child pornography or worse. For instance, parents have reported not seeing the clues that late night unmonitored computer usage may have offered. Others were so happy to see that their kids had made some friends, no matter that they were Internet friends, that they neglected to inquire about the friends, reach out to their families, or ask their kids what they were discussing with their newfound friends; friends who could very well turn out to be abusers. Is unfettered computer usage a problem? Is your teen waiting until you go to bed to hop on the computer? Keep the computer in a public, busy area of the house. Know why and with whom your kids are communicating on the Internet and when they are doing it.

Real-life peer examples are not the only examples teens with AS are likely to mimic. Therefore it is important that you monitor the information coming to your teen from his auxiliary world. Pay close attention to his TV, video, books, audio recordings and telephone habits. Help him to avoid violent content and content that exemplifies improper behaviour of any kind. Look instead for outside influences that can teach social lessons about making friends, what is inappropriate behaviour and how to recognize the difference between the two. And while you are at it, talk early and often about sex, drug, alcohol and crime issues. Although difficult, it is important to speak to your kids about these issues. Know what their views are on these subjects. Not talking about these issues or assuming that they hold little interest for your child is a mistake that parents of AS kids who have been involved in criminal activities have reportedly made.

Some behaviour rules are basic and should be made clear during the teen's earliest social training. Set out the basic rules: don't touch, hit or strike others, touch or destroy property, or threaten that you are going to do any of these things. Teach that the consequences for those that choose to do so will be arrest, jail, and loss of freedom; contact with family, friends and those who care. Create reward systems in which teens with AS can earn rewards for controlling themselves.

When your teens go out, set time for their return home. To increase communications, consider providing a cellular phone and ask your teen to call at regular intervals or you call them. When your kids are out with their friends, ask them where they are going, why they are going there and agree on times that they can phone home. Contact the parents of your kids' companions to share what you've agreed to with your teen. You're not big brother watching when you show a genuine interest in your kids' activities. It sends a message to them and their friends that you care and are interested in their welfare. It can also give your child an excuse to not give in to peer pressure: you will catch them!

Try to model appropriate social behaviour at home. When you're smoking, drinking, doing drugs, watching violence-laden or sexually explicit movies in front of your kids, can you really expect them to model appropriate behaviour? Of course not, but we sometimes need reminders that it isn't an inclusive school environment, workplace or community environment that will provide the best models of appropriate social behaviour for our teenagers with AS. Parents, caregivers and families will. When we don't ask the tough questions, monitor who our kids are with and what they are doing, when we don't discuss sex, drugs, alcohol use and criminal behaviour with them, can we really be surprised when others step into the gap and lure our kids into these activities? Those with AS are as susceptible to environmental factors as anyone else, probably more so. When brought up in an atmosphere of crime and with poor moral and social examples, people with AS may very well model these behaviours. It may be true that only a minority of teens with AS will become involved in these risky activities, but even one is too many. Teens on the autism spectrum will need more parental involvement and understanding at home, at school and in the community than the typical teen.

Stranger confrontations and personal security

Criminals are adept at noticing and selecting victims who appear unusual. They look for persons who appear to be unfamiliar with or new to their surroundings, those who may dawdle or move slowly or too quickly. The criminally bent individual becomes skilled at finding the perfect victim among those who appear timid, who wear clothes that are unusual to the area, who may speak with an accent, who are people watchers, who gawk, who have no eye contact or unusually long eye contact, who appear overly friendly, or whose appearance or behaviour is different from the crowd (Debbaudt 2002). Whether they recognize that the person has AS or not, they've learned through their criminal experiences that people who display these behaviours are easy marks who may not report the crime to the police or lack credibility as a victim when they do. Oftentimes the comforting accommodations that those with AS make to their stressful sensory environment can put them at risk.

Liane Holliday Willey described her feelings in *Pretending to be Normal* (1999) when she wrote about being confronted by a stranger during an early morning encounter in her Houston, Texas classroom. Driving a mini station wagon with no automatic transmission or air conditioning in the hot, humid Houston weather compounded the sensory overload of running the daily gauntlet of getting to work on time. She would invariably arrive on campus sweating, sticky, dazed and confused. In an attempt to avoid the heat and confusion of urban driving – missed exits, following confusing detours, getting lost in busy rush hour traffic – Liane decided to arrive at her classroom early that day.

But this day would be far different from the others. Arriving early to avoid the stress, and with enough time to allow her sensory system to settle in response to the silence her neatly arranged campus and classroom provided when there no students filling the physical and aural spaces with gab and shuffling feet, she felt safe and in control in the solitude. But the safety of that comfortable space was shattered when an uninvited stranger invaded it.

Older than most of the students on campus, the funky smelling and shabbily dressed man with the ashen, leathered face suddenly appeared in the empty classroom and slowly, methodically approached Liane's desk. Speaking in a monotone cadence, he inched toward her. As her sensory system was engrossed in his moldy appearance and she was curiously intrigued about the effect this man was having on her quiet, Liane heard in her mind the ringing of an intuitive bell of alarm when the man told her that he had just been released from jail.

Now too close, the man invaded Liane's personal space to the point where she had to move away from the putrid and invasive sensory input and the dawning reality that his intentions were probably not honorable that day. An early arriving student discovered Professor Holliday Willey in this confrontation and stepped in front of the stranger. It was only then that the intruder quickly disappeared, and Liane was able to make complete sense of the encounter and understand that she had been very lucky indeed. She knew then that her decision to arrive early at the virtually empty campus and classroom had left her vulnerable to unwanted situations that offer possibly perilous outcomes. Avoiding sensory input illustrates one of the many risks associated with the condition of AS that can put a person at risk of becoming a victim.

No one will ever know what the strange man's intentions were that day. Was it sexual assault? Robbery? Asking for directions? We all need to understand the vulnerabilities we have when making our way through everyday life. Advice for the AS teen who travels would include the following:

- Everyday driving and walking routes should be completed at a non-stressful time.

- Make note of any places to avoid, such as cul-de-sacs, dimly lit walkways and parking garages.

- Find out where the security office is, check in and ask about where and at what times they patrol. Let them know what your concerns are and ask them what are the best ways to reach them.

- Identify others at work or school who arrive at the same time. Park nearby or meet at a pre-planned location daily and walk as a group whenever possible.

- Always make sure that family members, friends, appropriate building or private security officers know your daily time of departure, arrival and the route that you take.

- When using public transportation, know the time schedules for buses and trains, then identify and use the safest nearby pickup zone.

- If possible, carry a cellular phone.

- When driving, carry a map, make sure the car is roadworthy, and lock the doors as soon as you get in your car. After parking the car and before unlocking the door and getting out, take a minute or two to look around and see what is going on around you.

- When walking, try doing what a good driver does when driving: take in the big picture. Make a mental note of what and who is on the horizon. Walk briskly with your head up. Consider your eye contact when walking toward strangers. Too much eye contact could be a cue that you want something or be taken as a challenge. Too little eye contact may make you appear scared or preoccupied target. Don't seek but don't avoid eye contact. Keep it brief and keep walking. Use well populated parking, walking and driving routes. Avoid unknown areas especially during 'off hours.' Do not wander or explore off the beaten path.

- If approached by a stranger or group of strangers who want your money or possessions, give them up. You can always replace them.

- Resist requests or attempts to go with strangers. Run away, carry whistles or other noisemakers and use them to make noise. Yell and scream. Get to a public place and phone the police.

Date rape and sexual assault

While stranger confrontations can lead to assaults, victims are more likely to report that the offender is someone who is known to them. Adolescents of either gender who have AS may be at risk from sexual assaults, commonly referred to as date rape. The adolescent years are tough enough without the added burden of dealing with one's AS. Teens are learning about and testing their ever-increasing awareness of their sexuality. Sexual experimentation is just one of many rites of passage that some succumb to during adolescence. Young boys may not take no for an answer; young girls may not know when to say no or fail to say it only in an attempt to fit in and find out. Adolescents with AS, too, are sexual beings who have the same desires, needs and feelings as their peers, but perhaps without the social awareness to recognize and inherently know what is – or isn't – appropriate behaviour.

For sexual assault such as indecent exposure, fondling, oral sex or penetration to occur, there must also be a lack of consent by the victim. Adolescents with AS will be asked if they truly understood the ramifications of and gave consent to another prior to a sexual encounter. Each person on the autism spectrum will have a different level of understanding, but the AS victim's conception of consent will come into question during investigations of non-stranger sexual assault or date rape allegations. Parents and caregivers must take a proactive role to ensure that adolescents and young adults are well prepared to determine what is and isn't an appropriate request from a friend or family member – or from a stranger.

Parents and caregivers

You need to know who your teen is going out with. Beforehand, contact their date's parents, learn where they live and their phone numbers. Agree with your teen and their date on the rules before they go out on a date. Provide a cellular phone and make arrangements for your teen to call or know that you will call them at pre-set times. Know where your teen and their date are going, why they're going there and when they'll return. Set a firm time for their return and agree about what the consequences will be if they miss the deadline.

Brief your teenager about date rape and agree about what is appropriate behaviour – holding hands, an arm around a shoulder or a kiss – and what isn't appropriate – touching, petting, and removing clothes. Clearly state what rape is – sexual assault – and reassure your teenager that it is OK to say no loudly and clearly to any advance, even when their date is telling them that it is OK.

Make it clear to your teen that while it's OK to be alone in the car when traveling to a location, it is not OK to stop, park and snuggle up. Nor is it ever OK to be alone in a bedroom, even when there are others in the home, say at a party or other gathering. Teach the differences of being safely alone with their date and being alone in a compromising place or situation.

Consider the ramifications of assault allegations. Parents should offer immediate support, understanding and comfort and listen carefully to any report or disclosure of possible sexual assault, but avoid the temptation to ask too many questions. If an incident has been disclosed that warrants notifying law enforcement, call the police immediately. Before any questioning, you should advise them of your child's AS. A good case could be lost if the law enforcers and prosecutors were unaware of the condition and did not make accommodations for it during questioning (See Appendix B for interviewing tips for law enforcers). Encourage law enforcers to ask your teenager to write down their recollections, or say them into a tape recorder.

Expect a savvy defense attorney to be well briefed by the perpetrator about the condition or any developmental differences the victim may have. They are going to ask what type of sex education the victim has had. If parents and caregivers haven't considered or inquired about sex education, or have never discussed it with their teenager, this too will come out during any investigation or trial surrounding allegations of sexual assault. Don't allow your teenager or anyone with AS to be victimized twice: once by the abuser and again by a system that lacks the ability or resolve to understand him or her (Debbaudt 2002, Chapter 4).

Critical life skills

When AS was included in our professional diagnostic manuals in the 1990s, parents held out hopes that earlier diagnosis would bring better educational services and awareness to their children. AS groups were formed and found some success in raising the level of AS awareness, advocating for better services, and offering innovative programs to our educators. But some parents are left in the lurch to deal alone with school administrators whose contact with students who have AS has been little or none. Some families have reported constant battles with school administrators who are reluctant to find good educational support for students who have AS. As the only way to receive ancillary services, other families report seeking an autism diagnosis for their kids. But, unlike obvious autism, AS is harder to see at earlier ages. When Asperger Syndrome is misdiagnosed in the younger child as ADHD, ADD or not seen and brought to the attention of diagnosticians, it is easy to see how parents, educators, and school districts are forced to play catch up when they do find out what they are dealing with. Parents and caregivers cannot take for granted that our educational systems recognize the need for safety awareness and law enforcement recognition and response training for our children and adolescents who have Asperger Syndrome. These systems are not ready for the many AS students who are now dependent on them.

Life skills training in general is often overlooked for the student with AS. The incorrect assumption is often made that these high-functioning, often academically proficient students don't need to learn basic life skills. Typically left out of the AS student's IEP is a plan to offer training and education about how to act appropriately when they find themselves in sudden interactions with a responding law enforcer or private security guard; identifying and appropriately reporting bullying and harassment; and recognizing the difference between a hug or a kiss, and sexual assault. Parents in the US have the power of the Individuals with Disabilities Education Act (IDEA) and Individual Educational Plan (IEP) provisions to request this kind of education for their loved ones. Would speech and language for 20 minutes a year be an acceptable service for an AS student's IEP? Ridiculous, we would say. Yet our AS students would be lucky to get a 20-minute training about safety and law enforcement. With the advent of zero tolerance policies in our schools, police as school resource officers have quickly become a permanent part of our educational landscape. Why not utilize their presence to educate our most vulnerable students? Like many creative ancillary services that have helped students with autism spectrum disorders learn, for instance, sensory integration therapy, the case for well-designed safety awareness and law enforcement education programs being offered to students with AS early and often can easily be made. It won't however, become reality until parents begin creating it at IEP meetings.

Conclusion

Those of us who live with AS understand that the behaviours and characteristics observed are part of the condition. But this is not yet the case within the general population. When research shows that persons with developmental disabilities are seven times more likely than others to come in contact with law enforcement (Curry *et al.* 1993), it should be no surprise to anyone that law enforcers who are trained to notice anything or anyone unusual and investigate it will take a second look at the AS teen.

In our increasingly security conscious world, it won't be just the police who are taking that second look. Teens and adults who have Asperger Syndrome have repeatedly told me that they feel paranoid that people are watching them when they are in public places. Paranoia? Maybe not. Signs at the Palm Beach, Florida International airport encourage travelers to 'Report Any Suspicious Person or Activity To The Nearest Security Officer or Airport Personnel.' If a traveler doesn't read the ubiquitous signage, the same message is repeated every few minutes over the airport's loudspeakers. Airports are not alone in advocating this kind of keep an eye on your neighbor program. In response to the 9/11 tragedies the US government proposed a new Terrorist Information and Prevention System (TIPS) as a way for workers such as truck drivers, utilities workers, train conductors and others to formally report suspicious terrorist activity. Now more than ever, people are looking at other people for signs of anything abnormal.

The following behaviours and characteristics associated with some people with AS, are often misunderstood by the general public and law enforcers as suspicious, criminal in nature or evidence of deception, drug use, or a psychotic episode:

- the inability to recognize nonverbal communications

- invasion of the personal space of others

- pacing and talking to self

- lack of or learned and fixated eye contact

- aloof body language and facial expression

- odd choice of clothes

- concrete expressive and receptive language of the literal mind

- perseveration on a particular topic

- vocabulary that may not match comprehension

- extreme distress over apparently trivial issues

- repeating other persons' statements
- reading signage aloud, such as signs in airports warning against making threats
- answers may be tactless or brutally honest
- may appear argumentative, stubborn or belligerent
- have difficulty recognizing jokes, teasing and the verbal/nonverbal emotional responses of others
- being unable to automatically deduce what others are thinking and why
- inappropriate social interactions
- the inability to quickly process and respond to urgent requests and commands.

When alone and unknown in the community, teenagers with Asperger Syndrome or any autism spectrum disorder will be noticed by a general public that is being urged to be on the lookout for suspicious behaviour and report it immediately to law enforcement authorities. AS teens need to be aware of this.

By the early twenty-first century, ASD training materials began to find their way into law enforcement publications such as the *FBI Law Enforcement Bulletin* and *Sheriff* Magazine. The ASD curriculum developed by the Maryland Police and Correctional Training Commissions in 1999 is now being modeled and reviewed by law enforcers in the US, Canada, Australia and UK. These materials describe and make a good case for basic education about the easily overlooked dilemmas that people with ASD present for law enforcement professionals in areas such as recognition of unique ASD behaviours and characteristics, response techniques and victim interview and interrogation room quandaries. Law enforcers are becoming aware that they are going to interact with developmentally disabled persons much more frequently than with other citizens. Police and private security officers are beginning to understand that these interactions can occur anywhere: in our neighborhoods, schools, workplaces, while traveling and shopping. When deinstitutionalization of persons with developmental disabilities became a reality a generation ago, more people with ASD began to get fair access to the community. Add to that an occurrence rate for those with ASD that has increased ten-fold over the past decade. It has become apparent that our loved ones are now being included in every aspect of everyday life and society, although not without a struggle to fit in. Without question, law enforcers are going to meet our sons and daughters, and we all want those meetings to be good ones.

Those who love, care for and advocate for adolescents with Asperger Syndrome are also beginning to recognize the need to form educational and awareness partnerships with community service providers such as law enforcement. Workshops that highlight the issues are regularly offered at AS conferences. Advocacy groups now include law enforcement awareness as a key element when considering services for people with AS.

In his (2002) report, *Taking Responsibility: Good Practice Guidelines for Services – Adults with Asperger's Syndrome*, Andrew Powell stresses making service development a priority for people with Asperger Syndrome, their families and practitioners, including training and awareness programs to increase professional understanding across a wide range of community services. The report also suggests education for forensic services (the use of science to decide questions arising from crimes or litigation) and practical advice for people with AS about crime prevention awareness, home safety, avoiding risk situations, how to explain AS to others, awareness of their own behaviours, reporting incidents, dealing with neighbors, and asking for help. Powell also suggests the development of crisis intervention services that are designed to be responsive to the specific needs of adults with AS who are under extreme stress, including working in a proactive way with police and other agencies through briefings about approaches that will enable behaviour to de-escalate, and by offering AS awareness and training sessions for local police, youth offending teams, appropriate adults, magistrates and other professionals in the criminal justice system (Powell 2002).

One example of mainstream criminal justice attention being paid to Asperger Syndrome issues is a report in the premier issue of the *International Journal of Forensic Mental Health* titled 'Asperger's Syndrome in Forensic Settings' (Murrie, Warren, Kristiansson and Dietz, 2002). This article reviews materials and issues in six case studies relevant to AS individuals who were criminal offenders, and highlights the role that Asperger Syndrome seemed to play in their offending and discusses the implications that features of the disorder have for decision-making in the criminal justice system as well as for disposition and treatment. The article also agrees with the Powell report and most conventional AS community thought that those with Asperger Syndrome are particularly vulnerable to victimization and that the vast majority of individuals with Asperger Syndrome do not commit violent crimes.

But all reports are nowhere near as promising. A report published by the US Council of State Governments is a fine example of what can be accomplished when all stakeholders come together on a particular issue and a sad example of what can happen when AS advocates are not at the decision-making table. The Criminal Justice/Mental Health Consensus Project is the result of grants from blue-ribbon organizations that include among others the US Department of Justice, US Department of Health and Human Services, Robert Wood Johnson Foundation and the MacArthur Foundation. This report is a 430-page comprehensive 'compendium of ideas that will help individuals identify and frame practices and programs that will improve the response to people with mental illness who are in contact with – or at risk of becoming involved with – the criminal justice system' (Council of State Governments 2002). Despite this document's attention to disabilities, autism and related developmental disabilities get short shrift. This should act as a wake-up call for all advocates of people with AS. With only a passing mention which suggests that trainers explain the differences between mental illness and neurological disorders such as epilepsy, Alzheimer's disease, Tourette's Syndrome, and autism and no reference to autism in the report's index, law enforcement and criminal justice professionals will clearly be left out in the cold if they rely on this report for information about people who have AS. Forget about Asperger syndome; it gets no mention at all. The AS community shouldn't feel sour grapes or outrage about this report, however. It simply illuminates the fact that without input from the AS and AS advocacy community – us – no one will toot our horn or represent our interests to the law enforcement and criminal justice communities.

The ramifications of these reports for the AS community are significant. We are best served when our advocacy groups permanently address the issues of AS and criminal justice, establish partnerships with our national and local law enforcement and criminal justice professionals, and encourage them to identify and develop AS resources that can be shared within their ranks and with the community at large.

It's never too late for Asperger Syndrome advocates to become involved by forming key partnerships. My book *Autism, Advocates and Law Enforcement Professionals: Recognizing and Reducing Risk Situations for People with Autism Spectrum Disorders* (Debbaudt 2002) presents guidelines that can be used in developing grass-roots partnerships between advocates, mental health professionals and law enforcement/criminal justice personnel. Once formed, these partnerships can then work to support training programs and understandings of each other's needs. These efforts offer us our best hope of lowering the risk factors that our loved ones will encounter during their vulnerable adolescence and throughout their lifetimes.

Appendix A

Parents may want to share the following information from *Autism, Advocates and Law Enforcement Professionals* (Debbaudt 2002) with retail security and the law enforcers who may be called to interrogate a teenager with AS who is suspected of committing a crime:

> Adolescents with AS that inadvertently display suspicious behaviour to police or security officers during questioning, for example, through a lack of eye contact or answers that are evasive or unconnected to the matter at hand, can easily become the object of increased scrutiny by the questioner. What started as a routine fact-gathering task may turn into an unnecessary interrogation when an officer, unfamiliar with the behaviours of AS, has their law enforcement instincts rightfully aroused.
>
> 'Without some elements of trickery, such as leading the suspect to believe that the police have some tangible or specific evidence of guilt, many interrogations will be totally ineffective' (Inbau and Reid 1967, p.196). 'Only one important qualification has been attached to the rule; the trickery or deceit must not be of such nature as to induce a false confession' (Inbau and Reid 1967, p.195). The person with AS through his or her responses, and the unaware interrogator through their beliefs, may become unwitting accomplices to continuing a faulty investigation in the best case or, in the worst case, to extracting a false confession, to say nothing of the often permanent psychological toll on the AS individual.
>
> A young man with AS recently stated: 'One area that would be a challenge is when to be honest and when not to. Sometimes, a

person with AS will admit to things that they have not done in order to please people.' The desire to make or keep a keep a friend may supersede their typical truth telling nature. 'If my new friend (the interrogator) wants to know about the shoplifting, then I'll tell him just to keep him around.' Rather than telling the truth, the person will tell his or her friend what he or she thinks the interrogator wants to hear.

Investigators interviewing or interrogating an adolescent with AS should be aware that the subject may have highly developed memory skills. There is the real possibility that a quick-to-memorize person will produce a very convincing regurgitation of hearsay facts. This could happen as the result of hearing a combination of details of the alleged offense from a by-stander or first responding officer and subsequently hearing more details provided by an interrogator who reveals some circumstantial evidence during questioning (by bluffing greater knowledge of the details of a crime). At the least, the suspect's seeming knowledge could be misconstrued as real familiarity of facts that only a guilty person could know.

The concrete-thinking ASD teen will expect others to be honest and they can become confused or disappointed when they are not. When an interrogator makes a promise, such as 'When you tell me about the (alleged offense), I promise to keep it a secret,' the person may believe the promise to be true. This person may not have a complete understanding of what is expected of them, or the consequences of their actions. They may not understand how serious the consequences of the confession will be for them. They may be led to believe that lying is what is expected of them. When the secret is revealed to others, the individual with AS may react very emotionally and even become verbally belligerent.

Typically, the teen with AS is a truth teller. While it is possible that this person has learned through example and experience to lie, his or her attempts to lie will be done poorly. An interrogator may seek an admission of lying about any part of the alleged offense. The friend seeker who has AS may respond with what the questioner wants to hear. The person may have made a mistake, but to the interrogator it was a lie.

When asked if he or she has ever thought about committing the offense in question – a standard interrogation technique – the honest-to-a-fault but innocent person may answer 'Yes,' as opposed to the characteristic answer of 'No' from an innocent person. While both persons only thought in passing about committing such an offense, the 'normal' person would not consider answering yes. The concrete-thinking adolescent with AS may answer the question as asked, causing the interrogator to continue the probe.

Interrogators would do well to consider the following when questioning the teen with AS:

- Be sure the subject understands his or her rights. Saying yes is not the same as understanding them.

- To avoid confusion, ask questions that rely on a narrative response.

- First ask a series of unrelated questions to determine the person's ability and potential for truth telling and lying.

- Ask a series of unrelated yes or no to determine the style and dependability of the response. Then ask the key yes or no questions.

- Prior to questioning, seek the advice of a psychiatrist or psychologist who is familiar with AS. Consider contacting a specialist from outside the criminal justice system. In the case of a minor, contact parents or guardians immediately.

- Seek the advice of a prosecutor.

- Follow procedure, but remember that the unusual responses from the person with AS may challenge all of your training.

- Also follow your gut instincts if you feel something isn't 'quite right' with your subject.

- If the confession or statement is 'too good to be true,' it probably is (Debbaudt 2002, pp.44–49).

Appendix B

Interviewing the witness information from *Autism, Advocates and Law Enforcement Professionals* (Debbaudt 2002, pp.56–59).

During the investigation phase, law enforcers can better interview witnesses with autism when they seek pre-interview assistance from professionals and/or advocates in the disabilities community.

Through this cooperative effort investigators can overcome the communications difficulties these cases present. At the same time they become more familiar with autism, thus increasing their own skills in dealing with these special members of the community. Such professionals can be as useful as having an interpreter present when interviewing a witness who does not speak the native language. Of course, the person assisting must realize that they, too, could be called as a witness in a court proceeding.

The following are tips for interviewers and bullet points suggested by curriculum collaborator writer and occupational therapist, Pip Farrar, adapted from her book *End the Silence*.

Preparation:

- Discuss with prosecutor any plan of action.
- Interview the caregiver or person who took the report first.
- Investigate possibility of multiple victims – interview others that the perpetrator might have had contact with.
- Review any records of assessment the person or their caregiver can provide.
- Ensure that assessment records are fresh, not outdated.
- Seek out from records communication strengths – goal is to prove competency of witness.
- Interview caregivers and persons who 'know' the victim for tips about how person gives and receives information.
- Investigators should get to know the person and their style of communication through casual conversation BEFORE they attempt to get any recollection from them. If they are not verbal, how do they communicate?

Videotaping:

- Consider videotaping interview (a good video interview with a victim that a perpetrator believes could not provide information may be a key to inducing the perpetrator to confess or plead guilty).
- Discuss with prosecutor an intention to conduct two videotaped interviews.
- If not considered prejudicial, proceed with preliminary videotaped interview to become acquainted with witness.
- Do not discuss the alleged offense during the first interview. Save direct questions of offense for the second interview. However, if witness makes a spontaneous disclosure of abuse, then proceed with details.

The interview:

- Carefully plan questioning based on person's ability level.
- Formulate and write down questions that are developed around the person's communication abilities.
- Consider having a trusted caregiver or autism professional at interview.
- Avoid all extraneous sensory distractions; person may be easily distracted.
- Avoid uniform or 'authority' clothing.
- Develop good rapport; use person's first name.
- Do not be condescending. If victim is an adult, do not treat the victim as if a child.
- Be careful to avoid witness burnout.
- Use simple, direct language. Deal with one issue at a time.
- Get the witness to recreate context of the event in his or her own words.

- Make sure your words and their words have meaning that you both understand.

- Be alert to nonverbal cues that suggest witness does not understand, is confused, or does not agree with the question you asked or the statement you made; for example, restlessness, frowning or long pauses between answers.

- Make sure that you and witness understand who is being referred to when using pronouns.

- Keep length of question short; avoid questions that suggest multiple answers.

- Be patient; wait for an answer.

- The witness or victim with autism may not want to answer any question more than once.

- Ask victim first if it is OK to repeat a question.

- Let them know it is OK to say 'NO' to your questions.

- Be convinced victim understands or is known to tell the truth.

- Carefully establish time lines.

- Avoid leading questions.

- Consider conducting interview in short time spans; person may have short attention span.

Acknowledgments

I would like to thank those that offered their time, suggestions, advice and assistance in the preparation of this chapter: Walter Coles, retired Royal Canadian Mounted Police; Jean-Paul Bovee; Jean Haase; Ellen Kerfoot, RN, BS; Lori Shery; Stephen Shore; Brenda Wall; and especially, Barbara Doyle, MS.

References

Council of State Governments (2002) *Criminal Justice/Mental Health Consensus Project.* Lexington, KY: Council of State Governments.

Curry, K., Posluszny, M. and Kraska, S. (1993) *Training Criminal Justice Personnel to Recognize Offenders with Disabilities.* Washington, DC: Office of Special Education and Rehabilitative Services News In Print.

Debbaudt, D. (2002) *Autism, Advocates and Law Enforcement Professionals: Recognizing and Reducing Risk Situations for People with Autism Spectrum Disorders.* London: Jessica Kingsley Publishers.

Doyle, E. and Iland, E. (2001) *Teaching Ten Important Lifetime Goals to All Children.* Springfield, IL: Doyle and Iland.

Farrar, P. (1996) *End the Silence: Preventing the Sexual Assault of Women with Communication Difficulties: Developing a Community Response.* Calgary, AL: The Technical Resource Centre.

Inbau, F.E. and Reid, J.E. (1967) *Criminal Interrogations and Confessions.* Baltimore: Williams and Wilkins.

Murrie, C., Warren, J., Kristiansson, M. and Dietz, P. (2002) *Asperger's Syndrome in Forensic Settings.* Charlottesville, VA: International Association of Forensic Mental Health Services.

Powell, A. (2002) *Taking Responsibility: Good Practice Guidelines for Services–Adults with Asperger Syndrome.* London: National Autistic Society.

US Department of Education (2000) *Joint OCR/OSERS Letter on Disability Based Harassment.* Washington, DC: US Department of Education. www.edlaw.net/service/harassment-disab.html

Willey, L.H. (1999) *Pretending to be Normal: Living with Asperger's Syndrome.* London: Jessica Kingsley Publishers.

7

When the Thunder Roars

Liane Holliday Willey

The more I am asked to remember what my life was like when I was young, the more I see things that look unpleasant to me now. Though I came away from my adolescent years fundamentally unscathed, I look back as an adult and wonder how that was possible. I know for a fact that my lifelong friendship with one of the most popular boys in school certainly helped others come to accept my eccentricities and uniqueness. After all, if the popular guy liked me, shouldn't everyone? But I also suspect I was a particularly strong Aspie teen, no doubt because I was fortunate enough to have a wealth of support at home, in school and from the medical community. These people who took a keen interest in my well-being and consistently provided me with the counseling I needed to stay on a reasonably solid course. With their help, I spent the vast majority of my adolescent years happy and content.

I did not remain so lucky forever. The hell of being different grabbed me by the throat when I was in my early twenties and it is with those distinctly sour memories in my mind, that I write this chapter. I doubt I could have handled life had my hellish nightmare began when I was an adolescent. As the mother of an adolescent Aspie and as a survivor of the kinds of cruelty specially saved for those with AS, I am consumed with sadness and worry when I think of the countless Aspie adolescents who are wandering through their teen years with more handicaps and less support than I had. Will they wake up from their own nightmare in time? Will they hang on to their integrity and their sense of worth? Or will they reach for answers that may well cost them their lives?

Life in the empty

I used to spend days comparing myself to others my age. I was clumsy, dizzy in my behaviour and rather daft when it came to moving through and alongside the crowds of other kids. I distinctly remember how hard it was to pretend to understand the various rituals and rites of passage that my peers seemed to enjoy when we were all teens. I knew enough to copy the actions of the few people I could trust. My formula was simple enough. When one of the friends I trusted laughed, I laughed. When they cried, my eyes welled up. When they expressed anger, so did I. Taking my cues on how to behave from those few friends, I was led to safe ground most of the time. Yet there were many, many times when I discovered, albeit too late for making mistakes go away, that I had stumbled from neurotypical land into Aspie land. Like Alice through the looking glass, I figuratively went through one dimension into another. It is odd on the other side of reality. On the other side, you can still hear and see, touch and smell, the conditions in the real world, but you feel as if time is slowing down and things are grown blurry. A simple blink, it would seem, would make me disappear all together, lost forever to the other side, the side of empty.

If neurotypical adolescent's emotions are crowded with noxious matter, Aspie adolescent's emotions spill over with the bad stuff, particularly when they are living on the side of empty. *Anxiety, anger, confusion, frustration* and *depression* are usually not far from the heart. When one or more of these emotions thunders onto the Aspie's center stage, nothing good can be produced.

Though I am skeptical when it comes to believing that all tough times can be kept from any teen, my personal experiences and research studies have convinced me that there are measures which can guard against the worst of the tough. What follows are the summaries of those experiences and studies.

Anxiety

It is my not so humble opinion that the effects of anxiety on the psyche, body and indeed society are completely underestimated. When the nerves rumble, so does everything else. I am always vulnerable to anxiety. Both good and bad things can bring it on. Parties, shopping, playing on the computer are all as anxiety provoking for me as traffic jams, long lines and bad news. I've been on and off various medications to deal with anxiety, but even when the anxieties are numbed, the reality is that I always sense I'm but one step ahead of the anxiety avalanche. This was particularly true when I was an adolescent and more prone toward anxiety-producing behaviours. For instance, I was completely disorganized and hardly ever able to remember what project was due when, where my books were, which class followed which, and what time the school bus would arrive at my street. Most days I scrambled till the very last minute shoving things into my backpack, tying my hair into some sort of knot or tail to cover the fact I hadn't washed it in days, and reaching for clothes – rumpled or not – that I had stuffed under my bed or in the corners of my room. I was constantly forgetting things and, no matter how many notes I wrote myself, I could never keep up. Maybe it would have been easier if I had been able to find the notes, but then everything seemed perpetually lost to me – even my baby-blue car which should have been easy to spot in parking lots filled with the more popular colored white, black or red cars. To make matters really tense, not only did I lose things, I also lost my way every day. I was always lost as a teen, truth be told, and I follow this trend even as an adult. But as a teen, it meant I was constantly on edge, worried about being late for a class, not finding friends at lunch, losing my way in crowds, on field trips – everywhere. Consequently, I used to seek out refuges in areas I often visited that would be terribly difficult to lose, even for me. In high school I spent my free time in a loft our library had built for studying and relaxing. I often slept in the loft. I used to sleep all over the place in public – on benches, in fields, and more than once on the pavement of a parking lot. Stress puts me to sleep after it stirs me up and gives me stomachaches and headaches.

Some days I might have been able to convince myself that my lack of organization and orientation were merely a silly little blip on the day or the result of my not having gotten enough sleep the night before. Other days I was left feeling incredibly stupid and unable. Neither feeling is acceptable. Today I have learned how to reduce the anxiety in my life, even though I continue to be somewhat disorganized, typically on a hunt for lost things including myself! Age has taught me that some things simply aren't going to change for me. Age has also taught me that I'd better take care of the anxiety levels before worrying about where my keys are.

Only when I'm calm can I really think. Adolescents with AS need to discover the tricks to calm now, not later.

Neurosystem

Aspie adolescents have the deck stacked against them when it comes to anxiety. In addition to the AS spectrum variables (sensory integration disorder, leaky gut syndrome, poor executive functioning skills, etc.), their neurosystem is often joined by a variety of 'kissing cousins' as I call them. These 'cousins' may include obsessive compulsive (OC) behaviours, attention deficit hyperactive disorder (ADHD), separation anxiety, auditory perception problems, as well as a host of behaviour problems. When any mix of the cousins join forces, the Aspie teen is in for one heck of a hard time. Join the Aspie in studying her neurosystem as a complex whole and help her discover ways to relax the effects of all her issues on her anxiety. Remember, when the AS and all its kissing cousins are kept quiet, Aspie teens can work harder to push the anxiety away.

Relaxation therapies

Relaxation therapies are finally considered cool across public school and college campuses. Classes in yoga, aromatherapy, and expressive arts are becoming popular electives. Not only that, they are often taken by kids who have come to accept differences in people. This makes joining such courses even more beneficial for the Aspie adolescent. Other excellent albeit more private anxiety-reducing opportunities include water therapy, massages, music therapy, guided imagery, biofeedback therapy and meditation.

Stim behaviour

Many Aspies rely on stim behaviour to still their nerves. A stim may be defined as a self-stimulated repetitious behaviour intended to provide and regulate sensory infromation. A stim may include behaviours such as rocking, hand flapping, pacing, hand rubbing, spinning, jumping, echoing noises from the environment. I encourage my daughter and myself to practice our favorite stims when we feel the need. I tend to rely on my own stim behaviours when I am alone or in my own home. For me, there is nothing more calming than a drift in our pool. Floating under water like a lazy dolphin is a perfect tension releaser for me. I cannot do that in public pools, and before we had a pool of our own I used to float under the water in my bathtub. Things on land work well, too. I have Aspie teen friends who enjoy walking in circles, walking in squares or simply moving about as if they are floating on a cloud. Movement, it seems, free or regimented, often works well to release tension.

Self-analysis

I strongly suggest teens with AS realize that anxiety might be one of those things they have to deal with for a lifetime. Instead of trying to avoid it at all cost, it could serve them well to know how to help themselves while they are in the midst of an anxiety attack, be they in the beginning, middle or over the edge. Only then can they call on the controls that might help them move from edgy to smooth. I have always encouraged and led my girls to discover what their bodies are 'saying' when they are becoming or acting anxious. I ask them to self-analyze in terms of their heart rate, their general well-being (does their stomach or head hurt?), their rate of speech, their eye movements and even their eye gazes (are they able to focus or are things blurry?).

When I have the kids compare their anxiety state to their regular state, they can typically find and realize differences between the two. Then they can move on to decide which relaxation technique would help them the most. Yoga might help them through beginning stages, biofeedback information might be beneficial in the middle stage and stimming behaviours might help them through the worst bits. This kind of understanding is slow in developing. Only now are my young adolescent girls beginning to master their introspective abilities. But to my mind there are few things more important than self-knowledge and understanding the effects of life on one's general health.

Anger

Anger roars through every human being at one time or another. It rips through Aspie teens. It has to. Too many things come on at once to avoid a collision. I have had more than my fair share of angry episodes, so many I am embarrassed to recall them now. I will however say that when the anger comes on, it comes on strong and fervent. Few emotions tackle me as fast or as completely. Not even sorrow can compare in intensity with anger. When you are a teen with anger issues, things are particularly difficult. As an adult, I have the option to blow off steam or disappear for hours. Teens do not have that luxury. Their whereabouts are usually made to be more accountable and they do not have the authority to tell others to bug off or get lost, yet they will – and when they do, look out.

Self-knowledge remains an important element with the anger emotion. It will behoove the Aspie teen to know what kinds of things set their anger off and how to recognize when their anger is getting beyond their control. The suggestions below are very general and will need to be individualized to fit the Aspie's character and needs.

1.   Doctors and counselors advise parents to remain composed when faced with their Aspie's anger. All of my personal experiences tell me that is valid advice. Do not raise the voice. Do not escalate the situation with big movements and big expectations of immediate quiet and obedience. Never get physical. Realize the anger needs time to flow of its own accord and that in the meantime there might not be a whole lot the adult can do to facilitate immediate composure. Do, however, keep the Aspie from hurting herself or others, even if it means you have to gently but firmly restrain her.

2.   Use silly humor to ease the anger. Physical humor is often the most noticeable and easiest to laugh at. Word-play games might work, but only if the Aspie is ready and able to think semantically. In general, I find humor works best when the anger is beginning to ebb.

3.   Keep the environment calm and free from as many sensory violations as possible. It would be ideal to have a room, even a closet would do, reserved for anger or frustration control. The room could be filled with zero sensory violations (as defined by the Aspie herself) as well as safe opportunities for releasing the negative physical energy such as punching bags, big pillows for grappling and trampolines.

4. Experiment with the idea of writing or drawing the anger into oblivion. The visualization and then release of something has held a historically strong appeal for humanity through the ages. Ancient cultures have described sending a representation of their anger and worries into a floating object only to then send it down the river and away from the soul. It may be that when we personify the anger, we can then challenge it straight on. In the absence of a river, writings and drawings of the anger situation can be torn up, burned, flushed, or even folded into a paper airplane and flown away.

5. When the anger has subsided, discuss problem-solving skills that could be used to avoid similar difficulties in the future. Be certain the skills you teach are based on logic and not emotion. Use charts, graphs and other visual aids to illustrate the problem solving logic. 'If/then' sentences linked by arrows are a particularly useful strategy.

Confusion

The mind grows quickly confused when faced with irrational dilemmas, at least it should. Logic is the only thing one can depend on. It is the only thing that makes sense. Yet neurotypicals are ever bent on using words, phrases, looks, and even conventions that are not based on any set of logic I know. And even if I am to figure out what in the world it is they are trying to say or do, the next time a similar situation presents itself, the game gets changed and new rules arise. No wonder Aspies are said to be incapable of generalizing from one situation to another – when we do, we are surprised to find out we are still incorrect in our assumptions. I think we grow wise to them, so that when something appears to look like something we have previously mastered or experienced, we recoil in the fear that there is some subtle trick or event waiting to bite back and yell gotcha!

When I am faced with nonsensical situations, I cannot move forward. I get stuck in rewind position, constantly reanalyzing and refiguring the cause for my confusion, up until the time someone is able to relax me into believing some things will never be within my ability to understand. When I was a teen, these uncomprehensible things were the subject of great debate in my home and in my journals. My dad and I would go round and round the questionable reasoning behind everything from the latest political decisions to the high school's decision to have classrooms without walls. My journals would hold my questioning the whys and how-comes behind my peers' behaviours and my social inabilities. All the talk in the world never put an end to my confusion, but I do believe it kept me from exploding inside, especially when my father talked to me. His sharing of his own confusion on similar issues gave me cause to believe I wasn't all alone in the world.

I am convinced my therapist toyed with the idea that I had a paranoid personality disorder because my ramblings must have sounded just that, paranoid. Because I never really know what people are trying to say to me, I am often left to dissect the possibilities and it eventually comes out as, well, weirdly paranoid to the untrained ear. While I may never understand everything I wish I could, I have figured out what to do when I am confused. I wish I had known what to do about my seemingly constant state of confusion, when I was a teen. Here are some suggestions to alleviate confusion:

- I'm stating the obvious here, but it is important to keep statements and instructions as clear as possible – if not all the time, then certainly when confusion is occurring.

- Encourage the Aspie to make a list of all the things that are confusing her. Sometimes when the entire list is laid out, it is more possible to unravel where the source of confusion began, how it grew, and how to end it.

- Confide that it is virtually impossible to avoid confusion all the time. Share times when you too are confused about life, people, etc.

- Reassure the Aspie by listening to her ramblings. Don't take that moment to doubt what she is saying or tell her she is being ridiculous, paranoid, etc. That kind of talk will only complicate her ability to reasonably analyze. Listen, take notes, and when she is done talking, try to help her untangle the source of confusion.

- If the Aspie has strong echolalia powers, ask her to act out the situation that left her confused. I always do this for my husband, and he is almost always able to tell me where my interpretations went haywire.

- Practice reading others with the Aspie. Take observation field trips to the mall, train station or some other favored people-watching spot, and talk about what people are doing and why. Encourage the Aspie to come up with her own hypotheses too. They will give you insight into how she thinks and it will allow you the opportunity to keep her thoughts logical and germane.

- Talk about the most common idioms and colloquialisms that teens use today. Directly teach them to the Aspie, so she will be able to better understand the communication around her. You don't know any teen words? That's easy enough to fix. Rent current teen movies, ask the school counselor, talk to a neighboring teen or join a teen chatroom on the web. The more you know about teen culture, the better able you will be to help your Aspie teen understand it.

Frustration

How can Aspie teens not grow up with at least some degree of frustration trailing in and out of their days? The best analogy I have for explaining the rationale for frustrations is simple – people with AS report they never get over the feeling they are living in a foreign culture. Imagine going to China for a month with no guide, no how-to book, no translators and no previous history with anyone or anything from China. Can you imagine how difficult and peculiar your life would be for those 30-odd days in your foreign world? Imagine if you had to feel that way each and every day for the rest of your life. How long would it take before frustration came along for the ride?

All sorts of things beyond the rules and words that neurotypicals rely on can be incredibly frustrating to the Aspie: cafeteria noises; personal space issues in crowds, classrooms, and at social gatherings; non-verbal glances and expressions; changes in bodies and voices and hair patterns; changing environments; new classroom materials and homework demands; new teachers or administrators or lunch line helpers or bus drivers or librarians or students – the list goes on and on and on. New, different, stop, go, sit, stand, now, later, never, today you fit in, tomorrow you don't. Nothing is predictable, nothing has staying power, but frustration.

At its most basic, frustration is essentially a state of being that happens when we are kept from solving a problem, controlling a situation or achieving the goals we set. With that in mind, I offer the following suggestions:

1.   Give the Aspie teen opportunities to take control of something. Gardening, caring for animals, collecting coupons, planning and making meals one day a week, building a playhouse, picking the night's activities, managing a special bank account. Use your imagination and virtually anything can become something that needs to be controlled.

2.   When an Aspie teen is frustrated, additional or exasperated intolerance for any kind of change could well develop. Your job will be to keep things as they have always been for as long as the intolerance lasts. Depending on how rigid your Aspie is, any number of the following might apply:

  • Keep everyday routines as consistent as possible.

  • Do not make any household or personal changes. Keep the furniture in the same arrangement, do not change your hair color or style, don't try a new recipe, don't buy a new toothpaste and do not make any major purchases.

  • Remind everyone in the family to keep as close to the normal house rules as possible. Give special rewards if you need to, to encourage their participation.

  • Be particularly diligent in keeping the Aspie's favorite clothing and bedding available.

3.   Help the Aspie find success, even if it means you have to cheat. Let her win in a game, discover hidden treasures you've distributed throughout the house, find an item you've conveniently lost, put together a project well suited to her strengths, put on a puppet show or fix a problem on your computer. The key here is to set the Aspie up for good

things. This is often all it takes to leave bits of frustration behind.

4.   During a time when the Aspie is not feeling frustrated, role model how you handle your own frustrations.

5.   Keep track of the things that are likely to frustrate your Aspie, and avoid them whenever possible.

Depression

I hear it in the questions they ask: *'Why do kids think they should hurt me?' 'Why am I always the last person picked for everything?' 'How come I can't get a date?' 'Why don't other kids like me?' 'Will I ever be normal?'*

I read it in their eyes: *I don't want to be beat up anymore. The loneliness is killing me. It hurts to be touched. Please make the noise and lights and crowds and confusion go away. I'm ashamed of my AS.*

I find it buried in my heart from days long, long ago. *I didn't mean to say anything hurtful. Why can't people like me as I am? Life is too complicated. I don't know how much longer I can go on pretending.*

Depression can lull one into a false sense of tranquility. It can cast spells of sorrow that compel sleep and shut-downs. Depression can choke out other ideas. It can make the simplest of movements seem like they are sunk in quicksand. Yet it can also act like a wind tunnel to pull its victim into a vacuum in need of more air and more action and more energy. *Feed me,* it seems to say, *with all you can find – drugs, nicotine, alcohol, self-abuse, anger, tears. Feed me, until you pull out your weapon and take us both to the grave.*

Psychologists recommend teens learn how to recognize the difference between a general feeling of disappointment or sadness and major depression as early as possible. I have to believe such an understanding would have helped me yell for help long before I finally did. Today, in my parent role, I regularly discuss these depression warning signs with my own adolescents. Only if they are self-monitoring with correct and cohesive information, can they then decide if it is time for them to call for help. Here are some of the common markers of depression as provided by Psychology Information On-Line (2000).

You might be depressed if:

- You feel sad or cry a lot and it doesn't go away.

- You feel guilty for no real reason; you feel like you're no good; you've lost your confidence.

- Life seems meaningless or like nothing good is ever going to happen again.

- You have a negative attitude a lot of the time, or it seems like you have no feelings.

- You don't feel like doing a lot of the things you used to like – like music, sports, being with friends, going out – and you want to be left alone most of the time.

- It's hard to make up your mind. You forget lots of things, and it's hard to concentrate.

- You get irritated often. Little things make you lose your temper; you over-react.

- Your sleep pattern changes; you start sleeping a lot more or you have trouble falling asleep at night. Or you wake up really early most mornings and can't get back to sleep.

- Your eating habits change; you've lost your appetite or you eat a lot more.

- You feel restless and tired most of the time.

- You think about death, or feel like you're dying, or have thoughts about committing suicide.

Obviously, the major risk of depression is suicide. It's no secret among experts in the field of AS, that Aspie teens are more prone to thoughts and acts of suicide than their same age peers. While evidence for this remains anecdotal at this time, it is widely considered valid and reliable. No matter the statistics collected, it warrants serious attention. The American Academy of Child and Adolescent Psychiatry (1997) provides the following suicide warning signs.

A teenager who is planning to commit suicide may:

- complain of being a bad person or feeling 'rotten inside'

- give verbal hints with statements such as: 'I won't be a problem for you much longer,' 'Nothing matters,' 'It's no use,' and 'I won't see you again'

- put his or her affairs in order, for example, give away favorite possessions, clean his or her room, throw away important belongings, etc.

- become suddenly cheerful after a period of depression

- have signs of psychosis (hallucinations or bizarre thoughts).

Ideally, there would be a library full of materials specifically written on depression and AS adolescents. This is not the case. For now, the best we can logically do is adapt what we know about teen depression in general to the kids we shepherd and care for. For more information on this exceptionally important topic, the reader is advised to look far beyond this particular chapter – please refer to the Resources section at the end of this chapter. The following ideas represent the kinds of things my own counselors developed for me during my youth, as well as things my family's current counselors recommend.

Action

Psychologists agree that the two premier treatments for severe depression are appropriate counseling and medication. Never is it recommended that kids be left to deal with their problems on their own. Never should teens be told it is perfectly natural that they feel depressed or sad. While it might be a common feeling for many teens, it is neither natural nor OK to feel true depression. Depression is a sign that something has gone greatly amiss in the system and immediate action must be taken to help affected teens.

Communication

In our house, it is often too difficult to openly discuss how we are feeling. As an alternative to verbalizing, my girls and I will choose to instant message or email one another about the big and scary issues. Not only does writing our thoughts make them more clear, it also provides a record I can keep and share with counselors. In the absence of a computer, journals or notepaper could be used to exchange written communication of feelings.

Quantifying feelings

When we do discuss how we are feeling, my family often finds it helpful to quantify feelings by using a numerical scale. 'On a scale of one to ten, one being the worst and ten being the happiest,' I might ask, 'how do you feel about the fact that you weren't asked to the party?' or 'On a scale of one to ten, how sad are you today?' After the girls give me their numbers, I can then form the right kinds of words to respond with. Low numbers will cause me to be more pedantic and exact in my thoughts, advice or questions. High numbers make me stop everything I am doing to concentrate instead on the girls' crisis. Short answers by the girls often mean they are more depressed than they would probably realize. Long answers tend to tell me my girls are at least able to talk, express and contemplate. Those actions lead to knowledge and understanding, two places that are centered more in good mental health than in bad. I worry less when the answers are long – unless they become rambling or incoherent. If the girls become too foggy in their communiques, I have to suspect they are headed for unsafe emotions.

Medication

When it comes to medication choices, the best recommendation is simple. Consult your family physican and prepare your adolescent for what might be a long course of trial and error, not to mention highs and lows. Discuss the changes that are likely to occur for your adolescents, the physical as well as the emotional. More or less sleep might be needed. Appetites will either wain or increase. Sensory sensations will be susceptible to great fluctuations. Some medications can make some adolescents more anxious, some more mellow. All sorts of odd, good and bad reactions might occur when any given adolescent takes any given medication. Hence it is only wise to prepare the adolescent for the possible realities, unless of course your physician and you decide it would be in the best interest of the adolescent to keep this information at bay. Each case is, of course, unique and worthy of extensive analysis far beyond these words. However, it will always be important for the adolescent to fully understand that under no circumstances can she mix any other drug, either prescribed or not, legal or illegal, with the medications prescribed for depression or mood disorders. This point cannot be underscored enough. The wrong mix of meds can be lethal.

Don't mess with depression

The bottom line is don't mess with depression. If you only slightly suspect your Aspie teen is coming near depression, seek professional help immediately. And if you are certain your teen will never become depressed, think again. Even if you are correct, there is no harm in understanding and realizing the signs of depression and more importantly, suicide.

Early intervention

When I initially met with my Aspie daughter's team of educators, I introduced the session with what I think laid the facts of Aspie adolescent life right out in the open. I said, 'If you all help me help my daughter, she will go on to do and become anything she wants to. If you do not help her, if you let her slip through the system, she could very possibly seek suicide as a release. Will you help her or let her die?' I am told I am a humorous woman. That day, there was nothing funny about one thing I had to say. Thankfully, my daughter's team saw the seriousness of my statement. There was no time for joking and playing with words. Troubled emotional states are not anyone's idea of a good time. Depression is not a game. Suicide is the end. It is essential to realize that adolescents with AS are especially vulnerable to relentless and severe depression which is at least partially related to the complications that come from not being able to plug into the regular teen society. But all is not lost to chance. When Aspie teens are supported through the tumultuous stages of anxiety, anger, confusion, frustration, and depression, they will be far more apt to recognize when they are going too far off the deep end of good. This early recognition leads to early intervention which is the real key to keeping the thunder from roaring.

References

Psychology Information On-Line (2000)
    http://psychologyinfo.com/depression/teens.htm

Teen Suicide # 10 Facts for Families© series. American Academy of Child and Adolescent Psychiatry (1977) Washington, DC: Academy of Child and Adolescent Psychiatry.

Resources

American Academy of Child and Adolescent Psychiatry
3615 Wisconsin Ave. N.W.
Washington, DC 20016-3007
USA
Tel: 202-966-7300
Fax: 202-966-2891
www.aacap.org/

American Academy of Pediatrics
141 Northwest Point Boulevard
Elk Grove Village
IL 60007-1098
USA
Tel: 847-434-4000
Fax: 847-434-8000
www.aap.org/default.htm

National Institute of Mental Health (NIMH)
6001 Executive Blvd
Rm 8184, MSC 9663
Bethesda, MD 20892-9663
USA
Tel: 301-443-4513
TTY: 301-443-8431
Depression info: 800-421-4211
Anxiety info: 88-88-ANXIETY (269-4389)
Panic info: 888-64-PANIC (64-72642)
Fax: 301-443-4279
nimhinfo@nih.gov
www.nimh.nih.gov

Suicide Information & Education Centre
201 1615-10th Ave. SW
Calgary
Alberta
Canada T3C 0J7
Tel: 403-245-3900
Fax: 403-245-0299
www.suicideinfo.ca/siec.htm

Suggested reading

Please keep in mind that these books are not written for adolescent Aspies. However, they are filled with general and useful information that can apply to our kids.

In addition to these resources, I advise the reader to contact their local health officials for more information.

Fassler, D. and Dumas, L. S. (1997) *Help Me, I'm Sad: Recognizing, Treating and Preventing Childhood and Adolescent Depression.* New York: Penguin Putnam.

Hall, K. (2000) *Asperger Syndrome, the Universe and Everything.* London: Jessica Kingsley Publishers.

Ingersoll, B. and Goldstein, S. (1995) *Lonely, Sad and Angry: A Parent's Guide to Depression in Children and Adolescents.* New York: Bantam Doubleday Dell.

Jackson, L. (2002) *Freaks, Geeks and Asperger Syndrome: A User Guide to Adolescence.* London: Jessica Kingsley Publishers.

Varma, V. (1997) *Troubles of Children and Adolescents.* London: Jessica Kingsley Publishers.

8

Settling into the Diagnosis of Asperger Syndrome

Rebecca Moyes

Ask any parent about the day their child was diagnosed with an autism spectrum disorder, and you will notice a cloud come over their eyes. For most, it is not a fond memory. Some may be able to tell you with exact clarity what date and time this life-changing event took place. For others, the details may not be so clear. But one thing is certain, usually every parent can tell you how they felt at that particular moment. Because many parents of children with Asperger do not receive their child's diagnosis until late childhood, they may have to develop a completely different 'game plan' than the one they originally had in mind when they thought their child was 'typical.'

Stages of Adjustment

There is no right way to feel when given the news that your child has Asperger Syndrome. All of the following stages are normal feelings at such a time and in the days and weeks following the diagnosis. More importantly, parents may move through and return to a variety of stages before finally 'settling in to the diagnosis.'

Doubt

The first stage of a parent's adjustment tends to be doubt. It is not unusual for parents of children with Asperger Syndrome to have concerns early on about their child's speech, social development, or behaviour. Often times, they may have spoken of them to their child's pediatrician, to a relative or even a close friend. Or, perhaps down inside, a nagging thought or twinge about their child's development had crept into the busy hours of childcare or the early elementary years. Was he/she responding appropriately to others? Was his/her language developing the way it should be? Did his/her passion for certain things extend beyond normal boundaries? Many parents report that they were concerned about little things here and there over the years, but their pediatricians or family members dismissed these concerns as trivial. Because developmental timetables have such a wide range of normalcy, parents' concerns can be easily explained away as simply minor worries or natural parent anxieties.

> Roberta was very concerned that her son was two years old and only said three words: light, fan, and water meter. He never said 'ma-ma' or 'da-da' or any of the words that typical children begin saying first. At her son's next doctor's visit, she reported this to the pediatrician. He turned out the light in the room to prompt her son to speak. At once, Roberta's son shouted, 'Ite!' The pediatrician said, 'I wouldn't worry about it. He says that word really well for a two-year-old.'

> Marsha and Jim, parents of seven-year-old Marc, became concerned with his lack of interest in what other children his age seemed to enjoy. When they took him to their local park to play, the other children would use the swings and slides and run and greet each other. Marc, on the other hand, seemed to enjoy examining the electric meter on the side of the park office building. Now, as a seventh grader, Marc still had no real friends. He is finding school to be exhausting socially and yet unchallenging academically.

For the parents described above, obtaining a diagnosis may validate their concerns. But for others, doubt may exist because the diagnosing doctor brought to light something they did not anticipate. They knew that something was wrong, but never expected this kind of diagnosis! Consider the following example:

> Joey's parents brought their son to a local hospital's child development unit. Their primary concern was the intensity of

Joey's anxiety and frustration levels at school. After a team examination, it was decided that Joey met the criteria for Asperger Disorder. Shocked, Joey's parents did not accept the team's decision and vowed to find another doctor.

There will always be parents who will go away from the diagnosis in denial and stay in denial. However, it is also important to recognize that during some periods of the child's life, when things are going well, parents may feel that they can put the diagnosis 'on the shelf' for a while – that the worst is over. Perhaps they may feel that their child has 'come out of it.' This can be dangerous. Autism spectrum disorders are lifelong. There will always be a new bend in the road to round or a new challenge which will present itself. Teaching the child social skills and everyday life skills is also lifelong. It is important for parents to understand that their child will always need some measure of support.

When the parents question a diagnosis, it is advisable that they get a second opinion as quickly as possible. Persistence on the parents' part not to accept the diagnosis only leads to a hindrance and delay in getting help for their child. Families and teachers need to be aware of this, too, when they are told about the diagnosis. Well-meaning professionals and family members sometimes make matters worse by actually talking a parent out of getting the help the child needs. Continuing to visit this stage of denial may lead to depression for the parents when they have to revisit the diagnosis over and over again. Worse yet, parents may later blame those individuals who built road blocks and made it difficult for them to initiate a support system.

> When Mrs Reynolds shared with one of her son's ninth-grade teachers the diagnosis of Asperger, the teacher replied, 'Don't worry. I've seen far worse. He will grow out of a lot of it.' Mrs Reynolds spent several days reconsidering whether social skills classes for him were really necessary.
>
> When Mr and Mrs Reynolds told each of their parents about the diagnosis, they got similar responses: 'Oh, I don't believe that. He's a boy; boys always develop later.' This only served to make Mr and Mrs Reynolds feel as if they were in a boat all by themselves.

If you are the parent of an adolescent with Asperger, and your spouse does not support the diagnosis, it is my recommendation that you should do everything possible to help him/her feel comfortable about it. Otherwise, time may be wasted in getting help because your spouse may be afraid of 'labeling' the young person. Time may also be wasted because you must devote more effort to convincing your spouse that the diagnosis is accurate, which, in turn, may exhaust your ability to build supports for your son or daughter, as well as your family. Sooner or later the child will begin to feel that one parent may be making more demands on him/her than the other. This is not healthy for the family unit. Learn about Asperger through conferences and books, or seek a second opinion.

Despair

For those parents who push and pursue because they are unsatisfied with the initial responses to their questions, there may come despair once they experience difficulty finding someone who is able to help or support them as they search for answers. Often the experts are not within their locality, take months to see, and the insurance phone calls and referrals become a real nightmare. For these parents, because they already suspect that something is 'different' about their child, the diagnosis may be easier to accept than for the parent who does not think anything is wrong and is just seeing the doctor 'because everyone is bothering me to do so.' The first type of parents will generally bring to the examination appointment a list of relevant questions and will leave with a validation of his/her inner feelings. The second type of parents may leave feeling as if he/she had the wind kicked out of him/her.

After the initial diagnosis, many families will begin to feel another type of despair. They may feel as if their lives are changed forever and that things will never be the same for them or their child. They may look at the 'normal' lives of other children their child's age and barely be able to contain their tears. Fathers may grieve for the loss of a boy that may never want to do the things that boys and their dads like to do together. Moms may grieve because they feel their child may never be able to develop meaningful relationships. There may be jealousy too, watching that parent next door with the perfect child go through a perfect life.

Parents may avoid interactions with other families because they are worried about their child 'sticking out' or having to explain to everyone what he/she has. They may feel it is easier not to participate in family functions. There will be fear of the future. They will begin to search for others who are 'in the same boat.' At times this grief may be overwhelming, and parents may need to seek professional help if they feel the majority of their days are spent in sadness and hopelessness.

Parents who harbor feelings of shame or embarrassment for their child or of their new plight especially need the help of supportive professionals to help them work through their feelings. These parents may actually impede their child's progress if they consciously or unconsciously communicate their feelings.

Anger

A big emotion involved at the time of diagnosis that isn't discussed much is anger. There may be anger directed at God. Why did He do this to me? What did I do to deserve this? There many also be anger directed at the diagnosing doctor, family and friends, as well as other professionals.

> One mother told another mother whose child was just diagnosed that 'God knew what He was doing when He gave you that child because I know you can handle it.' She replied, 'Please don't tell me that. I would hope that a loving God is not up there making decisions that nearly wreck my life because He wants to.'

The way in which the news is delivered will be forever implanted on the parents' minds. Doctors should make every effort to be as gentle and kind as possible and to provide some resources the parents can use when they leave their facility.

> Mr and Mrs Phillips were furious when the doctor gave them their son's diagnosis. They left the clinic with no information explaining what he had or providing them with any help to obtain treatment for him.

There may also be anger directed to family members and friends, especially when they are not sympathetic to their plight:

> When Mr Dale told his mother-in-law about his son's diagnosis, she said, 'Well, we certainly don't have any of *that* in our family.' Mr Dale never forgot that statement and has never really forgiven his mother-in-law for the comment.

Later, there will be anger at professionals who interact with the child. Parents may ask, 'Why do I have to fight for what my child deserves?' 'Why can't they just assign a teacher to my child who knows what she is doing?' 'Why does it take three months just to get an evaluation?' 'Why do I need to make five phone calls and wait three days to get a call back for one simple answer?'

Professionals need to realize that parental anger like the examples described above is normal and justified. Validating parents' anger can be a big step in building bridges with them. It should not be this hard to get needed help for any child. Any effort to ease the confusion and make the effort less frustrating will be appreciated. Providing a phone number of an organization that can help, matching them to another parent of an adolescent who is similar, or offering to attend a training or a support group meeting together can make all the difference in relieving frustration and anxiety for the parents. Many parents can then begin to reach out to locate support and information on their own once they realize they are not alone. This is a healthy step towards moving forward.

Fear

Anger can also be closely mixed with fear. When parents feel that they were not given accurate or detailed information about their child's disability, they may leave the diagnosis with much fear: 'Can my child die from this?' 'Does this mean he will be institutionalized some day?' Later, when they learn more, they may resent the doctor for not providing the information they needed to help them avoid those feelings. Parents who are experiencing much fear or anxiety concerning the diagnosis should arm themselves with as much information as they can. Fear is always easier to conquer when one's questions can be answered honestly and accurately. It may be beneficial to schedule a return visit with the diagnosing doctor a few weeks after the initial appointment so that new concerns and worries can be addressed once the 'dust has settled.'

Parenting and dealing with stress

When any child is diagnosed with a disability, the parents are bound to experience more intense stress levels than parents of children who are typical. One parent often takes on the extra burden of carrying for the child, finding help for him or her, becoming educated about the child's disability and about special education laws. This parent will soon discover that he or she then has to expend additional energy getting the other parent 'up to speed.' Parents should not fall prey to this habit. When one parent takes over completely, he or she will soon discover what 'burn-out' really means. This will only lead to further trouble for the family unit as he or she struggles to understand why the other parent 'doesn't really care' or 'just can't seem to get things done.'

It is recommended that parents share the duties of raising such a child and that they regroup at specified times to share information. While one parent learns about special education law, for instance, another can be researching qualified therapists and dealing with insurances. This way, each parent will feel part of a team. Their child will also sense this mutual support from both parents. The middle school years especially, when the child's social skills deficits become more obvious, can be very stressful for the family unit. Problems with other adolescents, with school staff and even in the family unit may surface and escalate to maximum anxiety levels. Both parents will need to be active partners in their child's education and in learning to provide support during this critical time.

Parents can deal with stress by joining a support group, or starting one of their own. Being with other parents in similar situations, laughing and even crying with someone who 'has been there,' can make all the difference. If parents, for one reason or another, are not the 'support group type,' they can find support in other ways: talking with someone on the phone or via the Internet.

The divorce rate in families of children with disabilities is very high. One reason for this could be the stress that these families must endure. Another could be the lack of time that partners have to spend with each other. When couples are alone, they should find things to talk about and do together that are unique to the two of them and do not have anything to do with the disability. They need to maintain their relationship as a couple and not merely as parents of a child with Asperger Syndrome. Too often, nights alone tend to be devoted to planning the next game plan for this child or commiserating on the latest problem area. This can truly exhaust and put strain on the relationship. Spouses should look for fun things to do together, make 'appointments' to be alone with each other, and keep their relationship a priority so that it will remain the strong foundation their children need. Perhaps even more importantly in this type of marriage than any other, scheduling time to be alone together is critical.

> Mr and Mrs Polino have a son with Asperger and two typical children. Early on, when their son was diagnosed, they felt the strain of all the added responsibilities beginning to take a toll on their marriage. After several sessions with a counselor, it was recommended that once a month, they hire a sitter for two hours. During this time, they were to leave the home and do something together (not a chore). Since they didn't have much money, often they would go and get an ice-cream cone and then go to the park to talk. Although, frequently, they talked about their children, they also would discuss other things. When their son with Asperger turned 13, and after several how-to lessons so that both he and they felt confident, they began to leave him in 'charge' of his siblings for short periods of time when they left. Today, Mrs Polino declares that those $10 dates (as she refers to them) saved their marriage, and their son with Asperger began to feel like a true big brother to his siblings.

Parents should also allow time for themselves and not give up all the activities they once enjoyed to manage their child who has a disability. They should keep their old friendships as they find new ones. Childcare is always less of a burden when parents can feel that there is still time to do the things that feed their souls.

Problems with one's employer can also bite into a parent's sense of well-being. It is vital that employers understand and support parents of children with Asperger Syndrome. There will be many school meetings and therapy appointments that will become required events for most parents of children with this diagnosis. Having an employer that makes things difficult in this respect will certainly add to the family's stress. Both parents need to understand that if each of them work, teamwork is still essential. The parent who has the easier time getting off work should not be the one who has the required burden in this area. Arrangements can frequently be made with employers to work through lunch hours, come in earlier, stay later or work at home or on weekends to accommodate their child's appointments. The important thing is that parents need to approach their employers with ways they are willing to make up lost work when they need to request time off. For some parents, it may be necessary for one spouse to work part time so that there are more hours to schedule these appointments. For others, it will require looking for a job with flexible hours and sacrificing larger salaries or benefits.

Empowerment

Eventually, some parents may come to the stage where they may feel empowered to make change in the Asperger community. They may take on administrative duties in the support groups in their area, arrange for a teacher training session, organize a fundraiser, or develop a community awareness program. This is a sign of adjustment and acceptance of their lives as parents of a child with a disability and a willingness to share what they have learned to make it easier for others. Those who are not at this stage should neither feel compelled to be like the type of parents mentioned above, nor obliged to participate in such activities that those parents may be organizing/promoting. Each individual knows what he or she can do. For some, donating their only free time to support the Asperger cause may be too overwhelming. They do not want to live and breathe every moment of their lives dealing with this diagnosis. For others, donating their spare time will be inspiring – meeting others and helping others is the 'vitamin' that keeps them going. Parents should be comfortable knowing what their role is and not feel forced to adopt a new one.

Accepting the gifts your child has to offer

There are many parents who feel that they need to spend a lot of time trying to 'change' or 'fix' their child. The symptoms of Asperger Syndrome are a facet of who he or she is. It is as much a part of our children as their physical qualities. We need to be careful that we are not overstepping the boundaries of our children's individualism to make them 'fit in' with our world as it is today. Many typical adolescents also have the qualities of other children. What parent of a typical adolescent does not experience mood changes, belligerence and explosive anger episodes at one time or another? Allowing them to be 'typical' is also important. If we don't, this may create feelings of self-loathing and depression as they struggle desperately to meet our expectations. A high percentage of adolescents with Asperger experience depression when they feel they are not accepted by peers and society in general. Home may be the only place where a child feels accepted. We need to acknowledge our children for the unique individuals that they are. Adults with Asperger who consider themselves to be happy and well adjusted frequently come from backgrounds where their individuality was applauded and their abilities were supported. The talents and passions of our children may be unusual, but they are just as important to them as ours are to us. Treasure your youngster's gift of individuality. It is a good idea to teach kids how to learn the 'game,' how to fit in when they need to, and how to find ways for coping that are socially acceptable for the times when they are in public. But, it is essential to always reassure your child that their uniqueness is a gift!

Find places in your community where your adolescent's talents can be utilized and appreciated. If your child is good with numbers, does your local library need someone to catalog their books? Many children with Asperger are computer 'experts.' Could your son or daughter start a home computer business in your neighborhood installing software or repairing hardware? If your child enjoys animals, does your local animal shelter need some help during the summer months? What about a child who is great in music? Are there any opportunities available through local music organizations where he/she can participate? Finding these outlets will provide an added bonus as your young adult will also find people who have similar interests.

Some parents may feel that their child's passions or talents are too unusual, but they need to be creative in their search. Discovering ways to support these passions may also lead to meaningful courses of study as the young person transitions to adulthood:

> Sixteen-year-old Joshua enjoyed looking through hardware catalogs and reading directions supplied with plumbing parts. A local plumber who was a friend of the family offered to take Joshua on a few of his house calls once or twice a week during Josh's summer vacation. That fall, Joshua enrolled in a local Votech program to learn plumbing and was the star of his class!

If you find these outlets for your son or daughter, you will be rewarded with an adolescent who values his or her existence and has a strong self-concept. A youngster who believes in him or herself and his or her talents as a child will be successful in whatever he or she accomplishes as an adult. Providing our children with the gift of self-esteem is always more effective than every dollar we spend on therapy and treatments to 'fix' Asperger Syndrome.

9

Families and Parenting
The Domino Effect

Jacqui Jackson

It is with much love that I have to thank Matthew, Rachel, Sarah, Luke, Anna, Joseph and Ben (though he doesn't quite understand such stuff yet) for their permission to open up their lives and use some of our experiences in the hope that we can educate, enlighten and even amuse others. I am very proud to be part of the lives of seven such special, unique and beautiful people and can only try my best to be a good parent and friend as we continue to learn together.

The domino effect

Gazing at my children all sitting happily together and watching a video, I sigh and wonder wistfully why it can't always be like this. These fleeting moments of family unity and contentment (and peace!) serve to alleviate some of the stress and anxiety which accompanies so many parents as they stealthily negotiate the minefield of teenage hormones coupled with the boisterous activities of the younger children.

In any household, each child, each adolescent, each young adult stands alone, precariously balanced but stoic and upright, making their own mark in their world but not yet fully aware of the effect they have on others. Like dominoes toppling, every word and action has a direct effect on not just one other person but, in my own family, another eight. Something seemingly as simple as asking for a biscuit can set off a chorus of 'can I have one too' and if there are not enough to go around, then World War Three breaks out! I am then expected to skilfully negotiate in a way that appeases everyone and prevents those all too precarious dominoes from crashing around me – a feat seldom managed! Often before I can intervene, someone has taken the last biscuit, sat in someone else's seat or changed the channel on the television and I am bombarded with a mass of 'Mum can you tell him' and 'it's not fair' as doors slam, voices raise and tempers fly.' I then stealthily move from room to room, negotiating, cajoling, explaining and comforting each one separately with the optimistic view that maybe I can educate each of them on how best to prevent such situations from being a regular occurrence.

Several times a day, those of us with more than one child perform an amazing balancing act in a bid to stabilize those wobbling dominoes and prevent each one from falling and knocking over the next. All too often however, there is nothing that can be done to prevent the inevitable and our job is to pick up the pieces, set them up and await the next fall.

One particular day illustrates the domino effect in its full glory. Ben has autism and many accompanying sensory problems so, at five years old, he had still never been to the cinema. Consequently for the last five years we had never gone to the cinemas as a family. However, as the children moaned about how bored they were, I experienced a dangerous mix of bravery and motherliness – some may say stupidity! I decided to venture out and take all seven of them to the cinema.

Making sure I wore one of my eldest son Matthew's coats which was large enough for Ben to crawl under, I began carefully covering every eventuality. An hour later, armed with a change of clothing, spare nappies, special yellow cup and dummy, blue beaded box, miniature house ornament and packets of gluten and casein free, colouring and gelatine free sweets, I was almost ready. All that was left was to prepare Ben.

I tugged at my ear to tell him to listen and with a mixture of signs, pictures and words I was pretty sure that he knew that we were going out in the car to see a very big television in a big dark room. Pocketing Ben's comforting goggles ready for entry to the cinema and donning the compulsory green earmuffs in preparation for the noise, he was at last ready to go. I took a deep breath and told myself that I had a group of teenagers to help with the younger two so how difficult could this really be? Insanity must have crept in that day!

On reaching the cinema, the first problem was that there was a queue. Knowing that there was no chance of the boys tolerating or even understanding the notion of queuing I barged to the front, carrying a squirming Ben and explained that we needed to get in and fast. Meanwhile the girls had skulked off in embarrassment. We were quickly issued with our tickets in a bid to move us on as soon as possible and Matthew battled uncomfortably with a cartwheeling Joe (who has AD/HD) whilst Rachel tried to tactfully extract Luke (who has Asperger Syndrome) from the side of an uneasy member of staff as he insisted on discussing the workings of the infrared scanner. The teenagers were now sulking and moaning and the younger boys were becoming more agitated – those dominoes were wobbling precariously!

Buying popcorn and sweets was the next step and the start of those dominoes crashing down. First I had to ask the staff if I could read the ingredients of the mints and popcorn, the only thing the boys, on the gluten and casein free diet, had any chance of being allowed. The girls cringed in embarrassment as Luke waxed lyrical about the benefits of a gluten and casein free diet and the hazards of gelatine and the first domino toppled, resulting in round shouldered and sulky girls sidling off to choose their own sweets. They were closely followed by a bouncing Joe who immediately saw their bag full of goodies and the next domino was sent crashing down as he shrieked 'That's no way fair' on seeing the chocolates and sweets that the girls dangled tantalizingly in front of him. Joe's bottom lip stuck out, his face turned red with anger and with one swift move his whole carton of popcorn was tipped all over the floor. Ben immediately wriggled from my arms, dropped to the floor and started crawling around on all fours eating popcorn. Screaming at Mat to pick up Ben, I instantly sent the next domino toppling. He shouted back that he was trying but there was no chance and that he didn't want to be there anyway and I only shout at him so he was going home. Off he walked!

Meanwhile Joe had put the empty popcorn carton on his head and was jumping up and down making monkey noises whilst Anna laughed loudly at him and Rachel and Sarah scuttled off in embarrassment. Bellowing at Anna for laughing and encouraging Joe sent the next domino toppling and she joined her two sisters in a bid to move as far away from us as possible.

Paying for another lot of popcorn and all of the sweets as quickly as possible and battling with a hysterical screaming Ben who wanted to carry on eating from the floor, we made our way into the cinema – the final straw and that which sent the last domino crashing to the ground! As soon as we walked in, despite the goggles and earmuffs, Ben became hysterical. It was too loud, too dark and he was terrified. There was no chance at all of him entering that room. To add insult to injury, I suddenly realized that the contents of his nappy had leaked and were smeared all down the front of my clothes. Joe was bouncing around, Luke was talking at great length about the pros and cons of surround sound and the girls looked ready to kill.

All dominoes had now toppled and the whole thing was an unworkable situation. I couldn't leave them in there on their own and I couldn't take Ben in. There was only one solution – to go home!

I am sure most parents reading this can substitute names and places and recall their own crescendo of toppling dominoes in agonizing and even amusing lucidity. In any family no incident stands in isolation and such incidents illustrate succinctly just how pervasive an autistic spectrum disorder really is.

Autism and adolescence

The influence of autism is something which we all take for granted and which impacts every member of the family. The boys have dyspraxia, dyslexia, Asperger Syndrome, AD/HD and autism between them. The girls, at their tender ages, don't fully realize the extent to which their outlooks have been broadened, their understanding deepened, by living each day in a way which takes into account their brothers' problems. Each one of the boys and their unique way of looking upon the world, enriches, amuses and often aggravates the rest of the family.

As the medicine cabinet emits a deafening buzz on opening, Ben runs around stark naked, Luke drones on and on about computers and Joe leaps around making monkey noises, the girls and Matthew don't bat an eyelid. Matthew (who is dyspraxic and dyslexic) at the age of 18, still insists on watching the same cartoon at the same time every night and asking how to spell the most simple of words. Yet the rest of the family merely accept him and each other for who and what they are – truly something to be treasured.

At 15 years old, Sarah, very different to Anna and Rachel, lacks confidence and experiences many of the same difficulties as Luke. Rachel tries in her own way to help Sarah and Luke with their difficulties in social interaction and communication and Anna tries hard to help with the practicalities of looking after Joe and Ben. Matthew struggles with the idea that he is the man of the house and therefore assumes responsibilities that he doesn't actually have. In fact, though several times a day they all clash dreadfully and I sit amidst the explosive combination of autistic and non-autistic teenagers and youngsters, I can fully appreciate how hard it must be for each and every one of them and applaud them for their efforts. Some days I sit in amazement and want to clap aloud as I watch the way Sarah automatically explains an idiom to Luke and Joe or Mat carries a fearful Ben around the garden and encourages him to negotiate his fears.

In many families, the words autism or Asperger Syndrome are to be ignored; a subject to be changed quickly. How often do we hear 'But they all do that' or 'Well he looks fine to me'? So many parents fight to get an accurate diagnosis in order for their child to receive the help that every child deserves. As parents, we are told time and time again that 'labels' are a bad thing and can create a stigma and a means of marginalization. What does that tell us about the society in which we live? If to have a 'label' which ultimately merely describes a set of characteristics, a unique way of thinking and viewing the world, brings discrimination, surely it is society as a whole that should be changed? Attitudes and opinions which uphold the ideals of the majority as the 'norm' themselves cause deprivation as they banish from our world the richness and fullness only created by a true acceptance of diversity.

Excuse me for one moment whilst I climb off my soapbox – indeed you may wonder what that has got to do with adolescence, families, parenting, Asperger Syndrome, or indeed dominoes. Simple. Parenting is about facilitating and encouraging a child to maximize their full potential, about teaching values and belief systems and encouraging a child to develop their own. It's about nurturing and educating and loving. That love is the driving force that keeps all of us parents fighting for acceptance and understanding for our children. It is also the driving force behind our desire to teach all members of the family values that even many professionals still do not seem to hold or understand.

As Ben giggles and crawls around licking everything in sight or strips his clothes off or smears the contents of his nappy everywhere, whilst Joe leaps around screeching like a monkey and destroying everything in sight, visitors often cast pitying glances and tell me how hard it must be for me. Those are the ones without teenagers! The physical exhaustion of being up all night, following them around, watching their every move and cleaning up after them is a breeze in comparison to living with teenagers and adolescents.

Adolescence. The very word is enough to bring most parents out into a cold sweat. Images of sulky teenagers, raging hormones, slamming doors, messy rooms and lengthy phone bills race around a parent's mind whilst memories of their own adolescent years flood back with uneasy clarity. As a parent of seven children, five of them at various stages of their adolescent and teenage years, I can tell you with great vigour that those images are right – and then some!

The hormonal changes, the worries about their developing bodies coupled with the need to assert their independence and individuality, make adolescence a difficult time for the whole of the family – when one suffers then boy do we all suffer! The presence of just one adolescent in the family is a sure-fire way of setting those dominoes crashing to the ground.

As a parent it is necessary to try hard to see past this apparent self-centredness and recognise that, as obnoxious as they may seem and as difficult as they are to live with, each adolescent is going through a difficult time as they learn to 'find themselves' in the world. Believe me, I know how hard this is to do, especially when you have been up all night with a small child and dealing with the endless snipes and mood swings of the adolescent seems such a thankless and exhausting task.

Living with Luke

'Luke, you are such a freak.' If I had been paid even the most miniscule amount for every time I have heard that then I would be one very rich woman!

Luke assures me that it doesn't bother him. If that is the case then it shouldn't bother me. It does. Luke doesn't recognize the scorn on his sisters' faces; he misses the raised eyebrows, the smirks and the knowing glances. Luke isn't good at reading facial expressions. Maybe ignorance really is bliss.

As brilliant as he is, as intelligent as he is, as funny as he is, sometimes Luke really just does not 'get it'. At this time in his life he is working so hard to understand the cacophony of hormones, emotions and bodily changes whilst also trying to negotiate and even bypass the many difficulties that Asperger Syndrome throws his way. No easy task and in our household, one that largely goes unnoticed by most.

Having someone with Asperger Syndrome as a member of a large family can cause immense friction. When Luke is following one of his sisters or Matthew around talking incessantly about computers or sitting a fraction of an inch away from them, they understandably turn and snap. Indeed they too are experiencing their own hormonal surges and their own particular brand of difficulties. All too often however, it seems to the others as if I am 'on Luke's side' when I try to explain that he genuinely doesn't understand that it is inappropriate to sit in between Rachel and her boyfriend or to comment to a new boyfriend that he is the third one that week!

Very recently, Rachel had been waiting for weeks for an important phone call from her work experience placement. When it finally came, Luke was the one to answer the phone. They asked 'Hello is Rachel there please?' Luke merely glanced quickly around the room, saw that no she wasn't there (she was in her bedroom!) and therefore answered, 'No, sorry' and put the phone down. The number was withheld and Rachel was understandably very angry. There followed a two-hour argument with me mediating in a way that would surely gain me automatic entry to the diplomatic corps! Though such incidents are commonplace when living with someone with Asperger Syndrome, our task as parents is to explain to our AS child where they went wrong (if indeed they did) in such situations, whilst also explaining to the others why our AS child does such things.

I have to say that a household of mainly adolescents and teenagers makes this very difficult as they are naturally self-absorbed, but even so I am immensely proud of the way all my children attempt to understand such things. Although 'Luke, you are such a freak' is heard regularly in our household, woe betide anyone else that calls him names. As they all grow older and it becomes obvious that Luke is always going to be 'different', his often infuriating ways are accepted and even smiled at far more than in recent years. On the other hand Luke and even Joe are struggling to understand why one week their sisters are in reasonable moods and at other times they turn and snarl at them for merely breathing! Part of living in a 'mixed' household means that all members of the family get to learn things that they otherwise may not discover till a much later age. In our family, issues such as puberty, masturbation, periods, sex and relationships are topics that are openly discussed by all members of the family (apart from Ben who is not at that level of understanding).

At 13 years old, Luke has begun to take an interest in girls. At 12 years old Anna has started to take an interest in boys. At 15 years old Sarah has had an interest in boys for quite a while. At 16 years old Rachel's sole topic of thought and conversation is boys. At 18 years old, the turn of his head and the light in his eyes as a pretty girl passes by shows us all that Matthew has had more than a passing interest in girls for quite some time! At the other end of the scale, Joseph is 9 years old and thinks that girls are for kicking and kissing is gross! Ben of course does his own thing.

For Luke, this is one area where I am sure, if he were honest enough, he is actually very glad to have an older brother and sisters. Rachel tries hard to advise Luke about talking to girls and ways in which to negotiate his AS so that he doesn't scare them off. She reminds him to clean his teeth and wash his hair and tells him when his clothes look odd. In other ways though, the presence of someone so eminently sociable serves to remind Luke and particularly Sarah of their own difficulties and gives rise to many a lengthy and heartfelt discussion about accepting oneself and others. I of course am the one to pick up the pieces when things go wrong for any one of them (and most of their friends too!) and I have to admit that this is the most exhausting aspect of parenting a 'mixed' household.

I have to say that anything I write about living with Luke and how his AS affects him and the rest of the family cannot be as clearly and succinctly put as when he does it himself, so I am loath to write much more. Luke has two books published so far, the latest being *Freaks, Geeks and Asperger Syndrome – A User Guide to Adolescence*. Luke covers topics such as bullying, morality, problems with school, language and many others, but the chapter he says he will keep referring to is 'The Dating Game'. His sisters played a large part in the advice given to AS adolescents and Luke himself says that, although as yet he has no experience, 'in true AS fashion he will persevere'!

Sibling rivalry

The many roles of parenthood really do make it the most diverse, multi-faceted job in the universe and all must agree that the rewards are amazing. Whilst most of us are used to and even adept at the roles of cook, cleaner, chauffeur, counsellor, nurse, teacher and many, many more – one role I for one would willingly give up instantly is that of referee!

From how many meatballs are on their plates to who is getting more attention from me than another, my children naturally compete over everything. 'It's not fair' is an all too familiar cry and I am sure I am not alone in this one. 'How come she can do that and I never could?' 'How come they are going out and we are not?' 'How come they go to bed later than me?' The stream of accusations seems endless.

Although 'It's not fair' would definitely win the award for the most commonly used phrase in our household (apart from 'tidy up'), a keen competitor and running an exceptionally close second is the all too familiar 'It wasn't me'. In my family it seems that not only have I got seven children, but I also have an invisible presence that takes the last biscuit, spills the orange juice, uses my make-up or walks mud all over the floor! Unfortunately, short of having CCTV in every room and playing back a video every night (and believe me I have considered it!), I am afraid there seems to be no solution to this one other than ramming home the importance of honesty and respect of others' property. In a large household there is always someone else to blame for any breakage, spillage or disappearance and with one younger brother who invariably breaks and spills things and another who cannot say whether he has or not, Joe and Ben get the blame for many things – though the girls do drawn the line at blaming them for using my mascara!

Although I do my best not to intervene unless I am sure of the facts and try hard to be fair, I am sure I make many mistakes and one or other of the children is wrongly accused or all are made to clean up a spillage because no one will own up to it. This naturally causes friction between them all and increases the amount of rivalry that is inevitable.

Sibling rivalry is an age-old issue and one that isn't exclusively a childhood problem. Many adults are still competing and falling out with their siblings, often till the ends of their lives. No one ever chose to be born into their family so it is logical that there is likely to be a certain amount of rivalry even within the most solid of relationships. Different sexes, ages, abilities and temperaments and the fact that they have to share their parents with each other are a certain recipe for conflict. When one or more children have special needs then even more pressure is added to family members. The sense of responsibility and often resentment of the older or more able child is not something to be ignored.

I cannot profess to have all the solutions to such rivalry and, until my children are all in adulthood and can look back and say that I did a good job, I have no definitive answers. I do have to say that although bickering and sulking go on between each of my children at some point every day, it is only of a very petty nature and usually driven by tiredness and hormones. Sibling rivalry is not a serious issue in our household but more of a tiresome inconvenience.

I am sure that there are many, many more ways to deal with sibling rivalry and each family has its own unique dynamics that affect the way each problem should be solved. However here are some tips that may just help to ease the endless squabbling.

1.   Although in my family this has never been an issue, a child's sex defines their activities to some extent. A boy may resent the fact that his sisters spend time with their mother putting on make-up and talking about 'girls things'. Likewise a girl could easily feel the same resentment when a boy seems to spend more time with their father. Try to accept this as natural and make an effort to redress the balance whilst explaining that such things are inevitable.

2.   Stick to your guns in the face of the 'it's not fairs'. As a parent we know that a younger child needs to go to bed earlier than an older one and it is our job to enforce such rules. Consistency is the key to success and acceptance.

3.   When one child has special needs it can often seem as if they merely get preferential treatment, so try to explain their difficulties in a way that all can understand. Acknowledge that you understand that some things really do not seem fair.

4.   Don't ever try to treat all children equally. Obviously that is not to say give one special attention for no reason, but each child deserves to be treated as an individual and some days

one child needs a hug or a treat or is ill and needs special care and the others have to accept that that too is 'fair'. The familiar 'it's not fair' will naturally bounce off every wall but to treat each one the same every time devalues them as individuals.

5.   Don't automatically take sides and punish the child who is seemingly at fault. There is often a lot more to any issue than one child lashing out at another. Investigate the reasons behind such problems and try to apply your skills as a mediator.

6.   Don't make comparisons between each child or compare your child with Asperger Syndrome or autism to a non-autistic child. Not only is each child unique, but they also feel unique and will very soon resent such comparisons.

7.   Teach your children that it is natural and acceptable to feel angry and resentful at times, but it is how they deal with and control it that is important. If they are angry with their siblings then that is perfectly normal and needn't be suppressed. Don't dismiss or suppress your children's resentment or angry feelings. Talk things through.

8.   As a parent it is our job to recognize how much of these feelings our children can deal with and be prepared and ready to intervene quickly and decisively before a child does something which they will later regret. I am often on the lookout for the warning signs of a major meltdown, particularly in the boys as they have more difficulty controlling themselves. Intervention before this happens means that they do not have to deal with guilt and embarrassment about their own actions.

9.   When possible let brothers and sisters settle their own differences, but keep a careful eye on the situation and be prepared to step in and mediate. Many siblings are unequal in terms of ability, age and strength and so it is often an unfair 'fight'.

10.   It is preferable to take action before the incidents of rivalry progress to physical or even verbal violence. Separate them

all and allow a 'cooling off' period. Then try to provide suggestions as to how they can handle the situation and what has caused the aggravation.

11. Don't ignore appropriate behaviour. All too often we only pay attention to the way siblings deal with each other when a problem arises. This is particularly important when one child has special needs. Acknowledgement of the effort that the siblings are making to accept and understand their brother's or sister's problems, goes a long way to increasing their confidence and self-worth.

12. Teach the child who is prone to teasing, ways to deal with it. When Luke has hissed at him 'You Asperger' or 'You freak' he now replies 'Why thank you' and it really does wash over him.

13. Alternatively, teach the child who is being teased to say firmly that enough is enough and to ask their parent or teacher for help.

14. To avoid the familiar fights over who sits in the front of the car, who does the washing up, who chooses the television programme, etc. try to devise a system of turn taking that is accepted by all as fair. When one child has special needs and is unlikely to accept or understand such things, then all family members need to understand that and be given appropriate concessions if the turn taking seems unfair.

15. Offer a treat or reward for an acceptable length of time without any arguing or fighting, though as the children get older ensure that they realize that this should be the norm and not done to earn rewards.

16. Try as hard as possible to give your children their own place – somewhere they can call their own and be alone. Respect their need for privacy. Find ways to prevent siblings from entering their rooms, particularly, as in my household, those siblings who are likely to be destructive.

Mealtimes in a 'mixed' household

Mealtimes and indeed anything relating to food seem to be one area that causes even the most placid of children to sharpen their claws and fight. Maybe in a large family it really is seen as survival of the fittest! From who eats the last piece of cake to how many chips they all have on a plate, when those dominos stand alone, precariously balanced, mealtimes are a sure-fire way of making them topple.

Autism really is pervasive. It weaves and wraps its tendrils around every area of life and the issue of food is one where it stamps all over with hobnail boots!

Most of us with children on the autistic spectrum are fully aware of how potentially explosive any mealtime can be. Books have been written on the many, many difficulties so many of our AS and autistic children have with food. If a parent is lucky enough to have a child on the spectrum who does not self-restrict their food to any serious degree, then we are still fully aware of the implications of using the wrong colour bowl, sitting the child in the wrong chair, putting all the food on the plate together or being wicked enough to allow one piece of food to touch another!

The presentation of the food, the smell, the texture and the temperature all depict whether or not a child is willing even to try any of the meals that have been so lovingly prepared. Most of us know the frustration of having carefully prepared and presented a meal, trying hard to fulfil all of the 'rules' imposed on us by our children, only to have the food sniffed (if we are lucky!) and pushed away. The effect of all this on the rest of the family cannot be underestimated.

Now that Ben is beginning to talk, even something so simple as asking one of the older ones to get his breakfast causes all hell to break loose. The first indication that chaos is likely to overtake the house and the domino effect is going to be witnessed in full swing is the screech of 'I want *my* bowl'. As Ben has changed and become more sociable, more verbal and infinitely more able, the others are having difficulty adjusting to the idea that he is still autistic and needs his routines – indeed he insists on his routines. Breakfast time is fraught with grumpy teenagers rushing to get their own breakfasts or stalling for time in the hope that they can stay off school. I am usually in the throes of sorting out last-minute forms, reading books and packed lunches for Joe and Luke and just scream to one of the bigger ones to sort Ben out. Will I ever learn? There follows the predictable 'not *that* bowl' and a crash as the cereal gets hurled across the room. If, on a good day, they manage to give him the right bowl, then invariably the wrong spoon is given and a familiar 'he *needs* the yellow one' rings out just before the inevitable crash.

Mealtimes are particularly difficult in our household because this is one area where I really do have to manage a 'mixed' household. All of us with children on the autistic spectrum, indeed those of us with children, will do anything and fight tooth and nail to enable our children to be happy, fulfilled and to maximize their full potential. There are many 'therapies' which purport to bring about all sorts of miraculous changes for people on the autistic spectrum and the controversy over this is ongoing. My personal opinion is that if something works for you, your child and your family as a whole then keep tight hold of it and run with it for all you are worth.

One such intervention in our household that really has resulted in miraculous, positive changes is a gluten and casein free (GF/CF) diet. My family has a history of problems with the immune system and multiple food allergies and intolerances. There is eczema, asthma, hay fever, diabetes and coeliac disease in our immediate family and in mine and many other families, biological intervention plays an important part in my children's physical and mental well-being.

I am not going to harp on about the GF/CF diet and the part excito toxins, food additives and phenols play in our lives and the changes that have occurred. All I will say is that the benefits have been so great for Luke that he has written a book (*A User Guide to the GF/CF Diet for Autism, Asperger Syndrome and AD/HD*) detailing how much it has changed life for him and his brothers and how to embark on this particular path.

However (isn't there always a however?), mealtimes, birthdays and indeed anything where food is involved is one area that sends those dominoes toppling fast and furious. The boys' diet has a knock-on effect on every aspect of not only their own lives, but their brother and sisters' too.

The kitchen is split into two halves, rather like a kosher kitchen. One side is completely GF/CF and egg free with its own breadbin, toaster and utensils, whilst the other side has regular food. This is the only practical solution to managing the different diets but it is not without its drawbacks. Often the girls or Matthew will grab a slice of their bread, slap it down on the boys' work surface then clear off. This not only results in contamination for the boys but also the need for me to begin the same old speech whereby I explain how unfair they are being and how they can see the effects on the boys. Consequently the non-gluten free children sulk and mumble about how spoilt the boys are, I get annoyed and tell them how selfish they are and any chance of harmony evaporates with the morning dew! Furthermore the non-gluten free members of the family, often resent the fact that the evening meal is always GF/CF. When they have had a bad day at school, when they are premenstrual or are merely in a typical teenager mode, the fact that they are being given a tasty, healthy, nutritious meal is inconsequential and, spoiling for a fight, the fact that they are being given 'the boys' food' is cause enough to sulk, moan and argue. I often tell them that they are eating wheat pasta when in reality it is gluten free and not one of them realizes (now I have blown my cover!).

When their hormones are giving us all a break and I have my pleasant reasonable children to live with me for a short time, then they fully understand the reasoning behind the diet, see the amazingly miraculous changes in the boys and are fully supportive. Indeed they are the first ones to moan if Joe turns back into the pre-diet, destructive little animal or they are required to change an endless stream of Ben's dirty nappies. I firmly believe that if they didn't have their brothers' behaviours and diet to moan about then their lives would be sadly lacking!

For any of you living in the same situation of having to cater to a 'mixed household' at mealtimes, I am afraid that I have found no perfect solutions to this problem but will gladly share those that help in my household:

1. As wearing as it seems, the most important thing to do is to keep talking. Other children have their own lives, own level of understanding and are not really interested in the complexities of the opium excess theory. Keep it simple and repeat it often.

2. Make an effort to give individual attention in some other way if it becomes evident that a sibling is resenting the special effort their brother's or sister's needs at mealtimes. Try to do this straight after the mealtime if at all possible.

3.   Another way I solve such feelings of jealousy is to involve the girls in the GF/CF baking. They enjoy the sense of responsibility and often produce some delicious concoctions. If a sibling is younger and you cannot leave them in the kitchen alone, then bake with them. This gives time and attention too.

4.   Make sure that if an infringement does occur then all the non-gluten people witness the reaction and explain to them very clearly why their brother or sister is behaving that way. Joe's swollen lips and hours and hours of screeching and barking as he leaps wildly around gives them enough of a reminder to be careful with their food and realize the necessity of the diet – at least for a few days!

5.   I have a video of Ben as he was before I put him on a gluten and casein free diet. When the girls and Matthew are being persistently sloppy and careless with their food, I sit them down and make them watch how he used to be and how he could be again if his diet was changed back.

6.   If your gluten free child is not about or you are out with only your non-gluten free child then indulge them in all the things that they do not have at home. If I have some time with only Matthew and the girls I buy them all fresh cream cakes and sausage rolls and they revel in the fact that they can eat them freely without having to hide them or watch for crumbs.

Without the added difficulties of cooking for different diets and different tastes in the same household, adolescent and teenage years often bring an additional worry – the worry of eating disorders. In an age where physical beauty is depicted as thinness and the emphasis in magazines and media is on exercise and dieting, I for one watch all of my children, particularly my girls, very carefully at mealtimes and though they may not realize it (they do now!) I carefully look out for any warning signs. I make sure to talk clearly and honestly about the dangers of taking diet, exercise or indeed anything else to excess.

More and more research is producing both qualitative and quantative evidence to indicate that there is a link between eating disorders and autism and, although the research is by no means conclusive, I for one am not taking any chances!

Self-preservation

Initially it can seem as if adolescents and teenagers have a self-destruct button and risk taking is noted to be a common part of the adolescent years. However, although many teenagers may experiment with fast cars, sex, alcohol, cigarettes and maybe even drugs, this does not necessarily apply to all. Nevertheless the worry of the 'What ifs?' is enough to take years off the life of any parent. I for one have spent many a night biting my nails and watching the clock, awaiting their return!

Parenting a teen with special needs is equally as stressful and the constant fight for services and understanding is both time consuming and exhausting. In a 'mixed' household where there are different ages and abilities, those stresses and worries are multiplied several times over and the weight of it all can be tremendous.

Although I fully accept and adore my children's differences, when I come face to face with a typically developed child or watch a 'normal' family it is sometimes very difficult not to compare and feel an immense sense of sadness. In fact, I often feel like a spy or alien invader placed here merely to observe and compare. I find myself furtively sneaking around watching typically developed children of the same age as my boys. This of course is closely followed by guilt at the fact that I am aspiring to have my boys any other way, and indeed that is not the case.

When I find myself staring as I discover that a child is the same age as Ben, Luke or Joe, I have to admit that I sometimes choke back tears. I am sure I am not alone in this and my advice to any parent in the same situation is to make sure you are absolutely sure who you are crying for. We are crying for lost dreams and hopes and aspirations but it is imperative to remember that it is *our* aspirations for our children that will not be realized, *our* expectations that we have to change and *our* hopes that have been shattered. Accept this grieving as natural and inevitable and, indeed, indulge in it occasionally (away from the children), but be sure to see it for what it is – our problem not our children's. Whilst we understandably feel pain as we watch our children being rejected or bullied by others or struggling to understand such a confusing world, I firmly believe that our job as a parent is to strive to make such things easier for them. This is not the time for pity and I personally take a deep breath, gulp back the tears and go in fighting!

Although we are travelling an amazing and exciting road with our children, it is not where we expected to be and I firmly believe that it is natural to ponder about and even grieve for where we could have been. The secret to dealing with such powerful emotions is to allow them to run their course without stifling them, then be sure to create a balance. If you are feeling negative then do a stock take of all the positives – believe me you will be amazed at how many you find.

If your children are desperately missing a service or therapy, then set out to fight for their rights. If you have tried unsuccessfully to 'educate' family or friends about the differences of your children, then merely release them to think what they like and accept that some people are unwilling or unable to learn. The key to self-preservation is your own acceptance, and that includes the acceptance of ignorance and intolerance in others. Some people we just cannot change. Some things we cannot change. The secret is to recognize this and move on.

This strain can take its toll not only on the individual parent but also on their relationships. Although I know that I may not seem an ideal candidate to advise on relationships, as a single parent with experience of counselling and, though I say it myself, a particularly good listening ear, I have spent many hours in the presence of couples whose relationships are suffering due to the stresses of parenting.

I have therefore included preservation tips for couples as well as single parents. Those that know me will be snorting with laughter as they read these for this is most definitely a case of do as I say, not as I do! I am working hard on applying some of these too (and I have to say thanks to the Chatters Gang for pushing me to do so!).

1.   If you have a husband, wife or partner, then find time to spend with each other. A relationship needs working at and keeping alive. (Easy for me to say as a single parent I know!) I know all too well how the stresses of life with any child, particularly those with special needs, can put a strain on a relationship.

2.   Remember to laugh together. In fact this applies to every parent and carer, regardless of whether or not they have a partner. For those of you with a partner, this is something

that can be shared. The ability to see the funny side of life is something to be cherished and I am certain that those of us with special needs children were also given an enlarged sense of humour. Make sure you use it.

3.   Learn to relax – maybe try meditation or yoga. I find this nigh on impossible but am endeavouring to snatch a few minutes here and there.

4.   Know your own limitations. There is no shame is admitting that things are getting too much. If you are stretched too far then the whole family suffers.

5.   Ensure that you keep tight hold of (or try to find) your own identity. All of us need to have a life beyond our children, even if it's just simply acknowledging our own desires and aspirations.

6.   Don't look too far ahead. I am often reminded by a very dear friend (thanks Jude!) that we need to take 'bite-sized chunks'. Valuable and important advice for any parent of a child with special needs.

7.   Plan a treat for yourself and make it your goal to achieve it, no matter how large or small it is. Personally my treats are to plan to sit down and have a cup of tea without interruption (rarely achieved I must say!) or to take a bath alone.

8.   If you have a partner, then mutually arrange a time where one takes over all responsibility so that the other can have their 'treat' and vice versa.

9.   If you are unfortunate enough to live with a partner who is unwilling to shoulder responsibility for childcare and other aspects of daily life, then my only advice is to make sure that you still allocate yourself treat times and stick to them. Try hard not to waste valuable time and energy on resentment but try to plan a constructive way forward. Resentment eats away at the soul.

10.   Count your blessings. Take frequent stock of the good things in your life and make a concerted effort to focus on all the positive aspects of your own and your family's life.

11.   On a contradictory note – allow yourself to cry. If you feel the need to lock yourself away and sob, whether from tiredness, at the injustice of it all or merely because you feel like it – then go for it!

The complex mix of age, ability, personality and gender all serve to provide a source of difficulty, enlightenment, amusement and joy as we strive together to learn and grow in realization of the way each member of the household impacts on the other. Indeed, as isolating as autism can seem, the reality is that 'no man is an island' and each and every one of us must mix with other people who are often very different to ourselves. Whilst the domino effect comes into play far more than I care to mention, as a parent my job is to maximize each and every child's full potential and enable them eventually to stand strong and tall when they feel pressured and begin to topple.

Parenting does not come easily or is carefree for most, but the process through which we come to understand and accomplish the goals of parenting is something to be enjoyed and cherished, especially when one is parenting a mixed family!

References

Jackson, L. (2001) *A User Guide to the GF/CF Diet/or Autism, Asperger Syndrome and AD/HD*. London: Jessica Kingsley Publishers.

Jackson, L. (2002) *Freaks, Geeks and Asperger Syndrome – A User Guide to Adolescence*. London: Jessica Kingsley Publishers.

10

Starting from Scratch
Being Innovative in Finding Interventions for your Adolescent with Asperger Syndrome

DeAnn Foley

One of the most frustrating and mind-boggling aspects of being a parent of a child with a disability is finding the appropriate interventions and therapies for your child. With the advent of the Internet, parents can locate information on various types of interventions and therapies. However, when your child is diagnosed with Asperger Syndrome (AS), one also has to attempt to incorporate a social component to the interventions and therapies as much as possible. Many a parent has lost sleep trying to determine what are the appropriate interventions and therapies for their child with AS and who is the 'right' therapist to provide the interventions. I, as any parent, felt triumphant when I found what I thought was the right combination of appropriate interventions, therapy and great therapists. After several years, even though I kept a watchful eye on my son Ryan's therapies, I was almost complacent. Then something happened – we moved.

After two grueling days of packing and getting our belongings into the moving van, it was finally time to travel to our new home. As we drove past the familiar and comforting sight of cotton fields and oil derricks, I felt the combination of sorrow and excitement that most everyone feels when starting over. After eight years in West Texas, we felt it was time to move back home where both sides of our families lived. About the time we hit what is called 'The Big Country,' the reality of our decision to move and its impact on Ryan's interventions and therapies hit full force. Panic and dread ensued. We were moving from a relatively rural area in West Texas to the Dallas/Fort Worth Metroplex. I began listing the pros and cons of moving. We were leaving behind many friends who were like family to us, but we would be living close to our true families. Ryan would have more opportunities to lead an independent adult life in a larger city, plus he would have more career choices than in a small West Texas community. Additionally, we were leaving behind good therapists in West Texas but the Dallas/Fort Worth area would have an abundance of therapists. Since Ryan was now a teenager, I had to be aware that what I chose had to be age appropriate and preferably with other teens. I knew once our belongings were safely off the van and in our new home, I would have to start from scratch to rebuild Ryan's interventions, therapies and – most importantly – friendships. This meant I needed to come up with new ideas plus re-evaluate the effectiveness of what we had been doing to determine if it would still be beneficial for Ryan.

This move underscored what I have discovered from my search for interventions and therapies over the years. As a parent, I must be creative. Therapy is defined as a treatment or a curative and involves a certified therapist. Then there is what I call interventions. I learned over the years to think of interventions as more a means to help Ryan improve his skills in areas that were difficult for him. Interventions don't necessarily require a therapist but rather can build on therapies. Over the years, whenever possible I have attempted to incorporate social skills and motor coordination with Ryan's interventions. Some of the therapies I found were mainstream; some interventions were not traditional in the sense that neither a doctor nor a therapist recommended them.

I feel the need to caution that when a parent is first beginning to try and locate these therapies and interventions, it is important to rely on the knowledge and expertise of professionals and therapists whom the parent trusts. A good therapist will help parents acquire knowledge and skills to work with their own child. Talking with other parents is another good and reliable method of finding interventions, professionals and skills. After a period of time, most parents feel comfortable in expanding on their knowledge and exploring other types of interventions for their child.

A few of the standard therapies for children diagnosed with AS are speech therapy, occupational therapy, and physical therapy. Most of these therapies can be addressed through the public school system. There are many good therapists working in the school systems. However, it is paramount that parents keep in mind that under Federal Law in the United States public schools are only required to provide what is educationally necessary for the child. This means that some of the therapies which parents would like for their children might not be made available through the school system. An option available to families is to augment the therapies being provided in schools through the private sector. If the family does decide to use a therapist in the community, it is extremely important that the school therapist and the community therapist communicate with one another. This can be accomplished through periodic emails, notes and/or phone calls. I suggest that the parents check regularly with both therapists to make sure that the communication is constant and consistent between the two professionals.

The need for any type of therapy in the public school system is determined through an evaluation by the therapist who then recommends to the individual education plan (IEP) team the goals, objectives, methods of therapy, and duration. In my experience, the two most important therapies for a child with AS are speech therapy and occupational therapy. For children with AS, parents need to request that any speech evaluation includes an evaluation of the child's language skills. Areas of language that need to be evaluated are both verbal and non-verbal language skill levels. The therapist needs to observe the child in a wide range of school and community environments. These observations need to take place in the classroom, the lunchroom, the library, hall passing time, playground, physical education classes – in short, any class that might be extra challenging to the AS student's sensory system and emotional state. It is also important that the speech therapist acts as a consultant and is involved with the child's classroom teachers and parents to teach the adults in the child's life how to provide language interventions when teachable moments appear.

Parents also need to request that any occupational therapy evaluation includes sensory integration by an occupational therapist trained in sensory integration. (See Chapter 5 for a detailed review of sensory integration.)

Many children diagnosed with AS have behaviour problems because they have a tendency to go into sensory overload. Noises, smells, and other students standing too close are just a few examples of incidences that will set a child with AS into tantrums, physical aggression or complete withdrawal. An occupational therapist with a background in sensory integration can help teachers and parents build environments to limit sensory overload. The occupational therapist can also help parents and teachers learn to look for antecedents (what happens before the behaviour) to prevent the sensory overload. Additionally, the occupational therapist will help the child to learn to modulate his reaction to the environment, how to calm his sensory system and how to remove himself when he feels overloaded.

Assistive technology is an area that is sometimes overlooked. The literature and my own experience have taught me that many children with AS have a difficult time with handwriting. Some children never develop the motor skills necessary to make handwriting a practical means of written expression. Others draw the letters, thus taking a very long time to complete handwritten work. Still others are such perfectionists that their writings are like works of art to them – they cannot allow even the smallest mistake on the paper – thus it is not a practical or functional means of written expression. Many children with AS can benefit greatly from an assistive technology evaluation for learning computer keyboarding skills. The assistive technologist and the occupational therapist need to work together very closely when the child is first learning the keyboard. Because most children with AS have poor motor skills, the skill of typing will be very difficult in the beginning and take longer to learn than with most students. With lots of patience and practice, most children with AS should be able to master keyboarding skills under the tutelage of a good therapist.

Physical education (PE) classes are typically horrific for children with AS. Children on the autism spectrum have weak social skills and may lack the understanding necessary to be a compete team player. In addition, their gross motor and fine motor coordination tend to be weak – not a plus when teams are being chosen. Understanding and following game rules can be challenging for the child who has language processing and sequencing (being able to put a series of actions into a sequential order) and organizational problems. Additionally, during PE children come in to close physical contact with one another, thus invading the personal space of the AS child. Compound these problems with putting the child in a gym with several screaming children and the walls will begin to resonate with sound and the child will likely go into sensory overload. This can lead to a child who hits, kicks, bites, etc. If the parents feel the school coach is capable of working with the child in the environment, a minority of children with AS can flourish in PE. In this case, it seems a good idea to involve the occupational therapist and speech therapist who can help the coach to work with the child. For many children with AS, PE at school is best avoided altogether.

Most of the therapies my son enjoys occur outside of the regular school setting. I find that we can design some very creative and unique opportunities for him that incorporate every area we think he needs help with. For example, a swim therapist can help a child develop gross motor skills while in the water. Swim therapy involves a therapist who has been trained in swim therapy. Most children with AS are drawn to water, which makes this therapy very appealing and necessary when given safety issues. In our own case, Ryan's swimming skills were too advanced to benefit from swim therapy. Our alternative was to have the YWCA work with him on swimming skills. The occupational therapist worked with the swim coaches to make sure they concentrated on particular muscle groups. We had hoped that this intervention would develop into a sport for Ryan since it could involve him swimming with teammates of his age. Though he loved to swim, he did not demonstrate an interest in wanting to swim competitively. Ryan now has the skills he needs to allow him to participate in this activity throughout his lifetime, should he choose to swim when he is an adult.

Music therapy was extremely beneficial to Ryan when he was young. A music therapist I once heard at a support group meeting explained to me that the reason music therapy is beneficial for students with AS is because music travels differently through the brain than the spoken language. Children can develop language skills and social skills through the use of music. Additionally, they can be worked within a group of children to help illicit social interaction.

Of all the therapies, equine therapy has been my favorite. This therapy is provided through horses. Hippotherapy involves a therapist – usually an occupational therapist, speech therapist, physical therapist or counselor. For children with high needs in these areas, hippotherapy needs to be explored first. Equine therapy is different in that an individual who is certified in equine therapy usually administers the therapy without benefit of additional therapists. When a parent is exploring these therapies as an option, I cannot stress enough the importance of the therapist being an excellent horse person. The parents need to visit the facility and look at how the area and the horses are maintained. The facility should be clean as well as the arena where therapy is provided. This area should also be well organized. The horses need to act and look healthy. Furthermore, the horses need to have personalities conducive to working with children. If the parents are not confident about their level of horse knowledge, they should enlist the help of a friend with horse knowledge. Equine therapy can help the child develop skills in language, sensory integration, fine motor coordination and gross motor coordination. In addition, equine therapy can help with developing social skills. The therapist can teach the child how the horse talks with his body (non-verbal language), how to interact with the horse, and how to communicate with the horse. Ryan formed a very close bond with his horse, John. This is another intervention that can be developed into a sport for the child with AS. Once the child has acquired a level of riding proficiency there are all types of pony clubs and horse competitions in which he can participate with other peers his age without a lot of social demand.

Another type of therapy or intervention is a social skills group. Parents need to consider several components for these groups. The group needs to be small with no more than six students at a time. It needs to be structured with clearly defined rules for the students, preferably posted on the wall in the room. Some groups in our West Texas community worked on self-esteem instead of social skills. While this should be a component, there are many other skills that need to be taught. These skills should include facial expressions, body language, idioms, social manners, how to start and carry on a conversation. Parents need to make sure they are clear on what skills the group is actually working. Furthermore, the parents need to be comfortable with the professional running the group and the other students in the group. The professional should also talk to the parents to teach them how to work with their own child while out in the community. Since social skills development is such a new area for many communities, there are few professionals qualified to provide this type of intervention. To fill this void, with some research, some parents may be quite capable of running their own social skills group.

Videotaping the classroom, interventions and therapies can be a wonderful extension of the student's work in the environment. The video recorder needs to be in the environment several times to help the student and the adult learn to ignore the device. The adult and student then identify what target behaviour they will be working on. The adult first needs to establish that he/she is offering advice for the student to improve their skill level. It is paramount that this be an adult with whom the student is comfortable and from whom she can take constructive criticism. In the beginning, the adult needs to make a point of showing the student where she was successful. Once rapport is established, the adult can help the student to pinpoint when the target behaviours were occurring and offer some suggestions on how the student can alter her behaviour. Another advantage to videotaping is that the adult can also critique his own interactions with the student and thus improve as well. As adults, we sometimes forget that any social interaction with a student with AS is not one sided but reciprocal.

Dance was an area we happened to stumble across. Ryan and I became involved in Scottish country dance. It is an old form of dance that involves partners and is the precursor to square dancing. The dancer continues to switch partners until at the end of the dance you wind up with your original partner. This dance style requires that you give eye contact when you meet your dance partners. It has very clearly defined social rules, such as how to ask someone to be your partner, how to accept an offer to dance, how to hold hands, etc. It turned out to be a wonderful means to help Ryan with rhythm, motor planning, following directions and social skills. Though this particular activity is definitely not for everyone, it is one that we have thoroughly enjoyed.

Another intervention that has been very effective for Ryan is one he came up with on his own. Ryan loves to write creative stories. Fortunately, he learned keyboarding while in elementary school so he is very proficient at typing. These stories can take him days to complete. The rule is that if one of his parents can read the story and edit what he has written, he gets to count it as a home schooling credit. There have been several benefits to this: Ryan is developing better typing skills and written expression; he is learning how to organize his thoughts, which is a deficit area for children with AS; writing helps him to process his environment and his social interactions; it also serves as an emotional outlet.

We are sensitive to the fact that these stories are very personal to Ryan. They give us an insight into how he is processing and interacting with his world. Writing in a diary can also be very helpful for some children. However, parents need to respect the child's sensitivity when it comes to sharing what has been written.

The fine arts is another area that parents can explore for interventions. Theatre has many potential benefits. Stage movement and drama can help the child learn to proximate body language to express feelings. It can also help teach the child to watch for non-verbal cues. When reading a script, the interactions are structured and predictable, which is another advantage to teaching social skills. Puppet theatre can help the child who has stage anxiety. They can learn the same skills but without being on stage themselves. For adolescents, other avenues in theatre include stage painting, set building, and/or backstage work. These are areas where students can interact with others. As a theatre major, I can safely say that most people drawn to theatre are not mainstream and tend to be more accepting of differences. Parents can look at their schools, community theatre, and junior colleges for opportunities for their child in theatre. Almost all theatres need help with building and painting sets. Volunteering yourself and your child is a great way to get started in the theatre.

Music, gardening and art and crafts, such as weaving, beading and painting can provide other opportunities for increasing hand–eye coordination. These activities can also be very calming for individuals who have sensory integration issues. It is important that children with AS learn how to spend leisure time to learn how to unwind. Sometimes in the hustle and bustle of family life we all forget to take the time to slow down and relax at the end of the day or when life is just too stressful.

Sports outside the school's PE program can be a wonderful experience for children with AS. However, parents need to choose these activities very carefully. It is my opinion that sports such as basketball, soccer, baseball, etc. should be carefully considered before the AS child is encouraged to undertake them. I have heard of a few children who have been successful and enjoyed team sports. However, for many children with AS these team sports require too many social skills.

During a conference in 2000 I heard Dr Tony Attwood suggest that AS adolescents be encouraged to participate in sports that stress individual performances more than team efforts: for example, such sports would include swimming, golf, bowling and cross-country running.

Tae Kwon Do has proven to be another great intervention for many kids with AS. Many people have asked if Tae Kwon Do promotes aggression in children with AS. Our experience and that of many we have spoken to suggests that it does not. The activity is extremely structured and the rules of the sport are clearly defined. Tae Kwon Do requires the child to learn to pay attention, to develop self-confidence and self-discipline, to show respect and to learn self-control. In Ryan's Tae Kwon Do school, the students were taught how to remove themselves from a harmful situation. They were also told that if they misused their knowledge of Tae Kwon Do on another person (parent, child, etc.), they would have to leave the program.

An area of social interaction that we recently stumbled across was a local church youth group. Since we had just relocated, we started with my parents' church. The youth group leader is structured in his activities with the kids and has established an excellent rapport with them. The youth group leader chooses games that require teamwork and has taken a special interest in working with Ryan. The youth in the group seem to be very accepting of Ryan. This group has helped begin the process of developing friends of his own age in our new community. So far I have stayed, watched the activities and listened closely to the Bible discussions. On the way home, Ryan and I discuss the evening and share our opinions on religion. Through these discussions, I have discovered that Ryan has some very profound and insightful interpretations of religion.

Pets are another method of teaching social skills and learning to care for another creature. Fish keeping is another wonderful way to encourage the AS teen to incorporate his sensory information to increase his awareness of the needs of other living things. Something I learned the hard way, however, is to purchase a tank that does not require a great deal of periodic cleaning. The larger the tank, the less often it will need to be cleaned. I learned that while the affordable, small fishtank was very calming for Ryan, cleaning it bi-monthly greatly increased both our stress levels.

Initially Ryan disliked animals, particularly dogs. Their barking hurt his ears and their fur bothered him tactically. He also had a difficult time interacting with them. Pet therapy helped Ryan overcome these issues. He has a very close bond with his horse, John, and my parents' German Shepherd dog, Elsa. John and Elsa have very patient personalities, especially when interacting with Ryan and both animals are very calming to him. If a parent does decide to pursue pet therapy, it is essential that the right pet and the right therapist are matched to the child.

There are many naturally occurring opportunities for parents to provide interventions with the child. Once the parents have learned some skills from the child's therapist, they can also work on skills in the home. Games are good ways of teaching interaction skills to children with AS, particularly board games. Taking turns, reciprocity and teamwork are just some of the skills that can be taught. Games such as chess help with visual motor planning. I have a friend who had her daughter learn archery to increase her visual perceptual skills.

Watching videos with your child is another great way to improve social comprehension. The parent can point out facial expressions, body language, idioms and subtleties of language and discuss them with the child. With some videos, we also talk about what moral the storywriter is trying to convey to the audience. Recently, we were watching a video as a family. In the show one character responded to a question from another with an obvious lie. His facial expressions and body language were very subtle so I stopped the video. I asked Ryan if he thought the character was telling the truth. Ryan responded, 'No.' Excited about my successful tutelage, I asked Ryan 'How do you know?', expecting him to tell me about the character's body expressions. Ryan answered, 'Because you stopped the video.' When it comes to videos, I need to work on developing a more subtle approach. The lesson: never underestimate your AS adolescent's ability to outthink you!

When they start watching for teachable moments, parents will be surprised how much intervention they can provide for their child while in the home and out in the community. For example, a trip to the grocery store alone has all types of possibilities for teaching social skills. Outings such as to museums can be other excellent ways to integrate the child into the community. Museums tend to be very quiet and soothing, plus they schedule films, art exhibits, tours, etc. These are methods to expand the child's knowledge and to learn how to act in public. Another avenue to find creative ways of working with your child is to get information on home schooling from the Internet. Home schoolers list in great detail how to work with your child at home, from learning reading comprehension to getting the most out of a public outing.

Moving back closer to family was an adjustment for us. We left several friends whom we were very close to in West Texas. In many respects, they took the place of family while we were there. Whether you surround your child with your true family or adopt surrogate families, it is important that the child has a sense of family beyond his parents. We wound up moving two doors down from my parents, in the house that had been owned by my grandparents. The benefit for Ryan has been that he gets to see his grandparents, aunts, uncles and cousins almost daily. This has expanded his social circle and provided him with other folks who can assist him in finding answers to his social questions. This helps to extend what we are teaching him.

Ryan has been a learning experience for his extended family as well. Living so close to him has allowed them to see how AS impacts his life. Recently my father had Ryan get out of the car to help guide Dad while backing up the car. This meant that Ryan had to take the perspective of his grandfather sitting in the car and use hand gestures to indicate which way Grandpa should turn the car and how far to back it up. Needless to say, this is a skill area that we will have to help Ryan to develop. My parents have also learned that when they ask Ryan to perform a task they must explain every step. If a step isn't explained, the chances are it won't get completed appropriately. When Mom asked Ryan to feed the dogs and cats while they were out of town, her list was very detailed and took three pages. While this might have been a bit too much, no one went hungry while they were away either.

Recently my family learned another side of giving Ryan instructions. One day Ryan's aunt came to our front door while he was alone at the house. She knocked on the door several times and then went over to my parents' house. About that time, Ryan called his grandmother to inform her that his aunt was at the door. Both his aunt and grandmother were puzzled that he wouldn't open the door when he knew it was his aunt. Later that day my mother told me about the situation. It was obvious she was bewildered. I started laughing. I reminded her that both she and I had left instructions not to open the door to anyone when he was in the house by himself but to call his grandmother and she would come over to open the door for the person. I explained that he had done exactly as we had instructed. Kids with AS don't adjust the instructions to include a novel situation. Once a rule is learned, it is followed to the letter. When I explained to his aunt, who is a special education teacher, why Ryan hadn't answered the door, she started laughing. She then suggested that we add an addendum to Ryan's instructions. I told her we already had.

If you do decide to get your child involved in the community sector, I advise telling the instructor or youth group leader some information about your child. In general, I always make it a habit to stay and observe Ryan for the first few sessions he has with any therapist or at any intervention event. I do this for several reasons:

- to make sure Ryan is comfortable with the adult and other kids

- to debrief Ryan if I see a social encounter that needed some work

- to see how the other kids interact with Ryan

- to see if the adult seems to interact well with Ryan

- to answer any questions the adult may have about Ryan.

Finding good professionals is paramount for your child. Something that I have learned along the way is that a good therapist will make the sessions fun. The child doesn't realize it's work and looks forward to attending the sessions. If your child isn't enjoying them, this could be a sign that your child is not benefiting from this type of therapy or intervention with this professional. It could be an indicator that it is time to find someone else. One poor therapist can set your child back or you can lose valuable time in acquiring skills. My rule is to go with your instincts. If your instincts tell you that the professional is not a good match for your child, then you need to find another. A good professional will also treat parents with parity (not talking down to them) and teach them skills for working with their child. You also want to make sure that you are clear on what the therapist is doing with your child and what outcomes you should expect. If you don't see improvement after a period of time, then you need to talk to the professional or maybe find another provider.

One of the most important lessons I have learned during my quest to build a strong intervention system for my son is to recognize opportunities that come from unexpected sources. A very unexpected intervention came through the Garland Fire Department's Explorer's Program. The Explorers is a group for adolescents who want to learn the skills to become a firefighter. Ryan is a member of this group. One of the activities was to prepare the kids to participate in Garland's 'Burn Day' at the Dallas Fire Academy. To prepare for this day the Explorers had worked on how to go safely into a burning building and put out a fire. To participate in Burn Day meant that Ryan would have to put on a facemask, oxygen tank, and bunker gear – called 'bunkering out.' Then he would have to go into the burning building with three other kids, locate the fire, put it out, and exit the building. The second activity was to enter the 'Flash-over Chamber.' This looks like a big metal barbeque pit, with a fire built on one end. The firefighters enter and then the door is shut. They stay in the chamber and watch to learn what a flash-over fire looks like.

The first hurdle for Ryan was putting on the facemask and oxygen tank, and then breathing through the mask. The firefighters explained that when the mask begins to vibrate, there are only five minutes of air left and the person wearing the mask is expected to immediately get out of the building. All the kids took turns putting on the mask. The way to tell if the mask is properly seated on the face is to put a hand over the front vent while the person breathes in. If the person can't feel any air moving through the front vent and a vacuum is formed between the mask and face, then it fits correctly. Watching this, I knew that Ryan wouldn't do well with getting the mask on, let alone taking the test. I nervously watched while he put on the mask and went through the test unfazed.

As the kids got ready for the day's activity, I watched as various kids on his team made sure that Ryan was with them, helping him participate in the group. At one point, I noticed that the group of kids went off to work on something, Ryan just stood there lost, not sure if he should follow. About the time that I started to walk up to Ryan to prompt him, one of the boys noticed that he wasn't with the group. He turned around, walked back to about five feet from Ryan, gestured with his arm and said, 'Come on Ryan. Come with us.' It was all Ryan needed to catch back up to the group.

A little later, the kids had to put on the heavy bunker gear, boots, oxygen tanks and masks. I watched as a fire captain from another station patiently helped Ryan get bunkered out. Then the captain checked to make sure everything was working correctly. It was time to go into the burning building. It was a concrete building with a metal roof. Flames leapt out of one of the windows, while black smoke billowed out of the door and other windows. The first team of four teenagers took their fire hose, got down on their hands and knees and crawled into the burning building. Several firefighters went in with the kids. Just a few minutes later it was the turn of Ryan's team. Ryan was the last one on the end of the fire hose. I watched as all four teens got down on their hands and knees and crawled into the burning house. After what seemed an eternity, Ryan came out by himself. My heart sank. I worried that the experience had been too much for Ryan. As he took off his mask, he was visibly upset. The fire captain and I approached Ryan; he told us that his mask had started vibrating so he had left the building. When the tank was checked, it showed that it had plenty of air. Ryan was upset and said he felt like a failure. No amount of talking to him seemed to help him feel better. In his mind, he hadn't made it as long as his teammates so therefore he felt he had failed.

The next activity was the flash-over chamber. Once again Ryan bunkered out. Several kids went into the flash-over chamber where the heat is as high as 1200 degrees. I kept my fingers crossed that Ryan would feel successful this time. Again black smoke billowed out of the structure. I'm not sure how long Ryan was in the chamber but when he left and took off his mask he was grinning. He had made it longer than any of his teammates and even longer than some of the other kids. Then the captain walked up and told Ryan that the facemask he had been wearing in the burn house had been checked and found to be defective. He also told Ryan that by following their instructions he had done exactly what he was told to do when the mask vibrated. Later that afternoon, Ryan was used as an example for all the teenagers about the importance of following the firefighters' instructions. Soon after Ryan's grandfather, who is on the Garland City Council, told Ryan that if the city ever heard of a firefighter not leaving the fire when their mask vibrated, the firefighter would lose his/her job. Ryan beamed with pride. What had initially seemed like a failure to Ryan had turned into a success.

When I look back on that day, I think of how Ryan managed to overcome his sensory issues – bunkering out and going into a burning building – how his teammates included him in all the activities, and the patience of the firefighters working with Ryan and all the teenagers. Most importantly, Ryan felt that he had been successful. Ryan's words to his father and grandparents about how he felt about the day were that he felt as if he was a hero. I think there were several heroes that day. While we all feel after September 11 that our firefighters are heroes, I feel that day they were heroes all over again for helping Ryan feel safe, confident and successful. I know that this day is a memory he – and I – will always cherish.

We are still adjusting to our move and to big city life. Ryan goes back to visit West Texas with his dad quite often so he manages to keep his connections with his friends who are our West Texas family. He still visits with John, the horse, takes him for walks, and rides him. I'm still looking for therapies and interventions, trying to go slowly and gradually to integrate Ryan into each new activity, making sure it is a good fit for him. I know that I'll revisit some of the interventions that have worked for Ryan in the past while continuing to look for new ones that will be just as effective. I'll look for new professionals and role models who will work with Ryan. In many ways it seems like an unending quest, looking for professionals, therapies, interventions, friends and families who will help Ryan in the adult world. Recently, Ryan summed up the experience of parenting a child with AS and trying find interventions and therapies. He said, 'You know Mom,' life is like walking backwards.' Puzzled about this statement, I asked him why he thought that. He explained, 'Because you can only see where you've been but not where you're headed.' He's exactly right.

References

Homeschooling

Homeschool World. www.home-school.com

About Homeschooling. www.homeschooling.about.com

National Home Education Research Institute. www.nnheri.org

Home Education Magazine. www.home-ed-magazine.com

Sensory integration

The Ayres Clinic. www.home.earthlink.net/~sensoryint/

SI Network: Sensory Integration Resource Center. www.sinetwork.org

ComeUnity: Children's Disabilities and Special Needs.
   www.comeunity.com/disability/sensory_integration/

Center for Autism Study. www.autism.org/si.html

11

Education and the Adolescent with Asperger Syndrome

Lise Pyles

Procuring a successful school experience for the adolescent with Asperger Syndrome can be a patchwork affair. Ask 50 veteran parents for their views on what has or hasn't worked, and you'll get 50 answers. Ask those same parents every few months throughout their child's teen years what works, and you'll likely get different answers then too. Our kids change a lot during these years, and every semester brings new issues. Parents of teens often report that they've had to piece together workable solutions and make frequent adjustments, as opposed to being able to tap into ready-made programs that fit their teens. Then again, there are the exceptions – some of us find good schools and good programs that work throughout the secondary school years and few changes are needed. For all of these reasons, it's difficult to take the pulse of this challenging period of schooling, and there is no one answer. However I hope this chapter will give you a lot of clues to help you achieve a worthwhile education for your adolescent with Asperger Syndrome.

The first section of this chapter will cover some trends and tips that may help school go more smoothly in general. Some will probably be reminders of things that have helped your child in younger years, while others are pointedly aimed at junior and senior high school issues. The second section of the chapter will cast a wider net, and outline some of the more creative avenues that families have taken in their pursuit of a genuine and valuable education. It's important to note that while there are a few specific programs mentioned by name, the intent here is not to point you to a particular school or program, but rather to expose you to some ideas. It will be up to you to see how that can translate into a viable educational alternative for your own child.

Some trends

Our children benefit most from a hands-on approach by parents

Parents typically tend to back off when children reach teen years, feeling that parental input is less needed. One might make a case for that with so-called 'average' kids (though I have sincere doubts about even this), but it is especially untrue for our special kids. Secondary school brings on a host of new experiences that must be responsibly handled. We do want to gradually ease back on the reins as our children reach adulthood, but the fact remains that our kids are typically younger in terms of development than their same-age peers, and will have special challenges that will continue on into junior and senior high school. As Lynn, a New York RN says about her very bright but often struggling son, 'Just because our kids are 17, that does not mean that they are capable of doing what other 17-year-olds do. Much care needs to be given to all placements, jobs, teachers, etc. Failure simply means the structure is not right.'

Also, at the beginning of each year, parents should arrange for a tutorial in Asperger Syndrome for all their child's teachers plus any other key staff members. Often this means that you will need to prepare handouts and give a talk. Keep it short and give concrete examples. Then follow it up with periodic phone calls or emails to each of your child's teachers to see how things are going and if there are further questions. This is more difficult in secondary school because of the involvement of so many teachers, but there is no substitute for communication.

The bottom line is that this is no time for parents to stand on the sidelines. Stay involved and on top of things. Monitor how things are going, even when you think you don't need to.

Parents must stay informed about their child's rights

A father to a now adult son on the autism spectrum writes:

I served as my son's case manager and staunch advocate when it became apparent early on that schools at whatever level knew virtually nothing about AS/autism…and it showed. Therefore, I wrote every one of his IEPs (the required Individualized Education Plan) and ISPs (Individualized Service/Education Plan for those over the age of 18). I firmly believe that well-informed parents should serve these functions rather than turning them over to often quite uninformed (and unmotivated) school personnel.

This is not to say that he worked alone. He feels that the success of his role 'depended heavily upon the serendipity of finding absolutely wonderful, dedicated, and caring team members…to play the roles which they filled so very well.' I think the point he is making, however, is that parents need to take a proactive role.

The recent rise in children diagnosed with autism spectrum disorders is a double-edged sword. On the good side, more schools are aware of the diagnosis and what constitutes an effective response. Primary schools in particular are beginning to rise to the occasion. And that's where the ground swell of recently diagnosed children is – in the younger grades.

Kids who are pre-teens or teens today, however, are still ahead of the wave. They are the pioneers, the groundbreakers, and the guinea pigs. Junior and senior high schools haven't been forced to deal with it all yet, except in isolated instances – one student here, another there, which is all the more reason why parents need to network (on internet, through support groups, and through their input into books such as this one) so that we can all stay informed on what we have each discovered.

As for one's educational rights, these obviously vary from country to country and you need to learn them if you want to exercise them. The IEP process (IEP in the USA and Australia; Statement of Educational Need, SEN, in the UK) is probably one with which you are well familiar by the time your son or daughter is in secondary school. If not, however, it is the formal process for creating an individualized education for your child. Roughly speaking, it involves having your child officially accepted as a special needs child within the school district. It brings together parents, school staff plus anyone else who is pertinent (therapists, experts or advocates) so that together you may decide on goals for your child and how to reach them.

Even if you have been through the process before, it's a good idea to refresh yourself on what your child's rights are and spend time thinking about the process from new angles. Is your child old enough now that you would like him to sit in on the IEP meetings, or parts of them? Also, if your child is 14 or older, there are requirements to address transition issues (college, job skills, etc.). You may also wish your child to remain in school longer, even up to age 22, and there may be legal provision for that. Even what didn't seem relevant in earlier years, such as an extended year (summer school), might be more relevant now. For all of these reasons, you may want to reread this sort of information every few months. (Please see the resources at the back of this chapter for where to find this information.)

Our children benefit from attention to transition

Whether your child is starting middle school, heading for high school, or simply beginning a new year at the same old school, changes mean stress. Starting in the fifth grade, academics really begin to kick in, and junior and senior high school bring yet new worries: lockers, changing classes, larger campus, coping with multiple teachers, changing clothes for PE, handling new electives, meeting higher academic expectations, and of course enduring (if not necessarily fitting into) the whole teen culture – cliques, fashion, dating, etc. It's a nerve-wracking few years for any child but especially so for the teen with Asperger Syndrome.

That's why transitions are so critical. When my own son began grade seven at a private mainstream school, the school's special education teacher was experienced with Asperger Syndrome and began him in a 'Bridging Program.' This meant that he began the first week in a separate class with just a handful of special needs kids. The focus in the beginning was just getting used to the school itself. Once he was comfortable, she carefully prepared for him to attend one regular class in his strongest subject (math). This was done only after the math teacher was coached in the topic of Asperger Syndrome and made familiar with my son's issues. Because this transition was so smooth, my son was soon ready to take on another class, and then another.

This sort of transition may have different stopping points for different kids. One child may only ever attend one mainstream class and spend the rest of the school day in a resource room. Others may take on two or three classes. Still others may transition to all mainstream classes, or perhaps all classes except one. The transition may be done under a formal program as was the case with our 'Bridging Program,' or it could possibly reflect a verbal arrangement between you and the school.

Either way, this 'start small and add' approach is vastly preferable to the tactic that some schools take, which is to start the child in all regular classes and then adjust after fiasco strikes. The end result may be the same in terms of number of mainstream classes, but effective transitioning avoids trauma along the way. Other ways of transitioning at the beginning of a new school year include the following:

1. Before the school year starts, take a tour of the school. Find the cafeteria, bathrooms, nurse's office, library, etc.

2. Find the bus stop at both ends of the trip or walk the route from home to school.

3. Get a locker assigned early (an end one preferably). Have your child practice opening the lock. *Note:* It is usually better to get a lock with a key because bullies are notorious for looking over our kids' shoulders and memorizing combination lock codes. A spare key should be given to the homeroom teacher.

4. Have your child try on new school clothes ahead of time to reduce the chance of last-minute problems with texture or fit. Ditto with adjusting the backpack and fitting in notebooks.

5. It's usually better to have all subjects in one notebook, rather than separate smaller notebooks. This lessens the need to revisit the locker or the chance something will be forgotten.

6. Explore the lunch options. Find out what lunch items will be sold and discuss in advance what your child might like. Avoid the stress of your child going to the lunchroom on the first day and coming away hungry.

7. You may want to see if your child can start with a shortened day on the first day. Arrange to pick him up early.

8.   Have an aide or buddy (adult or student) assigned to your child to assist in finding rooms and getting around for the first few weeks.

Your child may not need all of these helps, but a little problem prevention in the beginning can really pay off. However, be careful not to make all of your precautions transmit a message of anxiety to your child. Try to be casual and reassuring.

Our kids uniformly seem to require a 'chill-out' place at school

An overstimulated child needs a way to regain control. For children with Asperger Syndrome, the best answer usually is to allow them to leave the classroom and find a refuge within the school walls where they can pull themselves together. It's a simple solution, it's free and it works.

For Mary's 17-year-old son, that place was the nurse's office, a place that she calls, 'a haven when things get to be too much'. Even though Mary's son, now graduated, didn't use it all that much and tended to hide out in the library, it was helpful to know it was there.

A 'chill-out' place can be any place where the child can destress and regroup. My own son used the special (bridging) room and also the library. At other schools it might be the resource room, counselor's office, teacher's lounge, or even just a beanbag chair in a quiet corner. Along with a place to destress should come a permanent hall pass, so that our kids can seek refuge whenever necessary. Often just knowing that they have 'an out' gives them a sense of control and fewer tendencies to use it.

For some kids, working off tension with physical movement works. When tensions rise, the teacher can send the child on an errand, even an unnecessary errand, to the opposite side of the building and back again. This defuses the situation and helps the child to relax.

Our kids need classroom modifications

Everyone's list will be different, but most students with AS need some adjustments to make school life tolerable. These may be the sorts of things that can be written into the IEP, or some may be achievable with just a word to the teacher. Ask your child what most bothers him about his school day and see if a few things can be changed. Even a small change can make the difference.

Karen R in Maryland reports that the most helpful accommodations for her 15-year-old daughter have been: 'Small classroom size, no students with behaviour problems, and a safe space to retreat when things become overwhelming.'

Sue's list is focused more on teachers and staff. She writes that the biggest helps for her tenth-grader have been 'a sensational full-time aide who really tries to teach him, not just support him; adapted homework, so he still gets the same grade as other kids for less work, but he knows he improves his grade if more work is done; recognizing his autism, and not getting upset when he gets nervous before a test and that radiates into behaviours.'

Marla credits a formal behaviour plan with being extremely helpful to her son: 'I had to insist on a behaviour plan to protect him from the standard methods of discipline. For example, most kids know that they can push his buttons and push him to blow up at them. He once told a kid, 'Shut up or I'll kill you.' A typical child would have been suspended for this. It was agreed with the team, that should Bobby say this, it is out of frustration and not a threat. He only did it once but I had to protect him from the kids who know how to manipulate him.'

Cassie, a mother in the UK, has a slightly different list:

> Anxiety has been a major problem…when stress has impaired his functioning, I have phoned my son in sick, or invented a doctor's or dentist's appointment. Most of the 'appointments' were on Games days [Sports Day or Field Day]. Also important is understanding from the teacher – making absolutely sure that if he is asked a question in class it's one he can probably answer; giving him the space to think through his answer before giving it; giving advance notice of anything unusual; being clear in instructions; and TELLING US AT HOME IF SOMETHING HAS GONE ON DURING THE DAY. ('Definitely a capital letters accommodation,' she writes.)

In addition, although no one will need every accommodation, parents may wish to consider one or more of the following suggestions:

- Have your child use a laptop computer or 'smart keyboard' instead of handwriting.

- Have a scribe take notes, or copy teacher's notes.

- Allow extra time during exams.
- Opt out of team projects or group work.
- Exchange one class for another, or for study hall (also see curriculum options, below).
- Reserve a particular seat on the bus.
- Allow child to leave class early to avoid crowds at lockers.
- Purchase two sets of books, one for school and one for home.
- Obtain a syllabus of assignments at the beginning of the year.
- Arrange weekly chats between parent and teacher.
- Allow in-class work to be finished at home.
- Have a communications diary, and require an entry each day.

Our kids benefit from social skills training

At a standard junior high or senior high, there is typically no social skills class in place, which is a pity because our kids continue to benefit throughout adolescence from opportunities to learn and practice social skills. Social skills classes do seem to be evolving in grade schools, but parents would do well to inquire at the junior or senior high school about them, and indicate that the need for social skills training persists. See if a counselor, school psychologist, or special education teacher might start a social skills class. This could be a lunch group, a regular class period, or an after-school activities group. It can be exclusively made up of kids with social deficits or can also include some kids with good social skills. Some of the benefits might include:

- making friends
- role playing social situations (defusing a bully situation, mediating an argument, resisting offers of cigarettes, drugs or alcohol, interviewing for a part-time job, etc.)

- understanding body language, facial expressions, tone of voice, idioms

- having fun in a safe and moderated atmosphere.

If the school does not step forward with a social skills class, you can either force the issue by going through formal complaint mechanisms, or you can simply make an extra effort to work on these sorts of social skills outside school. You can model and discuss social situations in the home and also in the community (errands, business calls, etc.). You may be able to get your child involved in community clubs, volunteer work, or other activities, perhaps with your involvement in them as well. I got my son interested in doing volunteer work for the blind by volunteering myself, for instance.

Our adolescents may be more resistant to special helps than in younger years

When kids are young, they have little say in what therapies they attend, which classes, etc. As they get older, however, they do voice preferences. Teens become increasingly aware of themselves. They may be more upset at the thought of looking different from peers, and may strongly resist the very accommodations that we work hard to put into place. It is common for parents of older children to lament, for example, 'After I worked like a dog to get a couple of hours of speech therapy out of the school, now my child won't go!'

One way of avoiding this situation is to include your child in the discussions. You can discuss what progress has been made in earlier years, where there are still goals to be met, and so forth. Although self-knowledge is often a distinct weak point among our kids, your child may know what goals or weak areas he would like help with, which accommodations he will at least tolerate, and which ones he absolutely does not want to have.

Beginning in middle school, many parents feel that it is a good idea to have the child sit in on the IEP meetings. I confess that this never felt right in my own personal situation, and I never had my son sit in on any formal meetings throughout his entire school career. However I concede that it may be a great idea for many kids and maybe I should have done so. Teens who have input to the process may be more willing to go along with any modifications. They may also have great ideas, and will learn self-advocacy through participation in the process. On more than one occasion, such a child has been the one to notice later when an IEP isn't being followed!

After that, if there are still deficits you want to see addressed but you are still meeting with resistance from your child, then you need to pick your battles and/or negotiate some alternatives.

If your child balks at a social skills group at school because it sets him apart, for example, then insist he work with you or join an appropriate outside club or group. If it's physical therapy that prompts a rebellion, look to alternatives that will help increase physical movement. Perhaps a track team, bowling league, karate lessons, or even an at-home fitness routine will fill a need.

If your child does not want to do speech therapy at school, perhaps hire someone to work with him privately, or work on various issues at home in the evenings after consulting with the school therapist.

Another suggestion is to re-evaluate the situation that is being resisted. Maybe there is something amiss with the current therapy or modification:

- Your child has outgrown the therapy or it is too repetitive, boring, unchallenging, or not truly suitable. If your child cannot skip or ride a bicycle, this may seem important to work on with a 7-year-old, but if your daughter is a teenager is it so important any longer?

- There is a personality conflict, either with the person leading the activity, or with someone else in the group.

- Your expectations are too high. The activity is at a higher level than your child is functioning, or (more likely) your child is already on the edge of his stress threshold from just coping with normal school activities and cannot handle one more added thing (either during school or after hours).

It's helpful to remember that sometimes less is more. It's better to have your child do fewer things and feel successful (so that he can build on this another day), rather than to be over-scheduled with more things and fail everything.

Our children need buddies and mentors

The needs were straightforward when our kids were little. They benefited from buddies – other kids to be their friends, to share common interests, and to model rudimentary social skills like standing in line at the drinking fountain. Because our children may have had difficulties making friends due to Asperger traits, parents or school staff often needed to arrange these buddies.

As our kids mature, the needs grow ever more subtle and complex. They still need buddies to share interests, but the need for these 'other people' takes on new dimensions. There is still the 'friend' component – simply someone to hang out with at school, pure and simple. Added to that, though, in teen years there is often a greater academic component – a buddy can help them stay on task, be there as a lab partner, or provide help in handling more abstract homework assignments, larger projects, and so forth. There is also an increasingly complex social component – how to better fit in (navigating a minefield strewn with artifacts of the teen years – fashion, hair, dance, music, lingo, and so forth); how to behave within a small group; how to solve peer pressure problems, and survive boy–girl issues. Finally, on an even higher plane, our kids need guidance in becoming young men and women, and they need someone safe and non-judgmental with whom to discuss the grown-up issues that are important to them.

It's fair to say then that sometimes our kids need buddies, and sometimes they need mentors. One person could feasibly take on both roles, or your child may do best with a few caring people who fill these various needs. Chances are that you as parent cannot fill all of these roles.

When my son entered seventh grade, he was given a peer-age buddy by the school staff to show him around during the first few weeks. This worked well, mostly because the peer was quite mature and kind, and also because my son was motivated. This buddy became a great friend in time. When I complimented my son on making and keeping this friend, he told me that he knew that he'd lost friends in the past because of irritating behaviours. So with this friend, he quite logically told the boy, 'I don't always know if I'm doing something annoying, so if something I do annoys you, just tell me and I will stop.' So, this was the arrangement that the two boys made. I was impressed that my son thought this up and even more impressed that he was so willing to make changes based on the opinion of this friend. He'd certainly never made that offer to me!

This illustrates the power of having someone *outside the family* as a positive influence. Parents still offer advice, criticism and praise, but I wonder if our message is received in a very diluted form – after all, today's message is only one out of thousands that we have transmitted to our kids over the years. It is easily lost in the noise. But when someone else, such as a buddy or mentor, makes a comment, our kids may well take notice. That's my theory, anyway.

If you want your child to have a buddy at school (more a friend than a mentor), you can ask a teacher to pair your child with someone else at school who needs a friend, perhaps for lunch, a field trip, or as lab partners. The teacher could also choose someone who is already quite popular but kind, and simply ask them to help your child as a favor or perhaps for extra credit; or a person can be chosen based on a shared interest – two science buffs, chess players, musicians, or what have you. Any of these pairings can work.

To find a mentor (as opposed to a social friend), think about individuals who are older than your teen. This could be someone such as a college student, teacher, pastor, counselor, tutor, older relative, or just someone in neighborhood. The important thing is that this person should genuinely like and respect your child. Whether this partnership is made formal in any way (with scheduled meeting times or even involving pay), or whether this is just a casual arrangement that unfolds more or less organically, is up to you.

For my son, his love of bowling meant that he was down at the bowling alley a great deal. He befriended the pro-shop owner, and benefited greatly from the camaraderie. Through these interactions, he was able to do a bit of work there on a casual basis. He learned practical things such as how to polish bowling balls and retrieve pins from the automatic pinsetters, but more than that, the pro-shop became a safe haven where he could hang out and be accepted, and where he could enjoy companionship with an adult who was not a parent. The pro-shop owner became a great mentor – coaching, cheering or commiserating on my son's bowling, showing him how to handle anxiety and disappointments during tournaments, and just being a good guy and a good role model.

The above mentorship was of a very casual nature, both in its goals and also in how it was arranged (it wasn't arranged, it just 'happened'). However, sometimes these mentorships are much more formalized and goal specific.

Eric H became a mentor for a young adult with Asperger Syndrome who was just beginning in an Arizona community college. With permission, I have reprinted parts of his letter to me because it illuminates many aspects of the mentor relationship:

> Gary and I took a class together and we sat next to each other... My first impression of Gary was a no real impression at all. He seemed distant as you can imagine. However, I treated him, as I hope I treat all human beings, with respect.
>
> I was very big on study groups... The study groups helped me with my focus and as an organizer allowed me to hand-pick participants so that they were all dedicated students who strived for the best grade possible without much of the competitive stuff.
>
> Gary's father somehow found out about my study group and asked if Gary could participate...the rest is history. I guess the study group idea for Gary helped a great deal. I believe that the repetitious and ritualistic nature of a study group was slowly instilling study habits into Gary. During the semester, Gary's father offered (insisted) to pay me for private tutoring sessions. Being a rather poor individual...I gladly accepted the task.
>
> The funds for my services came from a pot of money through some grant or benefit Gary was eligible for. I would occasionally be asked for progress reports etc. to meet the requirements of the allocation.
>
> My job as I saw it was to work myself out of a job... and I have to tell you that I felt it worked and/or Gary grew away from needing my services. His development and social evolution was remarkable, however its emotional toll on me was indescribable.

Author note: the emotional toll Eric mentions was mostly due to becoming emotionally attached and therefore involved with the bureaucratic upheavals that Gary's family went through as they tried to access services and fight legal battles.

As for what makes a good mentor, Eric has a few comments:

1.   They should be peers (parents and adults may not be as effective).

2.   They must be disciplined and consistent (this seems vital).

3.   They must maintain (as much as possible) an emotional detachment from the family to be effective after the initial learning/mentoring phases.

      If number three cannot be accomplished, a friendship with its social interaction, post-mentor, can and does seem to do as much or more for one with AS.

I think Eric's last statement is an acknowledgement of the idea that a person may be either a teacher and guide for a person with AS, or he can be more of a friend and role model. The emotional closeness of the relationship may determine which exact role is fulfilled, but either one is valuable.

Our children need to feel good about themselves

This is simply a reminder that although school features dominantly in the lives of most adolescents, we parents can help our kids to see the larger picture. Life is about learning (not grades) and success can be measured in a lot of different ways. Help your child find a special interest, special friend, interesting work, hobby or skill that will bring joy and passion. This will help him ride over the inevitable rough spots in his school career. Many parents report that a saving grace for their children throughout their high school years is a passionate interest in one particular thing – for some it is music, for others it is karate or bowling or chess, and for still others it may be civil air patrol, ROTC, drama, or something else.

We can change education for the better

Every time you get an idea from one parent's school district and introduce it to your own district, you have made a difference. Even if you don't get it fully off the ground, the seed has been planted and others will pick up the cause and run with it. Someone started the first social skills class somewhere, and now they are popping up in many areas. The same can be said about charter schools, homeschooling organizations, and so forth.

Don't forget the power of writing a well-crafted letter; of documenting your efforts and the school's response; of going to school board meetings, advocating for other parents; even effective use of media. For a great handbook on making a difference in your school, you may wish to read *Angry Parents, Failing Schools,* by Elaine K. McEwan.

Various school alternatives

Choices at your regular school

Your child is very likely in, or headed for, a junior or senior high school that is designated by where you live, and you are making the best of the situation with any accommodations you can – perhaps many of those outlined above.

The accommodations I mentioned earlier in this chapter are of the relatively small variety – generally things that can be done with minimal impact at school, and can often be arranged with just a conversation with one or more teachers. Even a child who is not formally designated as a special needs student might be able to benefit from those small changes.

However, there are many other larger options that can be explored. Not all will be feasible for your situation, but my research has shown that students with Asperger Syndrome have been involved in a dizzying array of arrangements. I'll try to at least briefly outline each of them, but I'm sure there are even more out there that I did not uncover.

Please note that it would take mountains of books just to scratch the veneer on this hefty topic and there is no replacement for doing your own homework. Within each section and also at the end of this chapter will be some resources for helping you determine which of these avenues may be open to you. Beyond that, there is no substitute for using your local organizations to glean information – your district education office, the library, special needs organizations, local autism/Asperger support groups, local homeschooling organizations and so forth.

In many cases, the various options are not mutually exclusive. A student may be involved in more than one program. Also, the labels for these various options can be tremendously overlapping and confusing. For instance, I have attempted to talk about charter schools, alternative schools, homeschooling, and cyber schools as separate topics. However it's conceivable that an alternative school or charter school allows and incorporates homeschooling and also offers online 'cyber school' classes. So what does one call it? Therefore, don't despair if you are not sure where the lines of demarcation are or if the names trip you up or sound near identical. It doesn't matter. What is important is simply to be aware of the sorts of things that are 'out there' and then you will need to research exactly what is in your area or what you would like to bring to the area and what it is to be called. This is all about ideas! Don't get too hung up on the names.

Curriculum changes

One of the easiest things to do is take care in choice of courses. It's easy enough to avoid certain electives that may cause extra stress and to purposely choose classes with maximum benefit. Here are a few suggestions:

1. *Music.* If your child has hearing sensitivity, you may wish to stay away from choir and band, (too many sour notes!) in favor of music appreciation.

2. *Physical Education.* If there is a choice in certain PE sub-topics, your child may be better off choosing an individual sport (track, swimming, weight-lifting) instead of team sports.

3. *Keyboard/computer.* Have your child take keyboarding or computer classes as early as possible. Many of our kids have fine motor issues (lousy handwriting!) and keyboarding will be a skill that will pay off for the rest of their lives. It will also lead to more effective use of special accommodations you may wish to ask for later – a notebook computer or 'smart keyboard' (such as Alphasmart) to take into other classes.

4. *Advanced coursework.* If your child can handle the academics, encourage him to take the higher placement classes. One reason is that the higher classes generally have a calmer atmosphere, although obviously the work is also harder. A second reason is that it may lead to being able to take classes that can also count toward college credit, or will

enhance chances of being able to obtain college credit later through proficiency testing.

5. *Study skills.* A study skills class may be good for kids who need help in organizing work or approaching subject matter.

6. *Drama. Our* kids are often great at memorizing lines, and drama class can be good for learning to read and emote body language and facial expressions and as a way to work off tension through physical movement. If you do decide the classes and/or performances might be too much for your teen, I'd still suggest you find a different way for them to appreciate the dramatic arts. For example, the teen could join in set designs and construction, costuming, advertising the plays, etc. The opportunity to watch people use their bodies, faces and voices to express emotions is just too great for our kids to miss.

7. *Foreign languages.* Don't shy from these because of your child's language pragmatics issues in English. Our kids may excel in foreign languages, memorize vocabulary with ease and can be quite captivated by rules of grammar and making word root connections to English. For any class, try to find out what it entails. Will it be mostly conversational work or written work, for example?

How, where, and when will your child be taught?

If your child isn't formally part of a special needs program, he will probably be in a regular classroom and receive only minor modifications, if any. However, if he is formally designated as needing special services (on an IEP or equivalent), there are other options to explore.

SELF-CONTAINED CLASSROOM

This can be good for kids who can't handle a larger classroom. Watch that the academic level is not too low since often these classes are set up for academically slow students. Also, sometimes the schools would rather put your child in a self-contained classroom than make a more inclusive situation work. Marla says she would have liked to have her son Bobby in an inclusion setting in middle school, but she could not get the support of the school. She writes, 'I ended up going with their recommendation of self-contained because I feared he would not get the necessary support to succeed if I forced the issue.'

A CLASS WITH A MIX OF REGULAR AND SPECIAL ED STUDENTS

This might be termed as 'inclusion.' Other terms might be 'class within a class' or other catchphrase. Penny K prefers to call this 'not excluded.' She dislikes the term 'mainstream' as though her son must either sink or swim within the stream of typical kids. However she feels that 'included' is a patronizing term, as though it's an extra favor or kindness.

WORKING IN A RESOURCE ROOM

Many of our kids follow this path. It is easy to set up from the school's standpoint, and from the child's viewpoint it's a time to get special one-on-one help, to catch up on homework, and to avoid the stress of the classroom. One only needs to ensure your child isn't spending voluminous amounts of time to himself in the resource room if he would prefer and can handle the classroom.

ATTENDING REGULAR CLASSES WITH AN AIDE

This may be a full-time, one-on-one aide, a part-time aide, or an aide who helps other students as well as your child. I recently saw a quote in a newspaper from someone who oversees special education for a large school district in California. The statement was (paraphrasing here), that a program such as a one-on-one aide probably isn't workable for teens on the autism spectrum because the students would become social outcasts. He wanted to develop a buddy system instead.

There's nothing wrong with buddies, but I think this man is missing something. I know of many cases of teens with Asperger Syndrome who genuinely like their aides and for whom having an aide has made the difference between failure and success. Many of our kids remain out of the social swim for the most part anyway, so an aide is not going to be what keeps them from being in the 'in' crowd. An aide can make sure our kids aren't bullied and keep the stress levels way down. Our kids may or may not be clued in to whether having an aide is socially acceptable, but they often have few people to talk to and enjoy talking with adults, so an aide can be great for increasing social conversation. Some aides are thought of as 'cool' and can actually increase a child's popularity. In short, please don't make the same mistake this man has. If you think your child needs an aide, don't discount the idea simply because when you were a kid you'd have been humiliated. We need to remember that our kids have been dealt a different set of cards.

WORKING ACROSS DIFFERENT GRADES

A student might attend one grade for most classes and another grade for a splinter skill. One child at my son's school took twelfth-grade biology but was in eighth grade for other subjects. All of it took place at the same school (ours goes from grades 7 to 12), but in other cases students have attended a different school for certain classes. A sixth grader might travel to the junior high for math, for instance. It's a great idea to tap into a child's gifts and build on his successes and a great way to build self-esteem too.

'Alternative' high schools

All of the schooling options discussed in the rest of this chapter are alternatives of one sort or another, but when I use the term 'alternative high school' in the next few paragraphs, I am referring to the type of school that has been around for years as a sort of 'second chance' high school.

In years past, 'alternative schools' have had a reputation for being the last-ditch stop for kids who didn't succeed in their regular schools, for whatever reason. Sometimes these schools are even colloquially called 'expulsion schools.' Obviously, many of the kids there have presented disciplinary or other problems at their prior schools. As such, an alternative high school has sometimes had a certain stigma attached.

Although worrying about appearances is of substantially less concern to us than providing a good school experience, the possible behaviour issues of the other students can make this one of the more tenuous choices for a child with Asperger Syndrome.

Our children may also have behaviour issues because of poor social or communication skills, high anxiety and extreme frustration. This can result in outbursts, rages, or aggression, or other problems. Our kids also sometimes get labels such as 'Behaviourally or Emotionally Delayed' (BED) or 'Social-Emotionally Maladjusted' (SEM), or similar label. However that does not mean that they have conduct disorders or belong with other children who have conduct disorders. Drs Ami Klin and Fred Volkmar of the Yale Child Study Center have called such placements 'possibly the worse mismatch possible, namely of individuals with a very naïve understanding of social situations in a mix with those who can and do manipulate social situations to their advantage without the benefit of self-restraint.'

However, one cannot dismiss this option entirely. Today in many places, the alternative school is putting on a new face. In forward-thinking districts, alternative schools are now trying to work with different sorts of learners, and are acknowledging the learning styles that reaching them may involve. The schools themselves are often small with a lower student to teacher ratio and more personal attention. It may be too simplistic to reject this option out of hand, based on past reputations.

For anyone researching this option, some of the attractions to the traditional alternative high school may be small school size, and an emphasis toward bare bones academics without much emphasis on the school social atmosphere – there may not be sports, clubs, class plays or other distractions. You may sacrifice things like labs, choir, sports and so forth, so decide if this is an issue.

Perhaps the biggest worry is that any problem behaviours may tend to be dealt with through discipline. The atmosphere may be tightly controlled, with a penchant toward rewards and punishment. The upside may be a calmer environment than even a regular high school and more clear-cut rules (which our kids may find easier to follow). The downside is that our kids most often do try to behave appropriately anyway, but need education (information plus skills rehearsals) rather than punishment. We need to keep in mind that the techniques that work for other kids are usually not the same techniques that work for our kids. Ensure that the school you are considering understands Asperger Syndrome.

Charter schools

According to the Center for Education Reform (CER): 'Charter schools are independent public schools, designed and operated by educators, parents, community leaders, educational entrepreneurs and others.' Since they are public schools, they are free to families. Since they are run by people other than the standard school district, that fact can 'allow them to operate freed from the traditional bureaucratic and regulatory red tape that hog-ties public schools.'

It sounds like the best of both worlds, and indeed, many parents have eagerly embraced this option today. Charter schools are not available everywhere, but as of this writing, 38 states have authorized their existence: Alaska, Arizona, Arkansas, California, Colorado, Connecticut, Delaware, DC, Florida, Georgia, Hawaii, Idaho, Illinois, Indiana, Kansas, Louisiana, Massachusetts, Michigan, Minnesota, Mississippi, Missouri, Nevada, New Hampshire, New Jersey, New Mexico, New York, North Carolina, Ohio, Oklahoma, Oregon, Pennsylvania, Rhode Island, South Carolina, Texas, Utah, Virginia, Wisconsin, and Wyoming. Across the country, there are roughly 2400 charter schools in operation.

Charter schools are always public and have a common theme of independence from traditional bureaucracies, but after that it's a potpourri of possibilities. Some charter schools are of the 'back to basics' variety, with heavy emphasis on fundamental skills and mastery of core knowledge. Others are bent on innovation and experimentation. Most have the benefit of being small.

Again, the crucial aspect of all of this is to research the individual charter school carefully. What is its main focus? Some cater to kids who have had trouble succeeding in other schools, similar to the 'alternative schools' of the preceding paragraphs and perhaps with some of the inherent problems. Some are very specialized. In Maumee, Ohio, for example, one family-run charter school is designed for autistic children from grades K-3. Another charter school began as a business before gaining school status, and focuses on hippotherapy (horseriding) as a way of teaching learning disabled or developmentally delayed students from grades K-8.

California alone has over 350 charter schools and, as an example, one charter school seems like a great choice for students affected by Asperger Syndrome, even though that is not the emphasis of the school. It encompasses kindergarten through grade 12 and serves 3000 students over a six-county area. However the strength of it is that it is built on a principal of personal instruction. Parents are heavily involved in the day-to-day school experience. In many ways, this particular charter school seems to encompass the benefits (and some of the parental workload) of homeschooling, but under the auspices and guidance of the public school system.

At the school, each student is assigned an Education Specialist (ES) and together the ES and the parent choose the teaching materials and curriculum that will best serve the child, semester by semester. Special education services are available and course materials are free, just as they would be in any public school, but there is a personal touch.

The mother I contacted reports that she does most of the teaching of her AS son, just as a homeschooling parent would, but she has guidance and support from the school and no expense. Also, accessing special education services has not been a problem. Khyraen A writes:

> There are regular special education services, only unlike with the district (i.e. traditional public school), they rarely fight you on them and they are always one on one. Before, the district had my son in speech twice per week but only in group lessons. That was it. Now, he has one-on-one instruction for two hours per week. He learns more in those two hours than in a whole month in the regular public school.

One potential fly in the ointment is that there is a political movement to reduce funding to charter schools, and it is possible that this sort of option will diminish over the years, but for now, it seems like a great choice and more than one family affected by Asperger Syndrome has thrived in such a situation.

The other fly in the ointment is that some charter schools have had a rocky start. Even the best ones are fairly new and can be somewhat disorganized. There are other interesting wrinkles for the charter schools to work out with the school districts – getting bus transportation to take children to all of these new facilities, for one. Then, there are funding issues, staffing issues, procuring materials, and everything else you can imagine with a start-up venture. Although special education is supposed to be a 'given' when attending public schools, the pragmatics of when and where and who will teach can be difficult.

So, once again, be cautious and do your homework well. As well as understanding what the overall vision of a particular charter school is, see how long the school has been in operation, what its track record is, if it has adequate staff in place, if materials are going to be available, if transportation will be there when you need it, and what the physical facilities are like. Ask the school specific questions about special education services you require for your child, such as occupational therapy, speech therapy or social skills classes. Since this is still public school, any special services or major accommodations may need to be written into an Individualized Education Plan (IEP) for your child. Speak with other families who are already attending the charter school and get their opinions.

Residential or private day schools for the autistic spectrum child

At the expensive end of the scale are private schools, either residential or day school, that are specifically designed for the child on the autism spectrum. Many have traditionally been tailored for the lower functioning child (classic or Kanner's autism), but some do cater to Asperger Syndrome, the entire spectrum, or a broader scope of developmental disabilities.

The price can seem prohibitive and out of the reach of most parents. Keep in mind that if there is no workable alternative available to you within the public school system, then the public school system is obligated by law to fund such an option for you. The rub here is in having everyone agree on what is or is not appropriate and what is or is not workable. The parents must be able to show that the normal options do not work, and must be willing to do the research to find a private school alternative, because that information will not normally be offered.

In the worst case, it can also mean subjecting your child to a dismal situation first, to prove to the district's satisfaction that what they provide will not work. In the case where the family is already in a dismal situation, there is little to lose. However if you are in this situation and the school system wants you to try yet another setting that looks equally poor to you, it's a hard thing to face. On a more positive note, some parents have been pleasantly surprised to find their school districts readily agreeing with them on the program needed, or even suggesting it, and those parents have encountered relatively little resistance to paying for out-of-district or private schooling. One never knows.

As for the benefits of a school that is specifically geared to a child with Asperger Syndrome, it may be useful to look at the situation of Marla, an Illinois mom with two boys on the spectrum. One son, Mark, is 12 and attends a private day school in the Chicago suburbs. The school serves children and adolescents, ages 3 to 21, with developmental, emotional or behavioural disabilities, including autism.

Her other son, Bobby (13) also has Asperger Syndrome and is in a traditional middle school but on an IEP. He attends a self-contained Learning Disabled (LD) class, but is mainstreamed for science, PE/health, and Independent Arts. He receives social skills work and occupational therapy.

What are the differences? Marla explains:

> The difference between the two placements is that with Mark in private school I do NOT have to 'train the professionals.' They know what to expect from AS. Mark is given much more social skill work at his school. They work with him on recognizing his frustrations and better ways to handle it ALL ACROSS his day. He has a job at school (collecting and crushing the aluminum cans) that he loves. They are given responsibilities in the classroom as well... There is a daily communication book that goes back and forth from home to school. On days that he has ended up having a meltdown (these are few and far between now) they will call me to give me a 'heads up' on his day. They do NOT call me to pick him up. They offer support groups, seminars, and guest speakers. They are very family-orientated.
>
> I have had to train Bobby's teacher, social worker and aide in AS. I have had to supply them with literature and have spent much time on the phone answering their questions. The difficulty lies in the changing of teachers with his mainstreamed classes. Bobby meets with his social worker once a week with a peer group that includes other children with social difficulties and children that don't.

Of course, this is only one mom's experience, but it may be representative. You would expect a private school focused on autism to better understand it, and to work on behavioural and social issues as an intrinsic part of the day. Conversely, it's no surprise to find that even in a well-meaning regular middle school with its greater number of children of varying abilities, any therapies may be fragmented and segregated, and true understanding of Asperger Syndrome may be the exception rather than the rule.

Does that mean that a private school for autistic spectrum children is automatically the best answer for your child? No. Every situation will be different. Besides the possible cost and/or difficulty of getting into such a school, there may be distances involved, the stress of a new setting and, depending on your child's issues, it may be more insular than is actually needed. Once again, you need to visit any school you are considering and weigh the pros and cons. If it's a residential school, even more careful consideration must be taken because then you are leaving your child in someone else's hands for days at a time. This is a difficult decision to reach emotionally as well, for both you and your child.

Home tutoring/homebound

If you and the school agree that it is the right thing to do, your child could stay home and have public school tutors visit for a short period each week, much the same as if your child were bedridden with an illness. This is usually known in the US as 'homebound status.'

Nance M's son with AS was on homebound status for his entire seventh grade year. She reports that she had to obtain a medical diagnosis for him to qualify – her son's psychiatrist pronounced that he was 'too brittle' to attend school. Because of that, her son received two hours of instruction on each of two days per week (total of four hours/week). Nance loved homebound. She says it works if the teacher is a good match:

> Rick's teacher really respected my knowledge of Rick and the autism spectrum. She taught him with an auditory method. They had discussions on history, math, English and even philosophy of life! She respected Rick's intelligence and understood his deficits but focused on his strengths. She was quiet spoken, gentle, non-emotional, and non-reactive – a very good match for Rick.

As for whether Nance recommends homebound status, she responds: 'I would recommend homebound for an AS student…unable to deal with the middle or high school environment. I would make sure the match between teacher and student was a good fit, that the teacher respected the student and was open to learning about AS.'

Sue G in Missouri gives homebound status mixed reviews for the five-week period she has been allowed to use it for her son Jason. However, alone it is not the answer she has been looking for – at least not the way her school district is operating it. She reports that she is disgusted that her son has been allowed to take only two academic courses through the homebound program and his other grades have simply been 'frozen' until he makes up all the work he's missed while being at home. Her frustration is that if they had simply offered him *all* the classes via homebound study or another appropriate forum, he wouldn't be missing anything!

So, will he soon return to regular school to resume his studies? Not if Sue can help it. She plans to convene an IEP meeting to talk about half school days and half homebound for next year. Full-time school has not worked, and with the homebound program, she sees a different Jason that she has not seen in a long time. 'Jason is now happier, joking, teasing again, and just relieved.' She also plans on meeting the special school district superintendent shortly along with some autism professionals to discuss the possibility of starting an autism school. 'I want him to know that Jason is a prime example of what they have not done for kids with AS – the need is there. Jason is only the tip of the iceberg.' She sums up by saying, 'Some kids with AS may not be meant for full-time public school. I am not losing my son emotionally over a diploma.'

Home-study / alternative school

This option is something that some schools are turning to, in order to capture back some of the families who have left public schools in order to homeschool. Some districts are trying to establish a relationship with homeschoolers and are offering a sort of hybrid. The students can still be part of the school system, and report to a teacher or spend a few hours of week at a public school, but otherwise spend most of the week at home. It is rather like the homebound status, except that you do not need to be on a medical excuse to take part in it, and instead of having a tutor come to your home, the student visits the school. Jessie G in Seattle has chosen this option for her children. She explains further:

> My two teenagers, both with AS, attend a school district alternative school for homeschoolers. This is a place where homeschoolers can come and take classes. Classes are offered in the basic subjects … as well as in many more interesting subjects. High school students can obtain a district diploma by meeting district requirements. They must have x amount of credits in each area. However, we the homeschool parent and student can decide exactly what will be studied. This is the blessing for our focused interest kids. Also the total number of students is less, so there is not the noise factor. The administration is responsive to each student's needs. IEPs are recognized and mostly adhered to. They

only have to spend five hours a week there. All ages are there at the same time. It has been an ideal set-up for my kids. And as my daughter said to me today, 'You know Mom, I still enjoy learning.' How many 17-year-olds say that nowadays?

Work–study

Carol L in Nebraska has pursued a work–study arrangement for her 17-year-old son, Theo, stemming from a job he has had outside school hours over the past year. Theo works at a rehabilitation hospital, two shifts every other week from 3 to 11 pm. Carol feels it has been an extremely positive experience: 'The work environment is stable, structured, calm, peaceful, the routine is predictable … and he has the best team of people surrounding him that we could possibly ask for. If only all of his future work situations could be as positive!'

I would add, if only his school situation could be as positive. School has been far less happy and more stressful for her son. Because of this, Carol tried to arrange a work–study program for him, with the hope that he could spend less time in school and more time at work. However, as Carol explains, 'The work study requirement at his high school is that he would have to work at least 20 hours a week *in addition* to taking a full course load at school. In order to do that, because of shift work in medical institutions, he would have had to work every single weekend plus one full shift during the week – and getting home on a school night at 11.30 pm would have made the next day a disaster.'

So the work–study program (as the school so rigidly defines it) did not work out, but Theo still works at the hospital. His school career may be a difficult one at the moment, but he gets satisfaction from the success he experiences at work. He has a licensed position and is doing very well, according to his supervisor. As Carol rightly says, ' I am very, very proud of him for this accomplishment.'

So how does this translate to your own child? First, be aware that formal work–study programs are out there, but they may be 'too much' for many of our special needs kids. But the flip side to consider is that our kids may profit more than financially from a nurturing and positive work experience, and it might even represent the most positive part of a teen's week. I confess that my first parental impulse to my own son was to say, 'School comes first. There is plenty of time for jobs later.' But each child is different and, as with so many aspects of Asperger Syndrome, we need to be willing to think 'out of the box' sometimes and seek positive experiences for our kids wherever we can. We have bright kids, and with the right structure and understanding environment they can make tremendous progress. The workplace can sometimes provide in ways that a school cannot.

How do we plan for life after high school?

A father recently made the comment to me that as much as we worry about our young charges on the autism spectrum through their school years, 'they all grow up.' We need to look at what comes next. Here are a few ideas.

TRANSITION SERVICES

In the US, if your child has an IEP, when he turns 14 there should be a statement included that covers transition services. These services can be any activities that ease the move from high school to whatever the goals are for after high school. Think large. Those goals might be college, employment, vocational training, daily living skills, job search skills or other. They should take into consideration the interests and preferences of the student, which means your child should be involved in this process. Any person in the community (potential employer, adult agency, etc.) that may be part of the goal can be invited to the IEP meeting. Be warned, however, that some parents have found transition services have consisted of a simple form given to their child so he can list his preferences for life after high school. Then, nothing more ever happened. Don't let this happen to you.

SCHOOL-TO-WORK PROGRAMS

Most of us are aware of vocational high schools (vo-tech is a common term for these schools) and some of us perhaps attended them. These are schools where typical kids are guided onto various career paths early in high school and take courses that will qualify them for a certain job by the end of their senior year. This may or may not work for our kids. If your child is already strongly interested in a career path, keen to pursue it and does not need many class modifications, it might be a reasonable option. However I see three dangers. First, such a program may thwart future acceptance at a college, so if college is a goal, proceed carefully. Second, it channels a career path extremely early in a child's life, and I feel that most of our kids with Asperger Syndrome may need more time in making such a choice, not less. Third, the vo-tech school may be unable to accommodate a child who needs extensive classroom modifications or special therapies.

JOB COACHING

Job skills are certainly a critical part of our children's learning, but unfortunately they are not often well addressed. Some job skills may be provided through the transition services listed above. Additionally, there are agencies that can provide such things as job-hunting techniques, interview skills, job coaching, and supported employment options. Not every teen with Asperger Syndrome will need all of these services, but you should know that they are out there. Talk with your school about what job-related goals might be incorporated into your child's education plan. Also, consult the agencies listed at the end of this chapter.

Home education / homeschooling

I've talked earlier about options that involve the school district, whether that means learning within school walls, or at home under school direction (home-bound or charter school options apply here). But there is also an even more parent-directed approach, poularly known as 'home education' or 'homeschooling,' that decreases or even severs ties with the school altogether and puts education duties squarely with the parent. Laws differ from place to place, and families often still need to file forms, have their child evaluated from time to time, or abide by other rules, but by and large the home-education program is parent-designed, led, and delivered. Families often really enjoy this option, and find their child blossoming in this nurturing environment.

Homeschooling isn't easy. It takes a lot of parental involvement. It takes a certain amount of money to buy materials (although probably not as much as you might think), and it takes time. I didn't homeschool my son during his teen years, but I did for several of his primary school years. I can vouch for the fact that it's a lot of work, but very worthwhile. We were glad to get away from a mostly negative school experience, and my son made tremendous academic leaps with one-on-one attention in a quiet kitchen.

WHAT ABOUT SOCIALIZATION?

Here is a short article that I originally wrote for the National Home Education Network, a tremendous organization that supports homeschooling families. The network may be found on the web at http://www.nhen.org/ but the article is reprinted here.

Socialization and children with Asperger Syndrome

Anybody who has been homeschooling more than 20 minutes knows that the most popular probing question from the masses is: 'And what about socialization?'

This is an especially bothersome question for families affected by Asperger Syndrome who want to homeschool. Since lack of social skills is one of the hallmarks of the child with AS, people naturally assume that keeping a child home instead of exposing him to the social climate of school will just worsen the situation. The reverse is true, in my opinion, for the following reasons:

1. *School has people, but that doesn't make it social.* In fact, it is usually fairly anti-social since kids can be very cruel and bullies seem to be an ever-present part of the school experience. What is social about exposing our children to daily torment? Nothing. Children with Asperger Syndrome are natural targets for bullies and the situation frequently results in a tantrum, depression or violence, all of which could have been avoided by avoiding this 'social' atmosphere.

2. *Homeschooling does not mean denying social experiences.* To the uninitiated, homeschooling conjures a picture of cloistering your child at home all the time. For most homeschoolers, nothing could be further from the truth. There are trips to the library and the park, gatherings with other homeschoolers, and lessons and clubs that tie in with the child's interests. And we still live in neighborhoods, still have extended family and friends, church, etc. Homeschooling does not mean restricted movement but rather greater flexibility.

3. *Social experiences tend to be more positive when done through home education.* As homeschooling parents, we can monitor social gatherings to keep them positive. That is, we can pick and choose the activities, watch for bullies and intervene, head

off other kinds of trouble, and teach our children with spontaneous social lessons 'in the moment,' (or make a note to discuss things later). In short, we are on deck. Finally and perhaps most importantly, we can steer our children gently homeward before sensory overload undermines the whole event. In school, our kids do not get the luxury of this kind of protection or customized teaching. It's usually a case of 'sink or swim.' Our kids tend to do more sinking than swimming.

4.   *Homeschoolers may get more social opportunities out of their day.* When we homeschooled, my son was in the comfort zone of his home surroundings for mornings of academic work, and that still left him with some energy in the afternoons and evenings to try other things. Parks department classes, bowling league, swimming lessons, and Boy Scouts were just some of the things he tried. When we stopped homeschooling and put him into a regular school, however, these fell away. He was too burned out from the school day to do anything else, and quit all outside activities. Although he'd wanted to try public school and did fine academically, the trade-off was that he gained some very negative social experiences and lost some very positive ones.

5.   *The idea that our kids need the classroom experience of having positive role models around them every day is suspect.* It's true that positive role models are better than negative ones, but just placing our kids alongside peer-age, so-called normal kids does not mean that they will intuitively pick up on proper behaviour. In fact, their condition of Asperger Syndrome *means* they will NOT pick things up intuitively. Things like social graces, body language and speech pragmatics must be consciously and deliberately and specifically taught, bit by bit. Unless the child has a one-to-one aide to provide full-time tutelage in these things and allow ample rehearsal time, not many social skills will be picked up. Contrast that with the home environment, where the parent does have the time and patience to teach these things and can provide a safe place for rehearsing them.

6. *Finally, we need to measure by a different yardstick.* Our kids
    with Asperger Syndrome do not typically need or want the
    same level of social interaction than their neurologically
    typical peers do. Not everyone wants to be surrounded by
    others all day long, have large parties, or a dozen friends.
    Many of us (self included) cherish solitude, are happiest in
    our own company and function better with fewer social
    interactions. This is not abnormal, only different, and it
    should be honored. It is far better to have a little
    interaction and look forward to more another day, than to
    have too much interaction and suffer devastating
    consequences.

In short, parents can rest easy that their home education program
is probably doing more for their child's socialization than a public
school counterpart could. The only dark side, and there is a dark
side, is that our children will probably never be totally at ease in
social situations and will always have a few challenges, no matter
what we do. Asperger Syndrome is, after all, a lifelong condition.
And because of that, there will always be someone ready to
explain why our child seems socially inept. 'It must be because he
was homeschooled!' they will cluelessly proclaim. Sometimes, you
just can't win.

WITH HOMESCHOOLING, CAN I TEACH ADVANCED COURSE SUBJECTS?
You don't have to know chemistry to be able to provide instruction in it
to your child. There are many ways to get around this bugaboo:

1. Have your child sign up with a correspondence school or
    take courses through an online high school. Switched-on
    Schoolhouse offers homeschoolers a complete package of
    high school courses on CDs. There are also many accredited
    high school diploma programs – American High School,
    Indiana University High School, University of Texas at
    Austin High School Degree Program are just a few of them.
    For an extensive listing, I highly recommend consulting
    Cafi Cohen's website (www.homeschoolteenscollege.net/
    diplomaisp.htm) and her excellent books on the subject of
    homeschooling teens (see the end of this chapter).

2.   Join a homeschooler group and swap expertise with another parent. Perhaps you can teach Spanish or creative writing, and another parent can handle math.

3.   Hire a tutor. If your child wants to learn guitar or the piano and you don't know how to play, you don't panic – you pay for lessons, right? You can do the same thing with algebra.

4.   Ask that your child attend certain select courses at the local high school. A friend's daughter homeschools but takes science and drama at the local private high school. I know another boy who took only computer and driver's education at his local public school and homeschooled for everything else. Success with this will depend on what the general attitude toward home education is in your school district, but it may be worth asking.

5.   See if your child can attend community college early. Many community colleges accept high school students these days, and students can earn early credits both toward high school and also toward college.

WILL MY CHILD BE ABLE TO ATTEND COLLEGE AFTER BEING HOMESCHOOLED?

Yes, hundreds of colleges accept homeschoolers these days. If your child attends an accredited correspondence or on-line high school for his home education, you will be provided with transcripts. If you use a more casual method of homeschooling with you and your child designing the curriculum, you will want to keep a portfolio and create your own transcripts. For either method, you will want to read up on the subject of college admissions for homeschooled teens. Two good books by Cafi Cohen are *And What About College?* and *Homeschoolers' College Admissions Handbook*.

COLLEGES

Many of our kids may be college bound. Finding the right college is the trick. For our family situation, the logical choice is for my son to live at home and attend a local community college for the first two years. My son has no wish to live on a large campus, is repulsed by the prospect of sharing a dorm room or an apartment with anyone else, but also isn't keen to be out on his own yet. Community college seems like the best fit.

Colleges do work with kids with disabilities, but services are uneven at best. Some of the more common accommodations seem to be in the areas of test taking (more time), note taking, and having a private dorm room. However, there can still be a tremendous number of challenges. Living on campus requires handling things like budget, food, and laundry, besides coping with the course load. The social life can be intrusive and the pressure intense. Even signing up for courses is tremendously overwhelming (and best done on-line if that's at all possible).

Speaking of on-line, one really good option for college is to explore on-line courses. Dozens of colleges and universities offer either a wide selection of courses or sometimes an entire degree program on-line. Some of these distance learning degree programs are:

- University of Phoenix

- DeVry University

- Penn State World Campus

- American Intercontinental University

- Kansas State University

- Indiana State University.

See the end of this chapter for some helpful websites.

Quitting school/GED

It's every parent's fear that their child will come home from school one day and refuse to go back. Try not to panic if this happens. You can always see if one of the above options may work for your child. If nothing else works, your child can seek a General Educational Development (GED) diploma. More than 800,000 people take the GED test every year, and one in seven diplomas earned in the US today is via GED. Your child will be in good company. Whether that is a great comfort to Lynn is debatable. She feels that the GED is the only salvageable piece of a school career that failed her son completely. Her harsh words:

> Our son…ended up in the GED program in a district close to ours. Nothing prepared us for the challenge we would have [in trying to get a decent education]. He is bright, loves music and may have true gifts in acting. However multiple failures in odd

jobs, writing, and test taking in NY with the Regents mandated classes left him deflated and feeling a failure. We all know this is false. He was labeled a behaviour problem and put in a class for ED students in the ninth grade that was wrong. Schools have much to learn. Once he turned 16 he got in the GED program. The GED program is only two hours per day and he feels that he is not really being taught enough. He has been robbed of an education, at least at this juncture. We will seek a community college for computer this summer and continue to encourage him. At some time he must decide he can do it. We know he can. Stresses of adolescence are so burdensome for these few that the concentration needed to just get through the day is exhausting. Schooling must be incorporated 24 hours a day with daily living skills such as driving, buying groceries, organizing time, etc. Traditional schooling did not work. Whenever I used creative arts in his education it worked. Teachers belittled him and peers ridiculed him, hence oppositional behaviour erupted. He shut down.

If your child is close to quitting school or has quit, you also need to look at *The Teenage Liberation Handbook* by Grace Llewellyn. Although it is not written with any disabilities in mind, it is aimed at the student who feels there must be more to life than school. The subtitle of the book – *How to Quit School and Get a Real Life and Education* – says it all. It is filled with ideas, resources, contacts, and inspiring anecdotes from kids who did quit high school and went on to better things (jobs, college, travel, entrepreneurship, etc.). It is well worth a look.

In conclusion, there is no one pathway for achieving an appropriate and worthwhile secondary education for your child. There may be several pathways, each one with benefits and drawbacks, and parents will need to determine the best route. Decide what you need first, and then go about trying to get it. Ask other parents in your area about their experiences. Do not be afraid to ask the school system for new options, rather than accepting the tried and true that perhaps worked for other children but does not work for your own. Once you obtain the best option you can, then monitor it closely, both to make sure that schools continue to do what they promised and also because our kids' needs change as they grow. You may need to revisit this issue a few times and make adjustments, but I hope you are now armed with options and ideas to obtain success.

More information

Individual Education Program (IEP) guidance

Individualized Education Program (IEP) Guide
Editorial/Publications Center
US Department of Education
PO Box 1398
Jessup, MD 20794-1398
USA
Tel: 877 4ED PUBS
www.ed.gov/offices/OSERS/OSEP/IEPGuide/

Special educational needs (SEN) guidance (UK)

Action ASD
Assessments and Special Educational Needs (SEN) statements Info
Tel: 01706 222657
Email: info@actionasd.org.uk
www/actionasd.org.uk/Education.html

This is a local Lancashire support group with helpful articles.

Charter schools

Center for Educational Reform (CER)
1001 Connecticut Ave. NW
Suite 204
Washington, DC 20036
USA
Tel: (800) 521-2118
www.edreform.com/charter_schools/

National Charter School Directory 2001-2002 contains school data enrollment figures, grades served, and a description of each school's program for the 2400+ charter schools in operation today. The price for the Directory is $39.95 plus $6 for shipping/handling. To order a copy from CER by phone, call (202) 822-9000 or order online at www.edreform.com/pubs/

Residential or day schools for autism spectrum

UK

Schools list for children with autism
National Autism Society
393 City Road
London ECIV ING
Tel: 44 02(0) 7833 2299
www.nas.org.uk/schools/

USA

Http://dir.yahoo.com/Education/Special_Education/
Schools/K_12/
Directory of Schools, Camps and Residences for children with autism
www.eparent.com/resources/directories/schools.htm

Homeschooling information

AUSTRALIA

Australia Homeschooling: A to Z Home's Cool
www.gomilpitas.com/homeschooling/regional/australia.htm

This site lists many support groups, legal information, supplies, curriculum and more.

Home Education Research and Legal Information (HERLIN)
Melinda Waddy
54 Pilbara Crescent
Jane Brook WA 6056
Australia
www.3dproductions.com.au/legal/index.html

CANADA

Canadian Home Based Learning Resource Page.
www.flora.org/homeschool-ca/

The site lists provincial information, support organizations, chat rooms, among other things.

Association of Canadian Home-Based Education (ACHBE)
C/o J. Campbell
PO Box 34148
RPO Fort Richmond
Winnipeg
Manitoba R3T 5T5
Canada
Email: homeschool-ca-admin@flora.org
www.flora.org/homeschool-ca/achbe/
(Please include SASE or $1.00 if you require a written response).

NEW ZEALAND

New Zealand Homeschooling: A to Z Home's Cool
www.gomilpitas.com/homeschooling/regional/NewZealand.htm

Homeschooling Federation of New Zealand
PO Box 41226
St. Lukes
Auckland
New Zealand
www.homeschooling.org.nz/

UK

Education Otherwise
PO Box 7420
London N9 9SG
Helpline: 0870 730 0074
www.education-otherwise.org/

This national charity offers local and national contact for home-educating families. The website provides access to legal, curriculum and other information.

Home Education Advisory Service
PO Box 98
Welwyn Garden City
Herts AL8 6AN
Tel: 01707 371854
Email: admin@heas.org.uk
www.heas.org.uk

USA

www.home-ed-press.com/HSRSC/hsrsc_lws.rgs.html

This site is a state-by-state look-up of legal information.

General information on curricula, unit studies, and lesson plans

www.thegateway.org/
http://homeschooling.about.com/education/homeschooling/

National Home Education Network (NHEN)
PO Box 41067
Long Beach, CA 90853
USA
Fax: (413) 581-1463
Email: info@nhen.org
www.nhen.org/

USEFUL BOOKS

Dowty, T. and Cowlishaw, K. (eds) (2002) *Home Educating Our Autistic Spectrum Children.* London: Jessica Kingsley Publishers. UK ISBN 1 84310 037 1.

Cohen, C. (2000) *And What About College?* Cambridge, MA: John Holt.

Cohen, C. (2000) *Homeschooling: The Teen Years.* Roseville, CA: Prima Publishing. ISBN 0761520937.

Cohen, C. (2000) *Homeschoolers' College Admissions Handbook.* Roseville, CA: Prima Publishing. ISBN 0761527540.

Job-coaching

CANADA

Mission Possible
Employment Services for People with Asperger Syndrome (private consulting firm)
1370 Danforth Ave.
Toronto
Ontario M4J 1M9
Tel: (416) 466-5498
Email: info@anythingispossible.ca
http://www.anythingispossible.ca/funding.html

USA

ARC, Vocational Services Division
603 Southlawn Lane
Rockville, MD 20850
USA
Tel: (301) 294-6840
www.arcmontmd.org/vocaopp.html

Vocational Rehabilitation
40 Fountain St.
Providence, RI 02903
Tel: 401-421-7005
1-800-752-8088 EXT. 2608
Fax: 401-421-7016
www.jan.wvu.edu/SBSES/VOCREHAB.HTM (state-by-state listing
of VR offices)

Colleges and distance education websites

http://distancelearn.about.com/library/blpages/blcollegedegrees.ht
m?PM=ss12_distancelearn

http://distancelearn.about.com/cs/bachelordegrees/index_2.htm

http://distancelearn.about.com/mbody.htm

GED information (US)

American Council on Education
General Education Development Testing Service
One Dupont Circle NW, Suite 250,
Washington, DC 20036-1163
USA
Tel: (202) 939-9490; (800) 626-9433
Fax: (202) 775-8578
www.acenet.edu/calec/ged/intro-TT.cfm (general info)
www.acenet.edu/calec/ged/disability-accom-TT.cfm (info for
disabled test takers)

Making a difference in your school district

McEwan, E.K. (1998) *Angry Parents, Failing Schools.* Wheaton, IL: Harold Shaw.
ISBN 0-87788-019-0.

12

Disclosure for People on the Autism Spectrum
Working Towards Better Mutual Understanding with Others

Stephen M. Shore

Introduction

Is disclosure more than just stating to another person 'I have autism' or 'I have Asperger Syndrome' and hoping that they will automatically make a needed adjustment or is there more to it? What are we actually looking for when we disclose something about ourselves with another person? What do we hope to gain? How can we make the world a better place for people on the autism spectrum and whom they interact with? When and how do we inform people of a need for accommodation in the workplace and in other situations? What makes autism more difficult to talk about than sitting in a wheelchair as a result of paraplegia? Here may be some answers, but more important, a glimpse at how to work with these important issues.

While this chapter is primarily aimed at adolescents with Asperger Syndrome, working through the issues laid out here with a trusted and knowledgeable adult may increase the utility of this work.

The 'What Does it Mean for Me' worksheets are intended to help the reader answer the questions of What, Why, When, How, and To Whom when considering disclosure of one's own position on the autism spectrum that are raised in this chapter. These worksheets can also be filled out on behalf of another person if the person filling out the worksheets feels this will help in organizing the thoughts of another considering the process of disclosure.

George: I, I, uh, um, I've got something that I've been wanting to tell you for a long time.

Ann: Yes? What do you want to say?

George: We've been going out for a long time now and...

Employee: Remember when I suddenly had to leave the room during that board meeting the other day and you found me sitting in the dark supply closet a few hours later?

Boss: I do. And for the life of me I can't figure out what got into your head.

Employee: Well...

Son: You know how when I was a little boy I used to do these strange things like screaming instead of talking, and spinning in circles?

Mother: Yes. Why did you do that? We spent thousands of dollars and years of psychotherapy and you are now 30 years later finally getting around to telling me what was going on with you?

I am only able to write about disclosure due to the willingness of many kind-hearted people who allowed me into their lives to gain a greater understanding of the process they went through in disclosing to others their placement on the autism spectrum. The personal experiences that I was privileged to contemplate and later discuss were obtained through interviews, phone conversations and communication via e-mail. The main source of other people's personal and other information was from the Conference on Disclosure hosted in Wellesley, Massachusetts by the Asperger Association of New England (AANE) in March 2000. Dr Daniel Rosenn, a psychiatrist who specializes in working with children and young adults on the high-functioning end of the autism spectrum, opened the conference with a presentation from the 'professional' point of view. This wonderful and educational conference continued with individual stories of disclosure followed by over a dozen small, intimate workshops for further in-depth discussions on particular aspects of disclosing one's position on the autism spectrum. Additional stories of disclosure were collected and published in a booklet that was distributed at the conference. (Additional copies are available from AANE at www.aane.org.)

What disclosure is

Disclosure for the purpose of this chapter means having to reveal information about oneself to another person. This information has the quality of being potentially discrediting to the revealer's reputation in the eyes of the person being told.

WHAT DOES IT MEAN FOR ME
Whom am I considering to tell that I am on the autism spectrum?
_____
_____
_____

Disclosure is much more than just stating to another person 'I have autism' or 'I have Asperger Syndrome' and hoping that they will automatically make an adjustment in the relationship with the person disclosing. Disclosure involves sharing with another person information that is potentially discrediting or stigmatizing to one's reputation. It is an interactive mode of communication with another person or persons with the goal of better mutual understanding. In order to effect this goal, the disorder being disclosed has to be explained as well as how it applies to the person on the autism spectrum. Each disclosure must be prepared for each particular situation. In the case of a person with a physical disability, say, one that requires a wheelchair, disclosure happens upon the initial meeting because it is clearly visible.

People with disabilities are often considered less capable and, according to Goffman (1963), have less of a chance to succeed than a person without the apparent disability in similar circumstances.

By taking a close look at this mode of exchanging sensitive information with others, I hope to arrive at a logical manner of explaining the reasons and procedure for disclosure. I myself am at the higher Asperger Syndrome to 'Autistic Cousin' end of the autistic spectrum. An 'autistic cousin' is a person who has enough autistic traits to affect daily life. Although these tendencies exist, they are neither strong nor numerous enough for the person to be considered on the autistic spectrum. (Autism Network International www.ani.ac/ ani-l-info.html). I would love to be able to present a tight algorithm of why and how to commence with the act of disclosure. However, since human emotions and interrelationships are involved, I know this is impossible. I will have to settle for a mere glimpse at the reasons and procedures. While the issue of disclosure is important to those with autism,it is also cogent to society at large.

> **Huh?**
>
> You and the other person will understand each other better.

The risks of disclosure

Everyone has grappled with having to tell someone something about themselves that has the potential to negatively affect their reputation. Balancing the risk of damaging a relationship with another person with the hope of reaching a greater interpersonal understanding is the dilemma that is part of every disclosure decision. What leads a person to take such a risk? A person may need to tell a prospective significant other about a run-in with the law, perhaps an abortion, or a person in the family has a disability 'that no one knows about.' Perhaps the desire for disclosure arises from a need to explain reasons behind difficulties in a school or employment situation. Two important variables that drive disclosure are a need to reveal something that may be damaging to one's identity in the eyes of another and a fear that letting another know this information will cause relational damage or stigma to be applied to that person by society.

Disclosing one's relationship with the autism spectrum is important when issues arising from this disorder affect one's relationship with another person, job performance, or academic success. The anxiety caused by disclosure will hopefully be outweighed by benefits of sharing one's humanity with another. Some of the challenges faced upon disclosure is that the information will be handled discreetly and that the person disclosing will still be seen as a human being and not a diagnosis or collection of issues. In brief, the goal of disclosure is to bring a better sense of understanding and trust with another person.

Persons at the high-functioning end of the autism spectrum are considered to have an invisible disability (Shore 2001). The invisible disability contrasts with visible disorders such as quadriplegia, blindness, deafness, mutism and physical deformities that are immediately apparent to another person.

WHAT DOES IT MEAN FOR ME
An effect of autism that has a significant impact on my relationship with this other person
_____
_____
_____

According to the work of Goffman (1963), those with invisible disabilities are not immediately discredited, but bear the burden of *becoming* discreditable. That is, persons with a discreditable disability often go about life keeping the disorder a secret while possibly revealing their disorder to a few select close others. Revealing an invisible disability to somebody else, particularly if the person has known them for a while, can often present greater difficulties than dealing with a visible disability that is 'up close and center' (Shore 2001, p.132).

The person on the higher end of the autism spectrum must often contend with being somewhere between the visible and invisible type of disability. Others may sense there is something different but they cannot quite figure out what it is. For example, after disclosing the reasons behind my unusually strong interest in autism to a colleague, she responded, 'I've had my eye on you and wondered what was going on.' This person had extensive experience in special education and so had an awareness of various disorders. Others, including my wife, 'noticed something' when we first met but could not determine what that 'something' was. Disclosure is usually best accomplished by the person with the disorder as they are the most aware of the issues. However, sometimes it is appropriate for another person who is knowledgeable about the situation to either do the groundwork for disclosure or do the disclosing itself. Reasons for having another person do the disclosure may be that the person with the disorder is for some reason unable to do it – perhaps the stress of disclosing would cause verbal abilities to be impaired or shut down (Shore 2001, p.132).

WHAT DOES IT MEAN FOR ME
What are the risks of telling this person?

Who to disclose to and management of information

Drawing on *Pretending to Be Normal: Living with Asperger's Syndrome* (Willey 1999), Dan Rosenn (2000), in the keynote address of the Disclosure conference, described three groups of people who can be disclosed to. The first group consists of people who need to know. These are people with whom the person has regular direct contact in such a way that interactions with them are affected by autism. As Robert Stuart writes about himself when he still lived at home: 'When it comes to family members, of course the parents should know along with siblings to offer support and understanding' (2000, p.7). Stuart was diagnosed with Asperger Syndrome at the age of 33 at the urging of his wife, who lovingly encouraged him to have his 'differences' (p.7) looked into. Others who need to know might include a supervisor, coworkers, and trusted close friends. However, disclosure, may be inappropriate if the information is irrelevant or will have a negative impact on the relationship.

Sometimes a negative impact on a relationship with another cannot be predicted so one has to take the chance. Philip Schwarz, in his mid-forties, only found out about his placement on the autism spectrum after seeing his son's diagnosis. While researching autism for his son and comparing his own childhood and current experiences, he suddenly realized that he too was on the autism spectrum. Schwarz disclosed to a coworker about his position on the autism spectrum because that person was looking for information about his own son's diagnosis of Asperger Syndrome. Schwarz's goals for disclosure at this point were twofold – a search for increased mutual understanding and wanting to help this coworker's son. Schwarz reports receiving an 'Oh' as a response from the coworker and to this day has regrets about his decision to disclose. The coworker 'tended to write me off as ineffectual more readily as a result' and the nature of the relationship grew distant. Fortunately, Phil reports that this was the sole negative effect out of several positive outcomes of disclosure which he's had in the workplace (Schwatz 2000).

Gerald Newport, an adult with Asperger Syndrome and staunch advocate for his peers, had a similar negative result when he disclosed about being on the autism spectrum. Knowing that his supervisor had a child with autism, Jerry felt secure in telling this person that he too was on the spectrum with the hopes of building a better mutual understanding. As Newport (2001) writes in an ironic tone, the supervisor sure knew all about autism and all the 'limitations' that go along with this condition. As a result, Jerry remained in a position way beneath his ability for the several years he was with this organization. Fed up with this now dead-end job, he left after ten years of employment for much more fulfilling work.

In contrast to the first group of people who have frequent contact, the second group of people to disclose to are those who *might* have direct contact with the individual on the autism spectrum on a frequent basis. This population includes family members who the person does not come in regular contact with along with friends, classmates, teachers and others that the person does not regularly relate to in a way whereby autism might create a problem.

The third group consists of people who do not need to know about the disorder. This might include the postman, neighbors, the cashier at the corner store, and acquaintances. Creating a hard and fast rule about whom to disclose to is practically impossible. More importantly, one must base decisions on how, when, and if to disclose by considering the effect disclosure will have on a relationship with another person or persons. Trying to determine the effect of disclosure on a relationship can be particularly challenging for someone with autism as difficulty in decoding data from social interactions is one of the leading traits of the disorder (Grandin 1995). Discussing potential disclosures with 'wise' people may help in determining when, how, and whom to disclose to. (Goffman 1963, p.29). Perhaps finding such a person would have helped in Schwarz's case. Schwarz felt that if it were possible to disclose more easily, it would make his life a lot easier.

WHAT DOES IT MEAN FOR ME
Circle the group this person falls into
1. Frequent, regular contact.
2. Varying frequency and regularity of contact.
3. Minimal non-significant contact.

Reasons for disclosure

The anxiety caused by disclosure will hopefully be outweighed by the benefits of sharing one's shortcomings with another person. Some of the challenges faced upon disclosure include being assured that the information will be handled discreetly and that the disclosing person will still be seen as a human being rather than a diagnosis or collection of issues. The goal of disclosure is to effect a change in the relationship with another person or persons to bring about a better sense of mutual understanding and trust.

WHAT DOES IT MEAN FOR ME

What change or changes are you looking for as a result of your disclosure effort?

_____

_____

_____

The effects of disclosure

Disclosure has a two-pronged effect. The first, and more obvious one, is the hoped for positive change in interpersonal relationships.

However, there is a more subtle, larger effect. That effect relates to the change in the societal construction of a person on the autism spectrum. Each individual disclosure works towards changing this societal construct one person at a time. This change in societal construction is evident over the long term. For example, during the 1950s and 1960s autism was considered to be of psychological origin, caused by a reflection by the child of rejection from the mother (Bettelheim 1967; Dolnick 1998). This belief was challenged in the mid-1960s and early 1970s by Bernard Rimland (1964) who set out to prove a biological basis to this disorder.

Autobiographies and accounts about people on the autism spectrum began to appear in the 1960s and 1970s (Kauffman 1993; Park 1967). These stories of disclosure began to move the societal construct of the person on the autism spectrum from the nonverbal, antisocial, self-abusive child flapping his hands in the corner to somebody who is capable of contributing to society. The 1990s brought an explosion of information about autism via the Internet and more autobiographies (Grandin 1995; Johnson and Crowder 1994; Sellin 1995; Williams 1992) by people on the autism spectrum. From 1935 to 1959 only three non-fiction books were written about autism. This increased to 24 for the 1960s, 78 for the 1970s, 129 for the 1980s and a phenomenal increase to 338 for the 1990s (Wobus 2000). This boom in nonfiction reading material on autism makes society more tolerant and appreciative of the contributions people with autism can make. This acceptance of autism in society in turn encourages more writing about this subject with a corresponding decrease in the stigma attached to the disorder.

The second effect of disclosure relates to society as a whole. Each disclosure about autism that results in deeper mutual understanding changes not only the disclosee's construct of the disorder, but potentially everyone else with whom the disclosee comes into contact. With luck, the disclosee can act as a sort of ambassador and relay this information to others. For the most part, disclosure is a one-to-one, personal event with the goal of better mutual understanding. Possibly the person who has been disclosed to can carry forward this information to others at appropriate times and in an appropriate manner. However, disclosure via articles, autobiographies, and presentations reach a wider audience more quickly. In short, disclosure defines for the public construct what autism is and how to have better mutual relationships with people having autism. The disclosure conference hosted by the Asperger's Association of New England in March 2000 was the first event ever devoted solely to the issues surrounding disclosure. More such 'mass' communications of this important issue will speed positive change in public constructs of the autism spectrum (Shore 2001, pp.124–125).

WHAT DOES IT MEAN FOR ME

What changes in society could happen as a result of your disclosure?

_____

_____

_____

The hallmark of a successful disclosure is a positive transformation in the relationship with another person and subsequently in society as a whole. More successful disclosures will enable the public to construct positive ways of relating to and working towards eliminating the stigma surrounding those on the autism spectrum and other disabilities.

> There is an insidious kind of disempowerment that results from defining the [autism] spectrum in such a way that if one is 'too

successful,' one cannot possibly be on it anymore, despite past history. What that does is siphon off those members of the population best able to articulate for the population as a whole, and best able to serve as role models for children in the population. And that produces a permanently disempowered population.

And perpetuates the negative image of that population in the society at large, and hence the negative self-image of the population itself.

And makes disclosure much much more of an issue than it should ever have to be. (Schwarz 2000, p.33)

WHAT DOES IT MEAN FOR ME

Aftermath: What Happened as a Result of your Disclosure?

The concern over being stigmatized still runs strong was evident upon my request for permission from 'Anonymous' to include his contribution to the Disclosure conference booklet in this book. 'Yes!' was his immediate response to the idea of including his work. The unbridled fear of the potential consequences of his employer finding out about his Asperger Syndrome diagnosis arrived immediately afterwards with the added statement: 'but please do not mention my name in your book. I am already in enough trouble at work as it is.' As mentioned in *Beyond the Wall: Personal Experiences with Autism and Asperger Syndrome* (Shore 2001), fear of stigmatization at my place of employment was also a major concern.

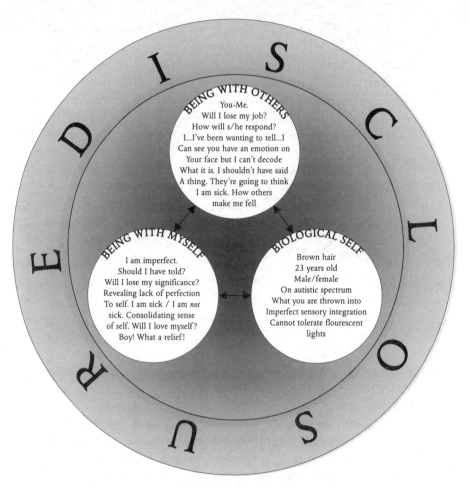

Figure 12.1 The three worlds of being as applicable to disclosure
Source: Shore (2001, p.119)

The three modes of being

The work of the existential psychologist Rollo May (1983) plays an important part in the disclosure process. As indicated in Figure 12.1, there are three simultaneous facets of human existence that come into play as one contemplates, goes through the act of, and reminisces about the disclosure event. The German words *Umwelt, Eigenwelt,* and *Mitwelt,* as used by Rollo May, may be roughly translated as 'biological self,' 'being with myself,' and 'being with others.'

Biological self

The biological self (*Umwelt*) refers to what each person is thrown into. This facet of existence 'includes biological needs, drives, instincts – the world one would still exist in if ... one had no self-consciousness' (May 1983, p.236). In other words it is 'the reality of the natural world' (p.126). For most people, this facet of being includes the color of their hair and eyes, gender, perceptual, cognitive and affective strengths and weaknesses. The person with autism will have additional components to this area. Some of them include sensory sensitivities and integration issues. The person on the autism spectrum may not be able to tolerate the humming and flickering of florescent lights in the classroom or the sound of the blender emanating from the kitchen of the restaurant they are in (Shore 2001).

> **Huh?**
>
> Who am I? Physically, cognitively, emotionally, and sensorially.

THE OUTER SENSES

Figure 12.2, the sensory star illustrates how I visualize the effect that sensory issues have on people with autism. The five senses of touch, taste, smell, sight, and hearing are known to occupational therapists as the *outer senses* and are located in the five points of the star. Just about every person I have met with autism has a variance from typicality in one or more if these outer senses. Some may be over-sensitive, whereas others are able take a lot of input before they register sensation. In addition, the information from one or more of these senses may be distorted.

1. *Sight.* A friend on the autism spectrum and I were in room with florescent lights. Upon my noticing that her eyes were vibrating at the frequency of those lights, she suddenly asked, 'Can we get out of here?' Not being a fan of this type of lighting myself, I immediately agreed. I asked her what she would have done if she had not been with me, but with a person who was unaware of the sensory issues of those on the autism spectrum. Would she have disclosed to them that she had autism and that this was the reason the lights affected her eyes, and thus she had to leave the room?

WHAT DOES IT MEAN FOR ME

What are my attributes or descriptions of myself?

Physically (What do I look like?)

Height? _____

Hair color? _____

Hair length? _____

Glasses? _____

Gender? _____

Likes and dislikes

What sense(s) do you like to learn which subjects with?

Sense	Topic
Ex: Sight	Geography
_____	_____
_____	_____
_____	_____
_____	_____
_____	_____
_____	_____

What is most annoying to my sense(s)?

Sense	Topic
Ex: Sight	Florescent lights
_____	_____
_____	_____
_____	_____
_____	_____

She stated that she would only have requested to leave with a possible explanation that she had sensitive eyes.

2.   *Touch*. Those of us who know people with autism may be familiar with the sensory 'violations' caused by haircuts. Haircuts and the shampoo that would occur afterwards hurt! My parents would explain that 'since hair is dead it has no feeling.' I knew that my hair had no feeling, but I just didn't have the verbal skills at that time to explain that it was the pulling of the hair on the scalp because of both the haircut and the following shampoo that was intolerable. For others with sensory sensitivities it may be the sounds of the electric haircutters or snipping of the scissors that cause sensory overload. For some children the sight of the scissors so close to the eyes can cause a problem.

3.   *Hearing*. A friend on the autism spectrum cringes and blocks her ears way before most people hear the siren of a fire engine coming down the street. Another friend actually feels pain at the sound of people clapping. For me, my wife has to place our wind-up travel alarm clock under the cushion of a chair to ensure domestic tranquility.

4.   *Taste*. Often we see people on the autism spectrum eating bland foods because of taste sensitivities as well as tactile ones. Others have a hypo-sensitive measure of taste and eat strongly flavored foods.

5.   *Smell*. I would not kiss my father for years, not only because his breath stank of coffee but also because his beard was painfully scratchy. Sometimes I have to leave an office or other location due to a perfume overload. Thankfully, my wife is perfume free. She was that way before I met her.

Most people are aware of these five senses of touch, hearing, taste, smell, and touch (see Figure 12.2). A theory mentioned by both Temple Grandin (1995) and John Ratey (2001) is that people on the autism spectrum are born with too many, yet immature nerve endings. This theory gives a possible explanation as to why most people with autism experience problems with sensory integration. Some or all of the five senses may be hypersensitive where as others may be hyposensitive. In addition, the data received from these senses may also be distorted. Some common examples of problems experienced in these five senses are listed in Table 12.1.

SENSORY VIOLATIONS

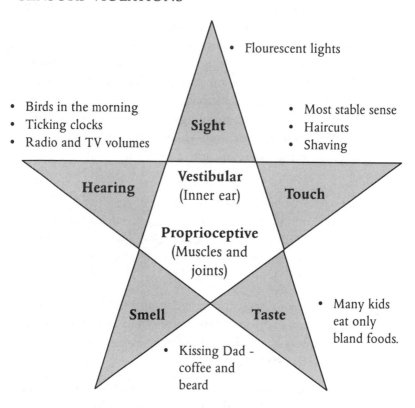

Figure 12.2 The sensory star
Source: Adapted from Shore (2003)

Table 12.1 Common Sensory Reactions of the Outer Senses			
Sense	*Possible Sensitivity*	*What it Feels Like*	*Common Reaction*
Sight	Florescent lights	The 60 Hz cycling of the lights is visible. Feels like sitting in a room with a strobe light.	Child may try to escape or have a tantrum.
Sound	Birds tweeting	Feels like birds' beaks scraping the eardrum (Shore 2001).	Child may cover his or her ears.
Taste	Avoidance of strong-tasting food	Tasting acid or other extremely strong-tasting food.	Child may spit food out.
Smell	Perfume	Feels like taking a deep breath from a Clorox bottle.	Sneezing, burning eyes, other allergic-like reactions. Child may try to escape.
Touch	Light touch	May feel like touching an open wound or getting an electric shock. May be overalerting.	Sensory defensiveness, brushing away light touch, jumping excessively at unexpected touch, seeks deep pressure.

Source: Shore (2003)

THE INNER SENSES

The *vestibular* and *proprioceptive* senses are often referred to as the hidden or inner senses (see Figure 12.1). The vestibular sense 'helps with movement, posture, vision, balance, and coordination of both sides of the body' (Myles *et al.* 2000, p.28). Proprioception informs a person as to where their body parts are in space and the appropriate amount of force needed to perform an activity such as picking up a glass of milk. As with the more commonly known outer senses, hyper- and hypo-sensitivities as well as distortions of these two inner senses cause challenges for those on the autism spectrum (Table 12.2).

Table 12.2 Common Sensory Reactions of the Inner Senses			
Sense	*Possible Sensitivity*	*What it Feels Like*	*Common Reaction*
Vestibular	'Low tolerance for activities involving movement' (Myles *et al.* 2000, p.29).	How most people would feel spinning around at high speed. Dizziness or lightheaded feeling.	Avoidance of any movement involving sharp changes in direction or the feet leaving the ground. Clumsy at team-oriented sports.
	Seeks vestibular stimulation.	Losing oneself in space: loss of coordination.	Attracted to roller coasters and similar amusement park rides.
Proprioceptive	Clumsy movements. Acts like a 'bull in a china shop.'	Having a body made of molasses. Movement is tiring.	Child often appears fatigued. Difficulty in modulating muscular force in everyday activities.

Source: Shore (2003)

Being with myself

Being with myself presupposes self-awareness, self-relatedness, and is uniquely present in human beings. But it is not merely a subjective, inner experience; it is rather the basis on which we see the real world in its true perspective, the basis on which we relate. It is a grasping of what something in the world – this bouquet of flowers, this person – means to me. (May 1983, p.128)

The 'being with myself' (*Eigenwelt*) facet of existence revolves around a person's awareness of self. The person has to deal with the fact that, indeed, they are imperfect as compared to what society might be considered 'normal,' and they are going to have to share that with another human being. This grappling with ideas of imperfection or differences can be enlightening for the person about to make their disclosure. While the primary goal for disclosure is usually to reach better mutual understanding with others, a better understanding of self also often occurs: 'Then I finally knew why some kids were mean to me ... I was going to get the help I needed to get better grades in school and get along in life,' wrote grade school age Ben Sawyer (2000, p.13). There may be questions about a loss of significance in the eyes of others. Essentially, when disclosure is concerned, it is a consolidation of self before sharing this self with the outside world. For Sawyer, this consolidation of self was a positive experience as he now had the necessary information to help himself!

> **Huh?**
>
> What are my strong and weak points?

Some people, after coming to terms with their own placement on the autism spectrum, develop a desire to use their experiences to help others with autism, for example Angie Guevara (2000). After one's own imperfection with another, the internal dialogue continues. 'Boy! What a relief! Why was I so apprehensive about revealing to my boss why I cannot have meetings in the boardroom with the florescent light?' Perhaps the person told will now wish they had said or not said some specific things.

Denial is another common reaction to both the facets of 'being with myself' and 'being with others.' Perhaps the person with autism is not aware enough of others in their environment to notice a difference. 'Nothing was ever his fault,' reports the mother of an adolescent with autism (Holzman 2000). Adolescence can be particularly challenging due to the difficulties of teasing out issues that are related to autism as opposed to those that arise out of this usually stormy time period of life. The adolescent just mentioned is now in his thirties and his difficulties from being on the autism spectrum have presented several educational, social, and employment challenges.

Successful efforts in the 'being with myself' facet are dependent on becoming aware of one's own awareness and striving to be driven by conscious choices rather than unconscious ones (Dewey 1944). Although I have not covered this here, a couple of other interesting areas pertaining to the study of disclosure include easing the way for people to recognize their own placement on the autism spectrum and getting points of view from people who were disclosed to.

Being with others

Being with others (*Mitwelt* or 'with-world') 'is the world of interrelationships with human beings' (May 1983, p.127). This term is more than the mere influence of others on an individual. It has to do with the 'meaning of others in the group [which is] partly determined by one's own relationship to them' (p.127). There is more than mere adjusting and adapting in the biological sense of the *Umwelt* or 'world around one' facet of existence. The word 'relationship' is a more apt description of the 'with-world.' In a relationship there is mutual awareness (May 1983, p.128). During an encounter with another human, both persons change as a result:

> 'Being with others' with mutual awareness can be the most difficult part of disclosure for the person on the autism spectrum. A lot of communication between people involves nonverbal communication such as eye contact, facial expressions and body language. (Shore 2001, 120–121)

Difficulties in nonverbal communication is one of the traits of the autism spectrum disorder (APA 2000). As a result, the person with autism may not be able to detect the very changes in a relationship they are trying to affect through disclosure unless the other person verbalizes in clear terms that the communication has been effective.

Three steps of disclosure as related to the three worlds of being

There are three major stages to the procedure of disclosure (Figures 12.3 and 12.4).

Step one

In the first stage, questions arise about the need to reveal potentially damaging information about the self. If the traits of a person on the autism spectrum do not interfere with the relationship with a person or persons, there is generally no need for disclosure. For example, nobody needs to be made aware of the fact that I am very poor at facial recognition unless it becomes a problem in a particular situation. Even when difficulties in recognizing people occur, it may be more appropriate to address the specific weakness rather than going into detail about the source of the problem. Another example might be a person who cannot tolerate florescent lighting due to sensory sensitivities. If, as a condition of employment, the person needs to come into contact with these lighting fixtures on a regular basis, then disclosure may be necessary. A decision should be made whether to disclose only the information that is needed – sensory sensitivity creating intolerance to florescent lighting – or whether also to disclose the *cause* of the intolerance. Disclosure is often best done on a need-to-know basis (Rosenn 2000). Robert Stuart, a person with autism, discloses 'only when [he] see[s] it becoming a problem' (2000, p.8). Referring to Figure 12.1, most of the interaction in the predisclosure stage is between the 'biological self' and 'being with myself' circles.

Other questions pertaining to the 'being with myself' facet of existence include dealing with imperfections in the self. Questions such as whether over-sensitivity to touch is really a problem of too many, yet immature nerve endings, or if there is a deep psychological reason stemming from childhood that lies beneath this problem may bounce around in one's head. Questions of imperfection haunted me as I wondered if I was just too stupid to analyze music of the Romantic era as I had seen so many of my classmates, including my wife, do. Would I lose significance in the eyes of my music advisor upon summoning up the courage to reveal the difficulties of analyzing relatively unstructured music caused by my relationship with the autism spectrum. When the decision is made to go through with the disclosure, it is time to move to step two.

Step two

Step two, the act of revealing the information to another with the intent of greater mutual understanding, is often the most difficult part to initiate. Through deep thought and introspection you revealed to yourself a weakness that you would rather not admit to – and now you are about to do the same to another person. The time and place for the revelation has been carefully chosen. Whereas up to now most of the activity has been between the 'being with myself' and 'being with others' circles, the difficult facet of 'being with others' now plays an important role. You wonder how the other person is going to react to you *and* how you will react to the other person and/or their reactions. Will you be able to go along with the carefully thought out script of possible reactions by you, the other person's reactions, and your reactions to those reactions? Or will something totally unexpected happen? And if so, how will you deal with it? Questions of one's significance to oneself and others and whether you will be able to accept the other person's newly defined sense of what your own self should be swirl about. Getting a reading on the other person's reactions is made even more difficult for people on the autism spectrum due to the challenges of decoding nonverbal communication and emotions. Perhaps there will be a sense of betrayal in the disclosee as new information is revealed. The disclosee may feel that the person disclosing did not trust them with the information until this time.

When I disclosed to my music advisor about my early childhood diagnosis of 'strong autistic tendencies,' I also told him, 'Although I can see you have an emotion on your face, I cannot read what it is.' That statement helped my advisor because it gave him an immediate real-life example of some of the challenges I confront on a regular basis. My advisor was very supportive and incredulous at my early diagnosis as being on the autism spectrum. I was genuinely surprised when he boomed out, 'I never would have known unless you had told me.' It seemed like a blatant statement of the obvious. You hope that the relationship with the other person has changed for the better as a result of this event. Time for step three.

Step three

Step three is the aftermath of the disclosure. There may be a great sense of relief. Or perhaps a sense that there was something you could have said to make the meeting with the other person easier, or something you should not have said. While some changes in the relationship with the other person may be apparent during the disclosure, other changes may occur either as a result of additional thought by the disclosee or as the information travels to others. Even though I sensed a positive change in my relationship with my advisor upon disclosing to him, I felt negativity from the chair of music theory. This reaction may have resulted from her receiving information about my disability from another source (Disabilities Office) before hearing it from me. Maybe she felt betrayed and thought I did not trust her with this information before revealing it to others.

The Three Worlds Of Being as Related to the Three Phases of Disclosure		
Rollo May's Three Worlds of Being		
Biological self	*With myself*	*With others*
What you are thrown into On the autism spectrum Imperfect sensory integration	Consolidating sense of self Will I lose my significance? Boy! What a relief	You–me How will she respond? I…I've been wanting o tell you How others make me feel

Figure 12.3

My application of these three steps

I go through a three-step process of unfolding my relationship to the autism spectrum when I discuss the content of my book, *Beyond the Wall: Personal Experiences with Autism and Asperger Syndrome*, with others. For example, one day my wife and I were at a party given by a professor I

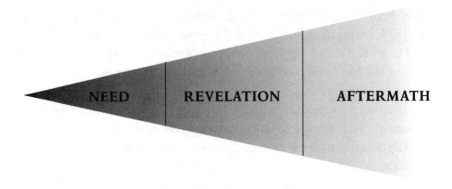

Figure 12.4 The three phases of disclosure

had for a class a few semesters previously. He graciously introduced me to other members of the gathering as 'a student of his at Boston University' and that 'I had recently written a book on autism.' A couple walked towards me and asked me what my book was about. When I don't know about another person's background, I usually say, 'It's about autism.' I quote the main part of the title, *Beyond the Wall,* and most of the time, people are satisfied with that and either change the subject or talk with another person. That is the first level of disclosure about my book. I have indicated an interest in this subject that was strong enough to write an entire book on it. Since these people could be classified as the third group – infrequent and/or insignificant contact – there is really no reason to go any further about my relationship to the autism spectrum.

In this particular case, the couple expressed further interest. At this point I indicated some of the areas of the book covering ideas for working with children on the autism spectrum and disclosure, as well as adult issues of relationships, employment, and education. Sometimes I will say that the book covers what it is like to be on the autism spectrum or even state: '*Beyond the Wall* is a text-based virtual reality tour of the autism spectrum.' Occasionally a person will understand the humor in that statement – since virtual reality is anything but text based. As I was in the midst of the second step of giving the full description of my book, my wife pointed to me and blurted out, 'He, he, he is autistic!' The couple were very surprised and I launched into the full description and disclosure of my placement on the autism spectrum. It turned out to be fine as the couple had a close friend with a child on the spectrum and were very interested in the subject.

Unless similar circumstances occur, I will wait until I ascertain that a person has a close connection or is 'wise' (Goffman 1963) before revealing my association with the autism spectrum.

It is interesting, and I consider fortunate, that my wife actually made that statement. Previously, she was very fearful of letting anyone know I was on the autism spectrum. She literally thought that people whose children I worked with and talked to at conferences would line up at the college president's door, causing me to lose my job. While this may seem paranoid, my wife did live through the Cultural Revolution in the People's Republic of China. During this time a person would indeed lose their job if they were connected to such a disability.

The Asperger Association of New England has developed a letter of disclosure that might be helpful in declaring one's position on the autism spectrum (Figure 12.5).

Conclusion and implications for the future

The act of disclosure merits serious thought for the following reasons. First, it involves revealing to oneself a lack of perfection followed by revealing it others. Sufficient psychic resources and self-esteem are needed to prevent a sense of inadequacy in the emotional, moral and possibly other domains. Once past the barrier of self-disclosure, the challenge is to impart this potentially discrediting information to others with the hope of better mutual understanding, trust, and minimal damage to one's reputation.

The study of how disclosure may be best accomplished for those on the autism spectrum has just begun. This research is merely the seed from which can grow further work on how to inform others of the needs people on the autism spectrum, along with developing a better mutual understanding, and deeper, richer, and more meaningful relationships with others.

References

American Psychiatric Association (APA) (2000) *Diagnostic and Statistical Manual of Mental Disorders of the American Psychiatric Association*, 4th edn, text revised. Washington, DC: American Psychiatric Association.

Autism Network International. *ANI-L Principles and Policies.* www.students.uiuc.edu/~bordner/ani/ani-l-info.html.

Bettelheim, B. (1967) *Empty Fortress: Infantile Autism and the Birth of the Self.* New York: Free Press.

Cottle, T. (2000) 'The beginning, end, and in between of adolescence.' Unpublished paper.

Dewey, J. ([1916], 1944) *Democracy and Education: An Introduction to the Philosophy of Education.* New York: Free Press.

Dolnick, E. (1998) *Madness on the Couch: Blaming the Victim in the Heyday of Psychoanalysis.* New York: Simon & Schuster.

Goffman, E. (1963) *Stigma: Notes on the Management of Spoiled Identity.* New York: Simon & Schuster.

Grandin, T. (1995) *Thinking in Pictures: And Other Reports from my Life with Autism.* New York: Doubleday.

Guevara, A. (2000) 'A pagan shape-shifter's lifeway.' In J. Goodman, D. Jekel and P. Schwarz (eds) *Disclosure and Asperger's Syndrome: Our Own Stories.* Newton, MA: Asperger's Association of New England, pp.16–17.

Holzman. A. (2000) 'My son's denial.' In J. Goodman, D. Jekel and P. Schwarz (eds) *Disclosure and Asperger's Syndrome: Our Own Stories.* Newton, MA: Asperger's Association of New England, pp.22–25.

Johnson, C. and Crowder, J. (1994) *Autism: From Tragedy to Triumph.* Wellesley, MA: Branden.

Kauffman, J. M. (1993) *Characteristics of Emotional and Behavioural Disorders of Children and Youth*, 5th edn. New York: Macmillan.

May, R. (1983) *The Discovery of Being: Writings in Existential Psychology.* New York: Norton.

Newport, G. (2001) *Your Life is not a Label: A Guide to Living Fully with Autism and Asperger's Syndrome.* Arlington, TX: Future Horizons.

Park, C. (1967) *The Siege.* New York: Little & Brown.

Ratey, J. (2001) *A User's Guide to the Brain: Perception, Attention, and the Four Theaters of the Brain.* New York: Pantheon.

Rimland, B. (1964) *Infantile Autism: The Syndrome and its Implications for a Neural Theory of Behaviour.* New York: Appleton-Century-Crofts.

Rosenn, D. (2000) 'Lecture on disclosure.' Disclosure Conference, Wellesley, MA.

Sawyer, B. (2000) 'One day in my life.' In J. Goodman, D. Jekel and P. Schwarz (eds) *Disclosure and Asperger's Syndrome: Our Own Stories.* Newton, MA: Asperger's Association of New England, p.14.

Schwarz, P. (2000) 'Personal account of being an undiagnosed university student – highlighting when disclosure might or might not have been helpful.' In J. Goodman, D. Jekel and P. Schwarz (eds) *Disclosure and Asperger's Syndrome: Our Own Stories.* Newton, MA: Asperger's Association of New England, pp.32–37.

Sellin, B. (1995) *Messages from an Autistic Mind: I Don't Want to be Inside Me Anymore.* New York: Harper Collins.

Shore, S. (2001) *Beyond the Wall: Personal Experiences with Autism and Asperger Syndrome.* Shawnee Mission: Autism Asperger Publishing Company.

Shore, S. (2003) *Beyond the Wall: Personal Experiences with Autism and Asperger Syndrome.* 2nd Ed. Shawnee Mission, KS: Autism Asperger Publishing Company.

Smith-Myles, B. Cook, K., Miller, N., Rinner, L. And Robbins, L. (2000) *Asperger Syndrome and Sensory Issues: Practical Solutions for Making Sense of the World.* Shawnee Mission: Autism Asperger Publishing Company.

Stuart, R. (2000) 'Disclosure: the big mystery.' In J. Goodman, D. Jekel and P. Schwarz (eds) *Disclosure and Asperger's Syndrome: Our Own Stories.* Newton, MA: Asperger's Association of New England, pp.8–9.

Williams, D. (1992) *Nobody Nowhere: The Extraordinary Autobiography of an Autistic.* New York: Times Books.

Willey, L. (1999) *Pretending to be Normal: Living with Asperger's Syndrome.* London: Jessica Kingsley Publishers.

Wobus, J. (2000, May 12) *Autism Resources.* www.vaporia.com/autism/nonfictionyears/index.html.

Employee disclosure letter

Dear Employer,

Your giving me the opportunity to work [as _____ at _____ company] is very much appreciated. I intend to do everything possible to succeed in this job. As you know, I have Asperger's Syndrome (AS) which is a neurological disorder. Even though I look like others, my mind works differently. Perhaps explaining some of my differences along with some of the things that can be done to assist me will be beneficial for both of us.

First, let me say that my disability means two main things:

- It is difficult for me to read non-verbal signals. Whereas most people can receive significant information through body language, facial expressions, gestures, etc. I cannot. I can determine when a person's face is expressing some kind of emotion but decoding what that emotion is presents a significant challenge to me.

- I have difficulty with the concept of "walking around in someone else's shoes" (putting myself in someone else's place).

Although these may seem like minor disabilities, they present a great challenge for me. As a result, I may do some of the following:

- Say things that are unintentionally hurtful or abrupt.

- Appear as if I am not paying attention when someone is speaking to me (as it is hard for me to make and maintain eye contact).

- Become easily frustrated if interrupted.

These are suggestions that will help me:

- Let me know as soon as possible if I have offended someone so that misunderstandings do not develop and grow.

- Understand that I am listening even though I may not be looking at you (remember, I cannot interpret non-verbal forms of communication. This is often the most difficult aspect of AS for people to understand, since this is something that most others do intuitively).

- Please do not interrupt me in mid-work, as it confuses and upsets me. (If an interruption is unavoidable, please allow me a few seconds to adjust and do not think I am being rude if I get momentarily upset).

- The more structure I have to my day, the better I will function. A written schedule with a timetable would allow me to concentrate more fully on my work (much like a school schedule, perhaps).

- Provide specific, detailed instructions of what I should do.

Having AS makes it difficult for me to socialize. As mentioned above, I may say or do the wrong thing at the wrong time, since I cannot understand all the subtleties of communication. Therefore, socializing is stressful for me, as I have to intellectualize subtleties that most people intuit. I may respond to this stress by sitting alone for a while. This does not mean that I do not like or appreciate fellow workers. Please continue to include me in the goings on of the workplace.

Asperger's Association of New England

1301 Centre Street, Newton, MA 02459

617-527-2894 info@aane.org www.aane.org

Figure 12.5

13

How Do I Be Me?

Mike Stanton

Patricia Howlin (1997) has written an excellent book, *Autism – Preparing for Adulthood*, which thoroughly deserved its prize as winner of the 1997 NASEN Book of the Year Award. It contains practical advice on a range of subjects:

- problems arising from the triad of impairments
- education
- employment
- psychiatric problems
- legal issues
- sex
- independent living.

Like most books on autism it is written for parents and professionals. It is sympathetic to the needs of autistic people and the difficulties and obstacles they have to face in their daily lives. Its emphasis on integration and normalization is much better than the social exclusion and institutional care that used to be the only option for many people with autistic spectrum disorders. It answers most of the questions that parents and professionals might like to put to an expert on autism.

However, the book does not answer what is for me the most important question of all, the question a young man with autism asked of his mother: 'How do I be Corey?' Corey's mom shared this question on an email list. They both gave me permission to share it with you. I do not know the answer for Corey or for anyone else, but I want to use this chapter to explore ways of helping Asperger Syndrome (AS) teens to find the answer for themselves.

Adolescence marks the transition from childhood to adulthood. In many cultures there is a definite ritual that marks the end of childhood and the beginning of adult life. It may involve tests of physical or mental endurance. Some ceremonies involve pain. They may have a religious significance. But in all these cultures the purpose is clear. The ritual marks a turning point in your life. Once initiated you are ready to learn the duties as well as the benefits of adulthood. In effect you become an apprentice grown-up.

I think that this sort of society would be amenable to young people on the autistic spectrum. As a child there is very clear information about what is expected of you. If you are unable to meet those expectations, society is typically forgiving and there is usually somebody on hand to happily instruct and show the way. When those childhood expectations are about to change to more sophisticated and adult-like expectations, the occasion is clearly marked. You are prepared for it in advance and a new set of expectations follow on from that.

In areas such as Europe, North America and the rest of the 'developed world' the old ways no longer hold sway. During the teenage years you no longer follow a clearly defined path mapped out by your elders. In fact the opposite is often the case. Teenagers, a word that did not even appear in dictionaries until 1961, are marked out by their conscious rejection of the values and standards of their elders. Their role models are no longer adult heroes and heroines but other teenagers: sports stars, pop idols, fashion models, TV presenters and minor celebrities who are only famous for being famous.

Instead of a clearly defined transition, teenagers face a long period of limbo. Adolescence is now a self-contained period in which you look to your peers and within yourself for guidance while resisting the advice of us boring old farts, the 'grown-ups'. This may be manageable for most teenagers but I can see how it creates real problems for those who are autistic. Put yourself in the place of a young person with AS:

1.   You have always looked to adults for guidance and may feel more comfortable with adults than in the company of other children. But now this marks you out as a 'geek' or 'nerd'.

2.   The adults you have relied on are changing. They are no
      longer satisfied with your well-practised responses. And
      they are no longer as willing or prepared to provide advice
      on society's expectations. They want you to 'grow up' and
      'act your age' but they never tell you how.

3.   Over the years you have worked out the rules of childhood.
      Now your peers are changing in ways you do not
      understand. You are missing the subtle indications of altered
      social rules and conventions. No one has told you what the
      new rules are, but you are punished by teasing and bullying
      if your inadvertently break these secret rules that everybody
      else seems to know about.

4.   Worst of all, you are changing as well. The physical changes
      are bad enough. But then you become aware of the
      differences in attitude between yourself and other children,
      differences that place you at a conscious disadvantage for
      the first time in your life.

The way out for many teenagers is to try and be somebody else. I know
how much effort my autistic son, Mattie, has put into 'pretending to be
normal'. But it placed him under a tremendous strain. Like Corey, what
he really needs to know is, 'How to be me'. At 17 he is beginning to
discover the answer, but this is only since he left school. He used to get
conflicting messages from his peers. Some were genuinely trying to help
him, but he always had to be wary of those who were trying to wind him
up and provoke a meltdown or setting him up for some ritual humiliation. Meanwhile an equally insistent teaching staff placed unrealistic
demands upon him to ignore peer group pressure and concentrate on his
studies.

Mattie is not the only one. I well recall reading on the Internet one
girl's account of how she deliberately adopted different roles. First she
copied the good girls and tried to be a model student. Then she got in
with a wild crowd and started breaking all the rules. Neither model
matched her true identity. Discovering her autism was the first step on
the road to self-discovery.

The pressure is always there to conform. But what if you cannot
conform because you are autistic and nobody has explained how to
conform? So you join the non-conformists, the hippies or the outlaws.

You conceal your autism by adhering to a group of outsiders. This behaviour seems to suggest you made a choice when, in reality, there was no choice at all. If you were a person with AS you would find it difficult to work out what other people expect of you. That is why people with AS often join the most tolerant, the least demanding and the most unthreatening teenage sub-culture they can find. Gunilla Gerland (1997) refers to a period in her life when she was involved with a dope-smoking crowd who were accepting of her peculiarities because they just assumed that she was as stoned as they were.

Some may join a teenage sub-culture with rigid rules that are clearly stated and expected; in other words, groups that lay the rules out there for others to learn and live by such as the army cadet force, college fraternity, boy scouts, cheerleaders, etc. Either choice, is really no choice at all.

A third way is to ignore peer group pressure because no matter how hard you try to conform, you always stumble and suffer ridicule and rejection. Instead you try to bypass adolescence and pass straightaway into the adult world. You will take your lead from adults and be what they want you to be. While this might provide some meaningful experiences, it is far more likely to encourage a lifetime of pretending and therefore a lifetime of unhappiness. Besides, no one can leap straight from childhood into maturity. Adulthood results from the successful negotiation of the trials and tribulations of adolescence. It is not possible to avoid these difficulties and emerge miraculously 'grown-up' on the other side.

Whichever path you choose, you are responding to the biological imperative – 'How do I survive?' – rather than to Corey's question of personal identity, worth and purpose. So, given the impossible demands placed on them by peers, parents and teachers, how do we answer Corey's question? How can we help autistic teenagers to discover who they are?

We can talk to them, explaining as best we can what society's general expectations are. We can tell them what neurotypicals (NTs) think they need, but most importantly, we can tell them they have a right to set their own expectations and the right to satisfy their own needs. When we close our eyes at night, we have to hope we all learn to meet somewhere in the middle.

You are autistic

First and foremost these young people have a right to know that they are autistic. This is not just about knowing why they struggle in matters that *seem* so effortless to their peers. They also need to know that the rest of us struggle in some areas that *they* take for granted. '*They*' is the key word here. Probably the greatest boost to my son's self-esteem came when he visited an autistic couple and was able to be himself and accepted for who he was. Spending time with other teenagers with AS has also helped Mattie tremendously. He has discovered a shared culture. He has also learned that other people with AS are unique individuals like himself.

Clare Sainsbury (2000) makes a similar point in her account of school life. Integration and inclusion are all very well and many young people with AS thrive in a mainstream setting, but there is always the feeling of being special. Spending time with other autistic people gives you the chance to be ordinary. My friend Kalen recently held a successful birthday barbecue. It helped that all the guests were trusted friends who understood her autism and many of them were also on the autistic spectrum. She described to me how it was all so 'normal' that she felt as if she was at someone else's house!

You are unique...

It is hard to learn that we are *all* individuals. The teenager with AS has one set of rules taken away with the onset of adolescence and responds by trying to develop and apply a new set of rules to human behaviour. Mattie used to think that everybody was like him. When he realized that he was different he thought that he was unique but the rest of us were all still the same as each other. We were just totally unlike him.

Mattie's contact with others with AS has taught him that all autistics have a unique profile of strengths and weaknesses. He is beginning to learn and accept that the NT people he knows are also unique. But the idea that the whole world is made up of individuals is scary. How are you supposed to know how to react with strangers? Best to ignore them and hope they ignore you.

…and so is everyone else

A young person with AS may believe that only he is unique and that other teenagers adopt similar dress codes, attitudes and tastes in popular culture because they are all the same. But one important motivation for this is to hide their individuality. Skinheads are a teenage sub-culture in the UK who favour cropped hair and heavy boots and have a reputation for racism, homophobia and violence. Yet I knew one skinhead who was homosexual and went to gay bars and another who visited Afro-Caribbean clubs because he liked black music and grew prize-winning flowers in his spare time!

These lads were pretending to be normal in the context of the inner city environment where they had to live, while pursuing their own dreams in private. They were NT. I cannot imagine a lad with autism maintaining such a double life. The nearest Mattie has come to learning this skill is to pretend to like football because that is what lads do on the streets where we live.

You have the right to happiness

Another aspect is believing that you are the only one with problems. Mattie was genuinely surprised when I told him that other people lead stressful lives as well. He was amazed to learn that I had problems too. If you believe that you are the only one with problems and everyone else is happy, it could make you quite resentful. Mattie, with typical stoicism, just accepted that his life was supposed to be miserable.

An important lesson for him was that he has the right to be happy. When he misreads the social cues, Mattie can be quite stunningly insensitive to other people's feelings. But the idea of the selfish autist locked in his private world is totally misleading. Mattie and people like him put immense effort into accommodating other people and putting themselves out on our behalf.

The best advice that Mattie got was from Dave, a clinical psychologist, who asked him to think about what *he* wanted. Prior to this Mattie had always been encouraged to meet other people's demands and expectations. Dave was the first person to give Mattie permission to put his desires before our expectations.

You have the right to privacy

My skinhead acquaintances represent extreme examples of a common phenomenon. Teenagers conform because they have to. It is the price of social inclusion. This does not mean surrendering your personal identity. My teen daughter, Katie, has a private life away from her peer group. She does not share everything with them. Some things she only tells her best friend. Others she only shares with her diary. There are even a few aspects of her life that she shares with her parents!

And so has everyone else!

Katie has to be very careful about what she shares with her older brother. He has Asperger Syndrome and has not yet learned when to keep quiet in front of his parents! Sometimes we have to remind him to be quiet and not share too much with us.

Honest to a fault

People with AS are often confused by this. It is not dishonest to fail to tell the whole truth all the time. When you meet someone new and they ask you where you are from, you probably tell them the town or the district. You would be foolish to tell a complete stranger your full address. Keeping things private is not the same as being ashamed of them. Certain things about your life are private for your own security. This obviously applies to personal details like PIN numbers and passwords for your bank account. It is less obvious when you are expected to observe different levels of disclosure with different social circles.

One reason for keeping quiet is that other people may misunderstand your intentions. I recently heard from the parents of a young man who, in common with many autistic people, has sensory sensitivities that make him very selective in his choice of clothes. In particular he does not like wearing trousers but will tolerate them in order to leave the house. But he does not understand that other people do not share his sensitivity so he does not explain it to them. Instead he sees nothing wrong in telling other people that he cannot wait to go home and get his trousers off. Then he asks them if they want to take their trousers off as well!

Lonely or alone?

Neurotypical folk sometimes struggle to comprehend the difference. They imagine the life of an autistic person from their own perspective as being unutterably lonely. They try to help AS teens get into the swing of things – discos, rock concerts, the dating game. This may be OK for some AS teens for some of the time, but they may not be able to keep up with the relentless pace of their NT friends' social life.

Once a week Mattie likes to have friends round in the evening. They talk, listen to his music collection, play computer games and surf the internet. We go out for the evening and leave them to it. At first we used to stay out as late as possible, but Mattie prefers us to come home at a fixed time. He likes to have friends in the house. He also likes to know when they will be going and our return is a signal for this. At first we used to worry in case they were merely tolerating Mattie and using our home as a youth club. But we were pleased that a core group of friends call round for him and include him in their activities outside our home.

Given that those with AS do struggle to cope with the social world, it seems a very good idea to me to help them discover and delight in the private world of their dreams and special interests. People are afraid to indulge someone's autism in case they encourage them to retreat completely into their private world. But if the world is so harsh that the alternatives are to retreat or to be broken, then retreating seems eminently sensible to me. I think that respecting the AS right to privacy, to an inner life that is hidden from the rest of us, strengthens people with AS and increases the social bond they have for people who show them such respect. This can make it easier for them to engage with the world.

I know this goes against the old wisdom that you have to constantly battle to drag autistic people out of their introspection and into the 'real world'. But it is old and outdated wisdom. You have to work with them, not against them. That means working with the whole person and respecting their right to be autistic.

Following your interests does not have to isolate you. There was a time during Mattie's early teens when he was isolated, not by his autism but by the behaviour of a gang of bullies who made it their business to torment him. At the time he was interested in railway modelling and I used to take him to a model railway club every week. There he found friends of all ages who were happy to answer all his questions and talk to him about their shared interest. He helped out at exhibitions and was delighted to discover that there was at least one part of the human race outside his immediate family where he found acceptance.

Conclusion

Peter Vermeulen (2000) has put together an excellent resource for professionals working with young people to explain their autism in a realistic but positive manner. Gunilla Gerland (2000) has written a very straightforward account that my son says would help any pre-teen with AS. There is an ever-growing number of autobiographical accounts that the person with AS can turn to for self-affirmation. Then there is the internet with all its web sites, email lists, news groups and chat rooms that offer support from AS peers. Information and communication technology has made such a difference to the lives of so many with AS that it justifies my friend Kalen's description of the computer as 'a wheelchair for autistics'.

But if Mattie and Corey and the rest of the teenagers out there are going to discover who they really are, there is no substitute for personal relationships. An important part of who we are is the contribution we make to the lives of others and the feedback we get from them. We all want to feel loved, wanted, needed and appreciated. This aspect of social interaction may be difficult for those with AS but it is not impossible.

Most of the time people with AS rely on logic and hard work to understand NTs and cope with our behaviour. Brain imaging techniques that are used during exercises to test responses to human faces show that those with AS differ from NTs in that they use a part of the brain typically used for recognizing inanimate objects, the Inferior Temporal Gyrus. In the rest of us NTs, it is the Fusiform Gyrus that is activated during these tests (Cowley 2000). But the most recent research by Karen Pierce of the University of California has found that the Fusiform Gyrus is activated in autistic subjects when shown pictures of their parents. (Nash 2002)

This suggests to me that (contrary to the popular belief that autistic aloofness arises from the fact that their brains are differently wired) positive emotional experiences may help to shape brain function. People with AS have brains that can work in exactly the same way as their NT counterparts. The fact that they do not respond to everybody in the same way just goes to show that their brains are just far more discriminating in the range of stimuli and experience that shapes their response. As ever with autism, the actual mechanisms are far more subtle than we first imagined.

It is exciting to think that by helping them to develop close relationships with a relatively small circle of family and friends, we can assist Mattie and Corey and the people with AS in all our lives to develop and discover their personalities and answer that question, 'How do I be me?'

How important friendship can be is shown by this letter from a young man on the spectrum to his NT friend. I find the level of self-knowledge and the degree of sensitivity he shows for his friend's feelings both marvellous and humbling. It is a brave letter and I thank Joel for his permission to reprint it here:

Dear Friend,

I want to thank you for being my friend. Your presence means a lot to me and I am glad that you have chosen to share your life with me. But, despite us sharing many things, and despite the amount of time we spend together, some things are hard for me to share with you. I'm sorry. But I do want to share them.

I appreciate your tolerance. But, even with your tolerance, it is still hard for me to be with you. This isn't your fault – it is my limitation. But, even with very tolerant people, I still have to put tremendous effort into every interaction. It is very stressful, and I never know if I'm doing it right.

When I spend time with you, I enjoy it. I wouldn't spend time with you if I didn't. But there are times when I go home upset simply because I can't figure out something about you. If you are upset, I assume it is something that I did but was unable to stop from happening. Surely there are times when you are upset at me and you don't speak, thinking that I will pick up the subtle hint. But, at best, I'll just pick up that you are upset and not know what I did wrong or how to fix it. Other times, I probably couldn't fix it even if I knew what was wrong. But when you are upset at something else – not at me – I still can be upset. Unless I know what is wrong, I can't rule out the possibility that it was caused by myself.

There are things I do which I know make people feel uncomfortable. My tics, for instance, are something that I try to restrain when I'm around most people (although that is usually a futile exercise). But, when I'm around you, I allow them to come rather then trying to stress myself out over something I can't really stop. I hope you don't mind. Other things, like my stims, I don't always realize that I'm doing. But when I do, I try to stop most of them whenever others are around. I allow myself to do a few of them around you, but even when I'm around you, I am fearful to do too many of them.

There are some things I can't control, like the loudness of my voice. Certainly, I can be loud or quiet when I'm trying to, but I can also be loud or quiet when I'm not trying to. Do you always think about the loudness of your voice? I have to, or even my friends will try to quiet me. But it is a lot of work. I understand the concern when I'm loud in a place where I should be quiet, and I feel bad when you point out that I am being too loud, but it is something I have little control over.

There are also some things I don't understand. I've lived nearly a quarter century with the fear that others would discover I don't understand some things, so it is nearly impossible for me to stop faking an understanding when I don't have one. The biggest example is with jokes. I probably don't understand half the jokes that I hear. But I'll still laugh, to cover up my lack of understanding. I'd like to be able to say, 'I don't understand,' but I don't know if I have the strength to do so.

I know you get sick of my endless conversations on only two or three subjects. I know you try to steer my conversation to something that interests you, too, but I don't let you. I'm sorry. But I don't know how to talk about anything else. I wish I could talk about the weather or your landlord or whatever else is important to you, but I don't know how.

I also know that I come across as a 'know it all' sometimes. It is very difficult for me to not speak when I disagree with you, even if it is just my opinion. I worked hard to reach my opinion and my initial instinct is that you haven't. I know that is often wrong, but it is a hard instinct to suppress. In fact, I do suppress it at great effort much of the time – but I can still annoy you even so.

I'm sorry that there are times when you feel bad but I can't console you or be there like some of your other friends are. I wish I could understand what you are feeling, but in those times your thoughts are very different from mine. I want to share something that happened in my day that is important to me, but you want comfort and someone to listen to you. I know that you probably don't care about my trivial thing, but I can't always see what is important – the little thing in my life seems just as important as your hurt. I wish it wasn't so.

What scares me is that these are a lot of reasons for you to not like me. Part of me knows that you probably really do like me as a person – otherwise you wouldn't want to spend time with me. But other parts of me are scared that you are doing it simply out of sympathy or obligation, rather then true friendship. I don't think I can read you as well as others can read you, so I can't pick up on the signs that you would be a friend for reasons other then friendships. So I worry about this – especially after I see you and I do something I described above. I don't want your sympathy, I want your friendship! I hope that is the basis of our relationship, but it is hard when you aren't able to know.

I have nothing to add to that except to give the last word, as ever, to my son, Mattie.

> My autism is not a problem. It creates problems. But it is not going to go away. I want help with my problems not with who I am. I want you to offer support but do not try and change me into someone else.

References

Cowley, G. (2000) 'Understanding Autism.' *Newsweek July 31.*

Gerland, G. (1997) *A Real Person – Life on the Outside.* London: London Souvenir Press.

Gerland, G. (2000) *Finding out about Asperger Syndrome, High Functioning Autism and PDD.* London: Jessica Kingsley Publishers.

Howlin, P. (1997) *Autism – Preparing for Adulthood.* London: Routledge.

Nash, J.M. (2002) 'The Secrets of Autism.' *Time July 15.*

Sainsbury, C. (2000) *A Martian in the Playground.* Bristol: Lucky Duck Publishing.

Vermeulen, P. (2000) *I am special – introducing children and young people to their autistic spectrum disorder.* London: Jessica Kingsley Publishers.

The Contributors

Tony Attwood was born in the UK and trained as a clinical psychologist, graduating from the Surrey University Masters Course in 1975. He then worked as a clinician, specializing in autism and intellectual disability in London and Herefordshire. He was awarded a PhD by the University of London in 1984. In 1985 Tony and his family moved to Australia. In 1992 he started a clinic for children and adults with Asperger Syndrome and in 1997 his book *Asperger's Syndrome* (Jessica Kingsley Publishers, 1998, London, UK) was published. The book has subsequently been published in ten other languages. He is currently working in private practice in Brisbane, Australia and is developing new diagnostic assessment procedures and modifications to Cognitive Behaviour Therapy to treat the mood disorders associated with Asperger Syndrome.

Dennis Debbaudt is a Florida based licensed private investigator and agency owner. He authored *Austism, Advocates and Law Enforcement Professionals: Recognizing and Reducing Risk Situations for People with Autism Spectrum Disorders* for Jessica Kingsley Publishers in 2002, the ground-breaking booklet *Avoiding Unfortunate Situations* (1994) and articles for the FBI Law Enforcement Bulletin, Sheriff Magazine, and newsletters of the Autism Society of America, Autism-Europe and TASH among other advocacy organizations. He was instrumental in the development of Maryland's Police and Correctional Training Commissions autism curriculum, an award-winning video and is involved in numerous grass-roots training projects. He presents autism recognition, response and risk management workshops for laww enforcement, criminal justice and education professions in the U.S., Canada and United Kingdom. Dennis reports and consults from Port St. Lucie, Florida where he resides with his wife, Gay, and 19-year-old son, Brad, who has autism.

DeAnn Foley has a Master of Education in Special Education. DeAnn and her husband, Matt, have co-authored several articles and presented lectures on education services and Asperger Syndrome. DeAnn currently teaches special education in the Dallas/Ft Worth Metroplex.

Steven E. Gutstein is a clinical psychologist and is responsible for developing Relationship Development Intervention (RDI), an innovative new treatment approach for people in the autism spectrum. He has founded the internationally known Connections Center for Relationship Development and the Monarch Therapeutic School with his wife Rachelle Sheely. Steven is the author of *Autism/Asperger's: Solving the Relationship Puzzle*, published by Future Horizons. He has also co-authored with his wife *Relationship Development, Intervention with Young Children* and *Relationship Development, Intervention with Children, Adolescents and Adults*, which are both published by Jessica Kingsley Publishers.

Isabelle Hénault is a PhD candidate in psychology at the University of Quebec at Montreal. Mrs Hénault is a sexologist and therapist. Her work deals primarily with sex education and social skills for individuals with Asperger Syndrome. Isabelle is the author of a specialized sex education curriculum for individuals with Asperger Syndrome.

Liane Holliday Willey is a doctor of education, a writer and a researcher who specializes in the fields of psycholinguistics and learning style differences. Dr Willey has a wonderful husband, three happy children, dedicated parents, some very special friends and an active social life. She also has Asperger Syndrome. A frequent guest lecturer on 'aspie' topics, Dr Willey is an energetic educator and advocate of Asperger issues. Her previous books, *Pretending to be Normal* and *Asperger Syndrome in the Family*, are also published by Jessica Kingsley Publishers. She is currently focusing on her life long dream of publishing a successful work of fiction.

Richard Howlin, PhD is a clinical child and adolescent psychologist. His central clinical focus has centered on the role of temperament and social understanding in children and he has recently been involved in a research project involving Asperger children with the National Academy of Child Development. In conjunction with clinical activities he has lectured in clinical child psychology at the University of Michigan for the past 13 years. Dr Howlin has worked and consulted with the Ann Arbor Public Schools since 1986. He was trained at the University of Munich and the Max Planck Institute for Psychological Research. Dr Howlin maintains a private practice in Chelsea, Michigan.

Jacqui Jackson is the mother of seven children, four of whom are on 'the Autistic Spectrum': Matthew, 18, is dyslexic; Luke, 13, has Asperger Syndrome; Joseph, nine, has ADHD; Ben, four, is severely autistic. Jacqui has been studying for the last ten years and has several Open University degrees, including a first-class honours in Social Policy. In addition to caring for her family, which includes preparing gluten and casein-free foods for some of her children, Jacqui volunteers at the Allergy Induced Autism Helpline.

Luke Jackson is 14 years old and has three sisters and three brothers. One of his brothers has AD/HD, one is dyslexic, one is autistic and Luke has Asperger Syndrome. He is the author of *Freaks, Geeks and Asperger Syndrome, A User Guide to Adolescence* and *A User Guide to the GF/CF Diet for Autism, Asperger Syndrome and AD/HD*, both of which are published by Jessica Kingsley Publishers.

Rebecca Moyes is a former teacher, and today works as an educational consultant for children with autism spectrum conditions. Her oldest child has Asperger Syndrome. She is the author of *Incorporating Social Goals in the Classroom* and *Addressing the Challenging Behaviour of Children with High-Functioning Autism*, which are both published by Jessica Kingsley Publishers.

Lise Pyles is author of *Hitchhiking through Asperger Syndrome* (Jessica Kingsley Publishers, 2002, London, UK), and is a contributing author for *Home Educating Our Autistic Spectrum Children* (Eds Dowty and Cowlishaw, Jessica Kingsley Publishers, 2002, London, UK). Lise is a parent of a child with Asperger Syndrome. Her family's journey has encompassed living on three continents and following several schooling options. Although she has been a freelance writer for several years, her primary concern is raising good, decent and happy kids.

Stephen M. Shore was diagnosed with 'atypical development with strong autistic tendencies' and was viewed as 'too sick' to be treated on an outpatient basis and recommended for institutionalisation. Nonverbal until four, but with much help from his parents, teachers and others, Stephen is now completing his doctoral degree in special education at Boston University with a focus on helping people on the autism spectrum develop their capacities to the fullest extent possible. In addition to working with children and talking about life on the autistic spectrum, Stephen presents and consults internationally on adult issues pertinent to relationships, employment, education, and disclosure as discussed in his book *Beyond the Wall: Personal Experiences with Autism and Asperger Syndrome, 2nd Edition* (Shawnee Mission, KS: Autism Asperger Publishing Company, 2003). He also serves on the board of the Autism Society of America, as board president of the Asperger's Association of New England and is on the board of directors for Unlocking Autism, the Autism Services Association of Massachusetts, and the Asperger Syndrome Coalition of the United States.

Mike Stanton teaches in a school for children with severe learning difficulties in the UK. Some of his pupils are children with autism, and despite the difference in ability he recognizes the similarities between them and people with high-functioning autism, like his son. Since Matthew was diagnosed with Asperger's Syndrome the whole family has been active in the National Autistic Society. Thus Mike brings both professional understanding and personal experience to the subject. He is, as he likes to style himself on Internet forums, 'a parent and a teacher and learning all the time'. His book, *Learning to Live with High Functioning Autism - a parent's guide for professionals* is published by Jessica Kingsley Publishers.

Marc Willey PhD, OTR/L is currently a faculty member in the Occupational Therapy Department at the University of Central Arkansas located in Conway Arkansas, USA. He has a special interest in pediatrics, hand rehabilitation and biomechanical research. Dr Willey also serves as a consultant at Arkansas Children's Hospital, located in Little Rock, Arkansas, where he directs a hand rehabilitation clinic.

Subject Index

Name Index